A FRANCHISE ON THE RISE

THE FIRST TWENTY YEARS OF THE NEW YORK YANKEES

DOM AMORE

FOREWORD BY JOHN STERLING

SPORTS
PUBLISHING

Sports Publishing books may be purchased in bulk at special discounts for
sales promotion, corporate gifts, fund-raising, or educational purposes. Special
editions can also be created to specifications. For details, contact the Special
Sales Department, Sports Publishing, 307 West 36th Street, 11th Floor, New
York, NY 10018 or sportspubbooks@skyhorsepublishing.com.

Sports Publishing® is a registered trademark of Skyhorse Publishing, Inc.®, a
Delaware corporation.

Visit our website at www.sportspubbooks.com.

10 9 8 7 6 5 4 3 2 1

Library of Congress Cataloging-in-Publication Data is available on file.

Cover design by Tom Lau
Cover photo credit Library of Congress

ISBN: 978-1-61321-947-8
Ebook ISBN: 978-1-61321-948-5

Printed in the United States of America

This book is in memory of the late, great Phil Pepe, who was originally to write this project. And it is dedicated to Bill Madden, who encouraged me to take it on.
First boyhood idols, then a young professional's role models, they became cherished friends.

———————————————

CONTENTS

FOREWORD

As I sit in the broadcast booth on a glorious midsummer day, I look up at Yankee Stadium and look at how *majestic* this ballpark is. That's the Yankees.

I suppose I ought to begin when I was a little boy and was made a Yankees fan by my dad. This was in the late 1940s. The Yankees' stadium was more majestic than the other ballparks, Ebbets Field and the Polo Grounds, and it seemed that the Yankees were, as they say, *across the tracks and up the hill*.

I listened to a game on the radio, I was in the car and the adults turned it on, and I fell in love on that day. You fell in love—I fell in love—with the Yankees and their uniforms and the stadium and all the championships. I was born at the right time, when they were winning championships all the time. I thought I was a Yankee, because I was a Yankee fan. I thought they were the classiest team.

Now, looking back, it didn't start out that way. When they established the franchise in 1903 as the Highlanders, it took them 18 seasons to win the American League, and then they wound up playing the team that was their landlord—they were tenants of the Giants at the Polo Grounds. It began with Babe Ruth in that ballpark.

That's the story Dom Amore tells in *A Franchise on the Rise*, the story of how the Yankees came to be and mean so much. If you look at the Yankees, they've been able to carry this banner of being the greatest franchise in sports through the '20s with Babe and Lou; and then the '30s with Joe D., the 1936 to '39 teams, the greatest teams that nobody ever talks about; and the '40s with Yogi, and then Whitey and Mickey. Then there are the George Steinbrenner "Bronx Zoo" days of the '70s—you can't even name all of those key players, from Thurman Munson to Reggie Jackson, Billy Martin, Graig Nettles, Bucky Dent, Willie Randolph, Ron Guidry—the list goes on. And then to the '90s with Joe Torre, obviously, my era in broadcasting. Anyway, that's quite an accomplishment, to keep that franchise up there that many years, as being "The" Franchise.

The Yankees symbolize something. They symbolize the best, the classiest. And that's why a lot of people have said through the years, when they put on the Yankees uniform they feel they have to live up to the Yankees standards.

As you will learn in this book, in 1923 owner Jacob Ruppert ordered that players wear clean uniforms every day. That sense of class has embodied the Yankees, and it's great for Yankees fans who love them, and it's great for everyone else who *hates* them. That's good for baseball.

The Yankees have been very lucky to have guys like Derek Jeter on their roster, and now Aaron Judge. Every time you mention to Judge how well he's doing, he tells you, "Well, it's because of my teammates." His character is very Jeter-like, it's very Lou Gehig-like, it's very DiMag-like.

You know, I don't believe that one job is better than another. Whether you're a broadcaster, a player, or a manager, it's all Major League Baseball. But it carries a little bit extra when it's the Yankees. And before I got this job, I didn't think it would ever happen, and now it's over 30 years that I've been broadcasting their games. I am so typecast, which you could understand by my having done so many games, but someone said to me once, "That's a pretty good thing to be typecast as." And it's true.

I love the history of all sports. And if Dom Amore wrote a book about the '32 St. Louis Browns, who finished sixth (I looked it up), I would love to read it. But to read about how the Yankees were formed? The story of how they began with nothing and, piece by piece, built the franchise and the brand name that we all know today? Well, you've heard me say many times, you can't predict baseball, but I can predict you will love this book and learn so much from it.

Enjoy the read.

—JOHN STERLING, Bronx, New York, July 5, 2017

INTRODUCTION
THE JOY CLUB

"God, what a way to run a ballclub!"

—Jimmy Austin, infielder, 1909–1910

Those who met Roger Peckinpaugh late in his life were impressed by his long, lantern jaw and his firm handshake. Everything about him suggested he was all business, especially when it came to baseball.

So in 1913, when a young, beetle-browed Peckinpaugh was traded to the Yankees, who used to be the Highlanders and whose manager Frank Chance thought hadn't done enough to earn *any* nickname, he was appalled.

"Hal Chase was the first baseman," Peckingpaugh told author Donald Honig for the book *The Man in the Dugout*. "Prince Hal. I was just a kid breaking in and Hal Chase had the reputation of being the greatest first baseman of all time. I remember a few times I threw a ball over to first base and it went by him to the stands, and a couple of runs scored. It really surprised me. I'd think, 'Geez, that throw wasn't that bad.' Then later on, when he got the smelly reputation, it came back to me."

Chase was later traded by the Yankees and eventually kept out of baseball on suspicion of fixing games. "Peck," the 22-year-old shortstop, was soon named Yankees captain.

"The Yankees at that time were what we used to call a 'joy team,'" Peck continued, "lots of joy and lots of losing. Nobody thought we could win, and most of the time we didn't. But it didn't seem to bother the boys too much. They would start singing songs in the infield in the middle of the game."

Hardly recognizable today, this was "Yankees baseball" for much of the first two decades of the 20th century. By comparison, the Mets, born with castoffs in 1962, were World Champions by 1969. The Yankees needed all of 21 years to reach the top.

The Yankees made Roger Peckinpaugh, at twenty-three, the youngest manager in major league history, a distinction he is likely to hold forever. *Bain News Service, courtesy of the Library of Congress*

There wasn't a comedian the caliber of Casey Stengel to ease the pain, but the journey, which began with a couple of well-connected New York pols providing what nobody else could—a suitable piece of land—was nevertheless fascinating and improbable, filled with colorful, sometimes unsavory characters, with would-be saviors. There was cheating, and brawling, and at times it seemed the American League franchise in New York barely existed at all.

"An impression once prevailed in this town that nobody loves the Yankees," wrote Heywood Broun in 1915. The New York Americans, the prevailing theory went, had few fans but did give the city's baseball fans a chance to see the American League's great stars, Ty Cobb, Tris Speaker, Smokey Joe Wood, Walter Johnson, and Connie Mack's famous "$100,000 Infield."

When Frank Chance was brought over from the Cubs to manage the Yankees in 1913, at astronomical expense and with wild fanfare, it appeared as though New York might turn a corner. But Chance's tenure brought more embarrassment, and finally he quit in a snit and handed the club over to Peckinpaugh, now 23, who managed the last 20 games of the 1914 season.

"The owners, what did they know?" Peckinpaugh told author Marty Appel in 1974. "They took the gate receipts and put them in a safe. They didn't know baseball. Anyway, Chance says he was going to recommend me to run the club for the rest of the season. 'Maybe you can get a little extra dough out of it,' he told me.

"The next day, [Highlanders owner Frank] Farrell says, 'We want you to take charge of the team for the rest of the season.' So I say, 'Yeah? What's in it for me?' So they offered me a little extra dough. And that's how I became the youngest manager in the big leagues at 23."

To this day, Peckinpaugh is the youngest manager in major league history. The Yankees were 10–10 and improved from seventh to sixth place.

"There wasn't much managing to do," Peckinpaugh told Honig, "other than selecting the starting pitcher and hoping we didn't get beat too badly."

Things began to change when an aristocratic brewer, Jacob Ruppert, and a bombastic engineer, Til Huston, bought the franchise in January of 1915. Piece by piece, they assembled the team and found both the right manager, Miller Huggins, and the right man to buffer the manager from ownership meddling, Ed Barrow. They also found a superstar to build around (Babe Ruth), the scouts, and, finally, the grand palace to be called Yankee Stadium. Within eight years of buying the team, the Yankees ruled the baseball world, and at the top they would stay for decades. Peckinpaugh, meanwhile, returned to his role as shortstop and captain and stayed long enough to play in a World Series.

Many, many outstanding books have been written on the remarkable history of the Yankees. Some have encompassed the entire history to whatever point they were published, some focused in intricate detail on just one year, or one era, including the early years, or one player, or one relationship.

In this work, I focus on the period from 1903 to 1923, the long road from a team existing only on paper to the first World Series championship. Through the modern access and digital-search capability to a wide range of old newspapers and periodicals, I have tried to find the characters' own voices and allow them to define themselves. In an era of not one, but a dozen papers in New York, it was possible at times to vividly reconstruct events of more than a century ago. Each paper, for instance, pursued a different angle of Ty Cobb's beating of a crippled fan in the stands at Hilltop Park in 1912. Assembled together, the full story emerges. I have endeavored to flesh out some parts of the story, tracing the day-by-day progress in the papers of the time. Some details made headlines at the time but were then buried in microfilm and forgotten, such as the snowy night Honus Wagner was offered 20 crisp $1,000 bills to join the new franchise in New

York; why there were holes punched in the outfield fence that facilitated the stealing of signs in 1909; that the Yankees' pursuit of a manager to succeed Peckinpaugh included a flirtation with Connie Mack; or that the team thought it had the next big superstar in a college football end named George Halas.

This is a story of the business of baseball, as it was done at the time and, in many ways, as it still must be done. There was no secret to building a winning organization. It took money and luck, but it also took a group of people working as a team, each allowed to do his job and each doing it superbly. Then, as now, a winning organization is an *organization,* one that makes a sound plan and sticks to it.

But then, as now, the human element should not be overlooked, and the forces of personalities on the course of history cannot be overestimated.

So this is meant to be a baseball story, the narrative of a sorry, sad-sack club that eventually grew to become champions.

CHAPTER 1

THE TENDERLOIN: UNEASY BIRTH OF A FRANCHISE

Frank Moss: I want to ask you a broad question: Do you consider the city wide open?
Bill Devery: It has always been wide open. I have never known it closed and I was born here.

When police chief William Steven "Big Bill" Devery was jostling around in his chair the way a heavy man does at the dusty, smoke-filled Tammany Hall in April 1899, he seemed to be defining New York City at the turn of the 20th century. When he answered the investigator's questions, before the Mazet Commission (not the first commission created to investigate and trap him) and declared New York City "wide open," he wasn't referring to a warm welcome for outsiders. The city, run for decades by Tammany Hall bosses, was a place where anything went—that is, if enough of it went into the right pockets.

And deep and bulging were Bill Devery's pockets. Those gathered snickered, sometimes roared at Devery's outrageously vague, evasive, winking, self-effacing answers, because that was Big Bill Devery and his relationship with the city.

Devery, born in New York on January 9, 1854, began as a patrolman with the New York Police Department in 1878 and by the 1890s was a captain, making the nightly rounds in The Tenderloin, Manhattan's Red Light District on the west side, dominated by pool halls, brothels, and saloons.

Most evenings, Devery's rotund silhouette could be seen on the corner of 26th and 8th, where patrons could come by if they needed his attention or wished to make a contribution. "Honest graft," Big Bill called it, the ultimate oxymoron, and he and his men would then "protect" the establishments that paid up.

Bill Devery, here with manager Harry Wolverton in 1912, was a "silent partner," but he was often visible at Hilltop Park. *Bain News Service, courtesy of the Library of Congress*

He was convicted on bribery and extortion charges in 1897, but it was overturned on appeal and he was restored to the force. Within months, when the five boroughs joined to form the sprawling New York City of the 20th century and beyond, Devery was named chief of police—to the horror of the reformers.

Sure, he made powerful, implacable enemies, but none was able to corral him. "He represented in the police department all that I had warred against as commissioner," wrote Theodore Roosevelt, whose warring went largely for naught.

Devery was questioned by Moss in 1899 for possible finagling in the Bob Fitzsimmons-Jim Jeffries fight at Coney Island, which he threatened to stop, then allowed to continue. There was the Lexow Committee, which uncovered bribery, extortion, counterfeiting, voter intimidation, and election fraud. And there was the Mazet Committee, established by Roosevelt to investigate Richard Croker's and Tim Sullivan's Tammany machinations, for which Moss cross-examined Devery about improprieties in the building department.

When Devery issued an order to his men to disregard the state's election bureau in November 1900, Roosevelt, now governor and vice-presidential nominee, fired off letters to the mayor, the sheriff, and the district attorney, warning he would hold them personally responsible for Devery's actions.

And yet Devery, lampooned in Harper's sitting on a fire hydrant scooping in gold coins from a "fairy godmother," broke the rules and lined his pockets with an insouciance that made him oddly likeable. Lincoln Steffans, one of the most celebrated investigative journalists of that or any age, loved sparring with Devery. "We'll have a fight," he told Steffans on the street corner one day, "and I hope you enjoy it as much as I will. I'll win, you know. . . .." Devery was known, in fact, to fill scrapbooks with the unflattering cartoons drawn of him, and his oft-used preamble to courtroom questions, "well, touchin' on and appertainin' to . . .," became a city catch phrase, especially in The Tenderloin.

"It was easy for the Christian ministers to hate Devery and reproach us for loving our enemy; they never met him," Steffans wrote. ". . . But as a character, as a work of art, he was a masterpiece. Every reporter I ever assigned to roast the man came back smiling, and put the smile in his report."

Devery laughed at the most dogged of muckrakers, stuck out his chin and dared them to take their best shot. "And," he chortled to one of Steffans's colleagues, "I'll shut the windows to keep th' noise out and go right on doing business just the same."

And for a time, he did. He got things done and the people were with him. The "Canyon of Heroes" parade route that has become a New York signature was originally laid out by Devery, for Admiral George Dewey's return from war in 1899.

By this time, Devery had made the acquaintance of Francis J. Farrell, a man who could help him navigate New York politics and who would lead him to baseball.

While Devery was big and boisterous, with straining vest buttons and a bristling mustache, Frank J. Farrell, a few years younger, stylish and natty, usually wore a serious expression, derby pulled down in front, and knew when to keep his mouth shut. As Devery was moving up the ranks, Farrell went to work tending bar for Jimmie Wakely at 31st and 6th, pouring the drinks for Tammany Hall's pols. When Wakely opened a new place on 42nd street, he sold Farrell the old saloon, according to the *Brooklyn Eagle*, "on friendly terms."

"Farrell made many friends in The Tenderloin," the *Eagle* reported, in a favorable profile in 1901, "and while his saloon was often the resort of many of the characters with which the district abounds, he never became mixed up with any scandals."

He did, however, become mixed up with Big Bill Devery. That was inevitable. "The acquaintance speedily ripened into friendship, and then Farrell, under the protecting wing of his patron, began to move up in the world."

Frank Farrell (bottom right) took his place among the AL's hierarchy, including Charles Comiskey (bottom left) and president Ban Johnson (bottom center). *Bain News Service, courtesy of the Library of Congress*

Farrell became the leading player in the legal, semilegal, and illegal gambling of the time, a lover of horseracing, and a czar of the Tenderloin's many pool halls, as many as 250 of them. One can easily imagine the nightly conversations between Farrell and Devery, in Farrell's dive, and on Devery's favorite street corner.

As the 1890s were coming to a close, it was but a matter of time before they would get together for a project, and only natural that baseball, quickly becoming a national obsession and burgeoning business, would sprout from their ill-gotten gains.

"There was one thing that all who have had confidential dealings with [Farrell] concur in saying," the *Eagle* concluded. "He can keep a secret and he is true to his friends. These qualities endeared him in the heart of Devery and when the latter rose, Farrell became recognized as his right-hand man."

Between the discreet Farrell's legal bookmaking and off-track betting operations in the neighborhood's pool halls and the blustery Devery's "honest graft," the pair were part of a syndicate, the *New York Times* reported, that raked in $3 million in 1899, the equivalent of more than $80 million in 2016 dollars.

Farrell's relative anonymity and behind-the-scenes influence were finally thrust out into the open during the 1901 mayoral campaign, when William Travers Jerome labeled his opponent, Henry V. Unger, a stooge of Farrell, "head of the gambling combine in this city."

On October 13, 1901, the *New York Times* charged, "it is vice itself in the person of Farrell that has brought about the nomination of Mr. Unger.. . . . Farrell wants a district attorney who will not make trouble for him."

Tammany Hall's candidates lost that election, but Farrell and Devery remained well-known figures in the city, at once admired for their audacity and power and held in contempt for their malfeasance. In their late-'30s, they "retired" rather comfortably. Leaving office, Mayor Robert Van Wyck, seemingly unaware of the irony, called Devery the best police chief the city ever had.

A baseball impresario would turn to such a pair only if desperate to get his show on Broadway. And Ban Johnson, who forged the American League and ruled it with absolute power, was becoming desperate. An Ohio native who by that time had moved from Chicago to establish an office in the Flatiron Building, just off the northern edge of The Tenderloin, the building where the successful business people of the day set up shop, Johnson found the city anything but "wide open."

Johnson was determined and shrewd. Like Farrell, he was often seen with slick hair, parted in the middle, a wing collar, and derby, earmarks of the day's dressed-for-success; ran the Western League in the 1890s, but rebranded; and the "American" League challenged the established National as one of baseball's major leagues. He was raised to be a lawyer but dropped out of the University of Cincinnati to become a sportswriter and gravitated to baseball, where he planned to make his mark by cleaning up the game's image, marred by gambling, drinking, and brawling.

Throughout 1901 and 1902, he signed star players from the NL, shattering the established league's cap on salaries, and assigned them to his teams. He also undercut the established league in ticket prices in Boston, Philadelphia, St. Louis, and Chicago. It was a smashing success. But he knew that "major league" status could not truly be achieved without a team in New York, and more specifically on Manhattan Island.

Nothing was happening in Manhattan without the Tammany machine's approval. The Giants were Tammany's team, especially while Andrew Freedman owned them. As Johnson schemed to bring the flagging Baltimore Orioles to New York, Freedman was there to thwart him at every turn.

Freedman and the ever-combative John McGraw, once a friend of Johnson and now a bitter enemy, took hold of the Baltimore franchise and began sending its players to the National League, in hopes that the Orioles would fold, wreak havoc on the remaining 1902 schedule, and destroy the image of the AL as a "major" league. Johnson foiled them, invoking rules in the league charter that allowed him to take controlling interest and compelling other teams to send players to Baltimore and keep the schedule intact.

Now, from the Flatiron, Johnson acted as owner and GM for a franchise that existed only in his mind and began collecting players. "I have been forced by circumstances to put the cart before the horse," he would say.

Johnson spent a frustrating winter trying to find owners, and a site for a ballpark to be built to replace the Orioles franchise with a new one in New York. But without connected men to own the team, securing the site was impossible. At Cincinnati in mid-January, NL owners met and hammered out a peace agreement with Johnson. The owners, so happy to have their league stabilized again and expecting stock to skyrocket, sang "In the Good Old Summer Time," the latest hit from Tin Pan Alley, the *New York Sun* reported on January 20, 1903.

John T. Brush, owner of the Giants, was not in the chorus, having left town quickly on other business, it was said. The NL, as part of the deal, agreed to allow Johnson to place a team in New York—meaning one of the five boroughs. Brush, who had acquired controlling interest in the Giants but still had Freedman as an ally, aimed to keep the franchise as far from Manhattan as possible.

New York newspapers of the day rarely carried bylines, but Joe Vila had nonetheless become one of the best-known sportswriters of the day. A Harvard man, Vila had been at the *Sun* since 1889 and was believed to be the first to take a typewriter ringside at boxing matches. As a result, he knew everyone and got involved. As he doggedly pursued information on the AL's plans for the city, he asked Johnson one January day if he had an owner.

Johnson, who had talked to a number of potential backers in the city, had nothing secure—no owner and no site for a ballpark. Vila suggested and arranged a meeting with Frank Farrell.

As Frank Graham, who later worked for Vila at the *Sun*, reported their conversation years later, Farrell offered to buy the team and told Johnson he had a site on 165th and Broadway. It was far uptown, but Farrell assured Johnson that soon the subways would make it accessible.

Then Farrell presented a check for $25,000 as a show of "good faith" and told Johnson he could keep it if he and his silent partner, Bill Devery—who was about a silent as one of his parades—couldn't make good on their promises. "That's a pretty big forfeit," Johnson said.

Vila laughed. Farrell was known to drop that, and more, on a horse race. Johnson knew he now had a fallback plan, at least, and that night he raised a glass at The Criterion Hotel, offered a toast in which he told a gathering of friends and sportswriters that the American League was coming to New York. They'd have to wait for the details.

Johnson still looked at more favorable options for a ballpark. Though the Tammany crowd had lost the election, Freedman remained on the board and effectively in control of the powerful Interborough Rapid Transit System, which was building the subway system. No one dared interfere with that project. Wherever Johnson thought he could build, there were road-blocks. When he looked upon a seemingly perfect, easily accessed site off Lenox, north of midtown, Freedman had the board claim the land for its needs.

According to the *Sun*, Vila reported that the truce between the leagues was teetering. "Although the National League owners formally consented to the invasion of this city, its agents are doing all in their power to block the deal," reported the paper on March 8.

"I decline to see any blood on the moon," NL president Harry Pulliam told Vila. "There has been no attempt by the National League to put the American League up a tree."

Then Johnson eyeballed a lot in The Bronx, just across the Macombs Dam Bridge and easily accessible from Manhattan—yes, roughly the spot where the future Yankee Stadiums would be erected. The Astors, the legendary New York real estate barons, owned the property, and Brush's agents, trying to lease it short term, were able to tie up the negotiations long enough so that a ballpark could not be built in time for the season.

No, if Ban Johnson was going to play ball in New York, he would first have to do so with its less-than-savory movers, and on their terms and turf—and this put the man who so wanted to make a fashionable thing of clean baseball in league with Frank Farrell, the pool room king, and Bill Devery, that collector of "honest graft."

To allay Johnson's misgivings, Farrell had agreed to keep his involvement a secret; Vila, who had brokered the involvement, had not reported it. Joseph Gordon, who ran a coal company and had been involved with the Giants in the 1880s, would be the president, the front man.

First week of March, 1903, Devery, still sparring in and out of court with the incumbent city officials, threatened to run for mayor as an independent, which turned out to be a bluff. Ban Johnson, on March 11, announced he was bluffing no more. "I know I have made many promises with regard to this matter which I have been compelled, through circumstances, to break," he said. "But this time, there will be no slip-ups. We have cleaned up the deal completely."

The location, like the Farrell-Devery connection, had been kept secret as they worked to lease the massive, 9.6-acre site, between 165th and 168th, from its owners, the New York Institute for the Blind. The papers were signed and building permits secured, when Johnson called reporters back to the hotel at 9 p.m.

The mystery was at last revealed, reported in the papers on March 12. Gordon would be president, and John B. Day—another with long, if peripheral, baseball experience—would be his No. 2 man. Johnson would not have a controlling interest in this franchise. As he explained, "it will be owed completely by New York men."

A tall, distinguished, white-haired man, Gordon appeared right out of central casting to be president of a company. He would make the rest of the syndicate known "in a few days," the *Sun* reported. In fact, only in 1909, after Gordon was pushed out and was suing Farrell, did the full nature of the dealings become public knowledge.

The 16,000-seat ballpark would be built in seven weeks' time on sprawling grounds bordered by 165th Street on the south, 168th on the north, Fort Washington Avenue on the east, and 11th Avenue on the west. The new subway, when completed, would stop at the northeast corner of the lot, but current trolley service could drop fans within a short walk of the grounds.

Johnson sold the franchise for $18,000, but the owners would assume the costs of building the park. The next day, Johnson took pols and reporters on a tour of the site, "the consensus of opinion being," Vila wrote, "that when completed the field will be the finest in the world for baseball purposes."

Johnson raved about the glorious views of the Hudson and the Palisades that this, one of the highest spots on the Island, would offer. The surface was horribly rocky, however, and a former police inspector, Thomas McAvoy, had the contract for building the grounds, the clue of a Devery connection. It would take $200,000 to clear and prepare the land for a baseball diamond, well over $5 million in 2016 dollars, and about $50,000 to erect the wooden grandstand, which would be very plain. Tammany's fingers would be in every slice of the pie.

Brush, Freedman, and their gang tried one more time to interfere, stirring up the neighbors and a local church to protest the building of the ballpark and the saloons that might soon surround it and calling for 166th and 167th Streets to be opened up to run across the middle of the lot. But whether they knew it or not, they were up against Farrell and Devery now. The opposition melted away.

Gordon announced there would be no liquor sold at the games. The Institute for the Blind had insisted upon that before leasing the property, and he wanted to have a contest where "small boys" in the city would submit suggestions to name the ballpark. The winner would get a season pass to the games.

McAvoy assured everyone that the park, which would eventually be called "American League Park," would be ready for the home opener on April 30, 1903, and drilling and blasting began immediately. American League baseball, which Johnson promised to be as American as apple pie, was coming to New York, the deal done as only it could be done in the Big Apple, "wide open" to those who dealt with the right people.

Day after day in March and April, the progress was reported in detail by Vila and the *Sun*. But it was another paper, the *New-York Tribune*, that reported, citing "reliable sources" shortly before the opener, that Big Bill Devery was seen inspecting the grounds and could have as much as $100,000 invested in the New York American League club.

"Me, a backer!" Devery roared, when the *Tribune* posed the question. "I only wish I did own some stock in a baseball club. I'm a poor man and I don't own stock in anything. What would I do with a baseball team? Me pitch with a stomach like this? Not on yer life!"

Beginning the next day, the *Tribune* winked back, repeatedly referring to the new team in game reports as "the Deveryites."

CHAPTER 2

YEAR ONE: BORN TO ORGANIZE

One thing is certain: New York will give the American
League a royal welcome. . . . Boston, too, will appreciate
seeing a fine team hailing from New York.

—Tim Murnane, *Boston Globe*, March 1903

By all accounts, April 30, 1903, was a near-perfect day to
play baseball on the northern tip of Manhattan Island. Brilliant
sunshine bathed the new ballpark on the bluff with spectacular
river views and a cool, comfortable breeze.

In 1777, George Washington and his army made their escape
through the neighborhood, fleeing across the Hudson River to
fight another day. Flash-forward nearly 130 years, and there was
red, white, and blue draped everywhere, plus a new wrinkle: blue
flags flapped atop the grandstand, carrying the name in white
letters of every American League city—Boston, Philadelphia,
Washington, Cleveland, Detroit, Chicago, and St. Louis—the

stable composition of the league, now that New York was at last in, for the next 50 years.

Thousands of small American flags, handed to spectators on the way in, waved in the stands as bandmaster William Bayne's 69th Regiment band played "Yankee Doodle," a prophetic choice, of course, that may have first planted the idea of the future nickname. The band also played "Washington Post March," "The Stars and Stripes Forever," and other popular patriotic songs.

And in the city that served as the nation's front porch for millions of arriving immigrants, many flags were in sight on this day. The *New York Sun* quoted a spectator: "Flags of all nations. That means that someday baseball will be played under every flag in the world and that baseball will be a world-wide game."

It was a day for global-scaled dreaming. Oh, the stands and clubhouses weren't finished, the roof wasn't up, players had to dress before coming to work, and the playing surface had a few hazards, including high spots and a swamp in right field that nearly swallowed the Highlanders' best player on the first play of the game. Nevertheless, papers rhapsodized, heaping praise on contractor Thomas McAvoy and groundskeeper Phil Schenk for getting a ballpark ready for a baseball game in about six weeks and praising the idyllic vistas for those who lifted their eyes occasionally from the diamond below.

Remaining work would be done during the first extended road trip, but in its 10 years of existence, American League Park, or Hilltop Park as it was more familiarly known, never seemed to be quite finished. It began as almost an open field, reported as 400 feet to the right field fence, 542 to center, and 365 to left.

Ron Selter, of The Society for American Baseball Research, later determined the original distances as 365 feet to left, 378 to left center, 420 to center, 424 to right center, and 385 to right. In June, a temporary fence was extended across right-center to keep the dangerous ravine out of play, shortening center field to 390 feet, right-center to 346, and right field to 300. The temporary fence was removed in 1904, then restored in 1907, shortening center to 395, right-center to 412, and right to 365. For the last two seasons, bleachers added to center field pushed the fence in to 370 feet in dead-center and 372 in right-center, very reachable even in the Deadball Era.

Over the years, as bleacher seats were added and the roof extended, the ballpark never really developed a signature or memorable feature. Like the team, it had a lack of a clear identity.

The Americans—or were they, depending on the newspaper one read, the Highlanders, the Hilltoppers, Griff-men, Invaders, or Deveryites?— had begun their existence with two wins and two losses in Washington, and two losses in three games in Philly. Now they were ready to introduce themselves to New York.

As the home team marched like rookie cadets out to the flagpole, with reporters within earshot, manager Clark Griffith called out, "I see three men in the grandstand with straw hats. That means warm weather is here, sure enough, so you fellows are due to find your batting eyes today."

The Highlanders, as they were more or less officially named because of the high ground on which they played, and because of the fact that the team's figurehead president, Joseph Gordon, brought to mind the famous infantry regiment "Gordon's Highlanders," were not simply an established franchise relocated from Baltimore. Nor was this to be a hapless expansion franchise, in the sense of the castoff-filled 1962 Mets. This was a franchise of established players, put together over the winter by AL president Ban Johnson, who threw out the first ball as Farrell and Devery discreetly settled into their box seats.

The expectation was success. To make it work would take a born organizer, and Johnson, before anything else was settled, had prevailed upon the Chicago White Sox owner, crusty Charles Comiskey, to grudgingly give up his successful manager, Clark Griffith, for this endeavor, for the good of the American League.

"Historic ground," wrote the *Sun*, "where Washington fought and where Griffith will now endeavor to lead his forces to victory."

Born four years after the end of the Civil War in Cedar Creek, Missouri, Griffith was two when he lost his father in a hunting accident. As a boy, he watched the returning soldiers play baseball in town, as they had to pass the time between battles. Raised by a widowed mother and plagued with chronic illnesses, Griffith grew to a frail but fiesty 5-foot-6 when the family moved to Illinois. He started as a bat boy for a local team but at age 17 was given a chance to try pitching. He became one of the game's first finesse pitchers—"The Old Fox," they came to call him—and was once handed a bill by the opposing team for 11 damaged baseballs, which he had gouged with his spikes and used to get them out.

Rising to the National League in the 1890s, he became one of the leaders of movements to organize players, and, as the league capped salaries, Griffith was sought out by Ban Johnson as the perfect guy to convince players to jump to gain leverage. He was savvier than the average player, and when he talked, they listened. In 1901, Griffith was pitcher/manager for Chicago, the first league champs, and Johnson consulted him frequently, especially when Andrew Freedman and John McGraw began sabotaging the Baltimore franchise in mid-1902.

Shortly after the season, Johnson made it known that Griffith, already popular with baseball writers around the country, would manage the team in New York, and they set about signing players. Griffith lured seven of the champion Pittsburgh Pirates—who went 103–36 in 1902—to jump to the AL and later said he got every player he recruited except one. During a snowstorm in Carnegie, Pennsylvania, Honus Wagner returned to his home riding a sleigh and found Clark Griffith waiting for him, and offering $20,000.

"I was making $3,000 with Pittsburgh," Wagner told the *Pittsburgh Press* in 1950, "and $20,000 seemed like a lot of money. I told Griff I didn't think there was that much money in the world. He calmly pulled out 20 $1,000 bills and I must admit it was tempting. But I told Griff I was perfectly satisfied and [Pirates owner] Barney Dreyfuss had treated me fine."

How much differently the first decade of the New York franchise may have played out if the finest player in baseball, Honus Wagner, had accepted the offer and played shortstop for them!

Griffith did, however, get Jack Chesbro and Jesse Tannehill, top starting pitchers. Catcher Jack O'Connor and third baseman Wid Conroy and outfielder Lefty Davis all jumped from Pittsburgh to New York, as well. Johnson and Griffith double-teamed Willie Keeler in a secret Chicago meeting to make the jump from Brooklyn for $10,000, plus a $2,000 bonus. The addition of a few other established players from elsewhere, and a handful of holdovers from the 1902 Orioles, caused the Highlanders to quickly boast a formidable roster.

Griffith didn't stop there. He even made a run (unsuccessful, of course) at the Giants' Christy Mathewson. Okay, now imagine Wagner *and* Masterson.

While Ban Johnson was making his way through New York's political jungle to identify owners and land for the ballpark, Griffith was settling into a hotel residence on 155th Street and Amsterdam Avenue. On the day the franchise was officially unveiled, March 12, Griffith and Gordon began "burning the wires," according to the *Sun*, to make a $10,000 deal for Ed Delahanty, one of the game's great sluggers. Johnson eventually slowed Griffith down, so as not to antagonize the NL and the Giants any further. Delahanty stayed with Washington, where he died during that season in a mysterious fall into Niagara Falls.

But by the time Johnson and Griffith were finished, Gordon told reporters the 1903 roster would command an estimated $80,000, twice what most NL payrolls were. The *Brooklyn Eagle* ran the story under the headline *"An Expensive Ball Club"*— helping to shelve the concept of capping salaries in baseball for the next century.

Griffith packed and headed for Atlanta, where he had arranged for the first training camp. The team grouped in Washington and on March 19, the Atlanta papers enthusiastically announced their scheduled arrival on the train at 3:55 p.m. "The aggregation is nothing less than a bunch of stars," the *Constitution* said, and their morning and afternoon workouts at Piedmont Park drew crowds.

Griffith's hands were on every aspect of the new franchise, with a free hand to spend the owners' cash and the league president's complete loyalty; he was now transitioning to the executive side of the game and had to work to hold salaries *down* after years of trying to organize players to demand more money.

He nevertheless won the confidence of players as well as the owners. As an experienced horse breeder, Griffith found common ground with Farrell, who was stepping out from the shadows as most active and demanding of the ownership group. Theirs was to be a stormy relationship, however.

Griffith's new team spent March and April of 1903 in Atlanta and New Orleans, playing Southern Association teams. They beat the Crackers, 9–0, in the first exhibition game at Piedmont Park on March 26, the first of three consecutive shutouts, then won three of five games against the Pelicans in early April. Griffith paid for a couple of New York writers to cover camp (this is the way things were done then), including Jim Bagley for the *Evening Mail*, and their stories began building interest for the team's arrival in New York.

The Americans, as they barnstormed northward, were wearing white flannel uniforms with black trim, black collars, and a black *N* and *Y* on the breasts in an odd, olde English, hook font. *Sporting Life* called the attire "the swellest thing in the business. Clark Griffith designed them."

For road games, the scheme was reversed. The black was changed to dark blue, the font slightly different. The uniform, like the ballpark, was adjusted nearly every season as the franchise searched for identity in those early years. The *N* and *Y* were interlocked on the left breast in 1905, then separated again.

In 1909, presumably at Devery's suggestion, the franchise adopted the interlocking *N* and *Y* designed by Tiffany in 1877 and presented as a medal of valor to New York police officers shot in the line of duty. The insignia appeared on the left sleeve and later on the left breast. Pinstripes first appeared in black in 1912 and reappeared in 1915, after Farrell and Devery sold the team. The iconic Yankees uniform at last was beginning to take shape and take hold.

"Griff" was a motivator. Ty Cobb, in a long Sunday magazine article of the period, noted the players' habit of overestimating the pitchers they hit well and Griffith's reputation for pushing the right buttons: "That pitcher must be pretty soft for you fellows to fatten your batting averages today, and they need it," Griffith would sneer. And if one of his hitters argued, Griffith would say, "When you fellows are hitting, the pitcher always has lots of stuff. That's old bunk."

On April 22, they dropped their first regular season game, in front of a large crowd at Washington. Jack Chesbro took the 3–1 loss. But the squad got its first win on April 23. Harry Howell, at 26, the youngest member of the first rotation, beat the Senators, 7–2. New York got 11 hits, and Washington made six errors.

In Philadelphia, the Highlanders squared off against Connie Mack's defending league champions. Griffith made his first start and lost a pitching duel to young star Chief Bender, 3–1. Only the last game was salvaged, as Jesse Tannehill took a shutout into the ninth inning and held on through a sloppy finish to beat the Athletics, 5–4. Then the team headed to its new home.

The crowd, reported as 16,243 by the *New York Times*, was gathering at the less-than-substantially-completed American League Grounds, with thousands sitting in temporary folding chairs or standing in roped-off sections of the outfield. Meanwhile, the team grouped behind home plate in what served as their warm-up jackets of the era—heavy, long maroon wool sweaters with shawl collars, leather elbow patches, and the same *N* and *Y*.

After his little pep talk about straw hats, warm weather, and finding their batting eyes, Griffith handed the ball to his best pitcher, Chesbro, and the Highlanders beat Washington, 6–2. The first batter, Rabbit Robinson, drove one over Keeler's head in right, the ball disappearing into the pond that was not quite filled in. Keeler, protecting his left shoulder, which he had injured in an offseason carriage accident, stopped short of falling down the ravine and into what writers began calling "Keeler's Hollow," and it went for a double. But Chesbro stranded the

Clark Griffith (right), the Yankees' first manager, ended up as the owner of the Washington Senators. After leaving the Yankees in 1908, he continued to play a role in the franchise's history from the opposing side. *AP Photo*

runner, and New York scored in each of its first two at-bats to take the lead for good.

The Highlanders won two of three from the Senators, and two of three from the A's. After losing, 6–1, to Hall of Famer Eddie Plank on getaway day, they boarded the train for Boston on May 6 to start a stretch of three weeks on the road as McAvoy's army of workers returned to finish the ballpark.

At 6-foot-1 and 195 pounds, first baseman John Ganzel, one of several ballplaying brothers out of Kalamazoo, Michigan, was strapping for the era in which he played. He was 24 when he broke in with the Pirates in 1898, and he moved from team to team, between the majors and minors, before landing an every-day job with the Highlanders, taking over first base as efforts to get Ed Delahanty failed.

On May 11, Ganzel was back in his home state, mired in a 2-for-23 slide, when he belted one of George Mullin's curve-balls over the outfielders and set out around the bases. When he reached home safely, the game was broken open, and Ganzel had etched his name permanently in the history of the franchise. It was the first home run in Yankees history.

William Edward Conroy, who went by "Wid," was manning third base for the Highlanders. At 25, he was one of the younger players lured from Pittsburgh, and one of the few to jump back and forth. He had begun as a major leaguer with Milwaukee in the American League in 1901, then moved to the Pirates, and finally returned to the AL. He had a reputation for taking unusually large leads off first base, and for his all-around aggressive play, resulting in a set-to with the Cubs' Joe Tinker in 1902.

Wid also etched his name on that same day when he added the second home run in the seventh inning as the Highlanders beat the Tigers, 8–2, to climb above .500. They would hit 18 homers as a team in 1903.

From Boston to Detroit, Cleveland, Chicago, St. Louis, and Philadelphia the Highlanders roamed, a month-long odyssey of the rails, during which they lost 12 of 20 games. When they returned to the hilltop, they were 15–18, and there Boston buried them, by scores of 8–2, 9–0, and 9–3.

The first manager was on the hot seat.

"Griffith has not given satisfaction as the leader of the team," Gordon, obviously goaded by Farrell, was quoted in *Sporting Life*. "But with the resources at his disposal, he must now see to it that the boys play winning ball."

Hmmm, an old, underachieving ballclub, wherein the owner calls out manager after a slow start. Does any of *that* sound familiar?

The team was old and banged up, and an embarrassed Clark Griffith now realized he had misfired on some of his vaunted acquisitions and he left the team to scout for new players. He tried again to acquire Delahanty to play first base, but Washington would not budge.

Herman "Germany" Long, former Boston National Leaguer, was the most acrobatic shortstop in the game in his time, but his time was the 1890s. He was now 37, hitting .188 with 14 errors in 22 games. With Johnson's prodding, Detroit took Long off New York's hands in a June 10 trade, sending their young, exciting shortstop, Kid Elberfeld, hitting .341, to New York for Long and utilityman Ernest Courtney.

The Giants had long been trying to land Elberfeld—McGraw considered him a young version of himself—and when he was shuffled to the other team in New York, the relationship between the teams deteriorated. The trade included "cash considerations," which prompted Gordon, in his short diatribe, to warn this was Griffith's last chance to turn it around. Norman Arthur "Kid" Elberfeld's stormy time in New York began on June 13. One of the writers—Elberfeld credited Sam Crane—dubbed him "the Tabasco Kid" when he got to New York, and it stuck. The Highlanders were 18–23 when he arrived and immediately tightened up the infield defense, helping Chesbro beat Detroit, 3–2. Then New York posted consecutive 1–0 victories over Chicago. A seven-game winning streak vaulted them over .500 in early July. As a long homestand offered a chance to climb back in the race, they lost nine of 12.

Keeler, his left shoulder barking, was hitting .313, the best of the bunch around him, but far below his standards—he began the season with a .371 lifetime average across a decade. In late July, the gossipy *Sporting Life* reported that Keeler was taking "inconspicuous roads" back to his home in Brooklyn after Highlanders home games, reportedly telling a friend, "Why, I am even ashamed to look my father in the face after the showing we have been making since the season opened. With such an aggregation of stars as we have, we ought to do much better."

By July 28, the Highlanders were 37–40 and 14 ½ games behind first-place Boston, having just lost another five of six to them.

A few blocks away, the Giants had the stars in their prime—McGraw, Mathewson, Iron Man Joe McGinnity—and were 13 games over .500. Fans were flocking to the Polo Grounds, not making the extra effort by trolley and on foot to get to American

League Grounds. And the Pirates, despite all those defections, again had a commanding lead in the National League as Wagner was having another of his monster seasons. Though Griffith remained a respected figure in national baseball circles, the Farrell-Devery syndicate was increasingly unhappy.

Farrell was seen around town with Ned Hanlon (also known as "Foxy Ned"), who, running his teams in street clothes, had been one of the game's most famous and successful managers throughout the 1890s. The most recent of his five first-place finishes with Brooklyn had been in 1900—though it would be almost 100 years before Hanlon's contributions were recognized with Hall of Fame enshrinement. Keeler had played for him in Baltimore and Brooklyn, as Hanlon perfected and unleashed his aggressive, exciting brand of baseball, which included the bunt, the "Baltimore Chop," and a lot of running. Perhaps he could light a fire under the franchise.

Nothing came of the socializing; perhaps admonished by Johnson, the Farrell-Devery syndicate allowed Griffith to continue. The Highlanders went 19–10 in September to improve the season only cosmetically, finishing 72–62, in fourth place.

Ban Johnson would never hesitate to throw his power behind any effort to make this new franchise a success, but for the moment his old nemeses, Freedman, Brush, and McGraw, had the better of him. Griffith, with Johnson's help, went to work to maneuver better players to New York, but with the leagues at peace there would be no more raiding of NL franchises.

Jack Chesbro started 36 games, completed 33, and won 21 in 1903. Griffith would count on Chesbro to carry the Highlanders to the top in 1904.

CHAPTER 3

WILLIE KEELER:
CATALYST AND CAPITALIST

Dear Sir; Have you any treatise on the art of batting written by yourself? If so, please inform me where I can obtain such and the price thereof. I enclose stamp for reply. . . .

—Fan's letter to Willie Keeler, 1901

If Willie Keeler could have had a dime for every old-timer who has said, "in my day, I would have played for nothing," he would probably have tucked them all in his pocket and kept them. He was a businessman, and his business was baseball. One of the most quotable athletes of his day, he was at his most eloquent when describing his theories of hitting or his motivation—"the good old coin, as doled out by Uncle Sam."

So Keeler, 30, was a contented man, his skills and earning power at their peak on the night of November 30, 1902, the Sunday after Thanksgiving, when he rumbled down a dark California road, in a horse-drawn surrey, with several other ballplayers on the way to do some duck hunting. Following the season, a large group from both American and National League had each invested $150 toward expenses and traveled out west to play a series of all-star games, a barnstorming trip that would pay off several times over.

More important was a business meeting Keeler had on his way across the continent, in Chicago with Clark Griffith and Ban Johnson, who had rushed out to meet them. Detroit had long wanted Keeler, and Johnson wanted him for the AL, but not even the good old coin, as doled out by Uncle Ban, could get him to venture that far from his beloved Brooklyn, where he still lived in his father's house at 376 Pulaski Street, across from a brewery.

But Keeler wanted to know if Johnson was certain he would have a team in New York in 1903 and beyond and was assured of the soon-to-be-Highlanders' existence. "Well, then I'd be interested," he said. Keeler agreed to a two-year deal, a $2,000 bonus, and a $10,000 salary. Brooklyn thought its current agreement with Keeler extended through the 1903 season, so there would be controversy. Keeler wanted it kept quiet until he got home.

Now, the barnstorming tour was a rousing success, pouring money into Keeler's pocket. He was negotiating to go back for a second lucrative year of coaching baseball players at Harvard—not bad for a high school dropout—a three-week crash course on hitting before spring training. He would then stay close to home and play for a big raise the coming summer, a win all around.

Keeler, who used to infuriate his teachers at P.S. 26 by bringing bats and balls into the schoolroom, never denied he was blessed, indeed, to be able to make a living from something "I'd rather do than anything else—play ball," but make a good living

Wee Willie Keeler's skills were fading by the time he joined the Highlanders, but he still "hit 'em where they ain't," to coin his famous phrase. *Bain News Service, courtesy of the Library of Congress*

he would, monetizing his skills and building his brand all the while.

"We can count on our fingers the number of years we will be able to play," Keeler was quoted in the *New York Clipper* in the spring of 1898, when he was in a dispute in Baltimore. "At the end of that short period our ability to earn money as ballplayers is ended, how do we find ourselves? Why, we have spent the best year of our lives on the diamond, those years usually employed by young men in acquiring commercial and professional knowledge that will prove lucrative to them for many times the period usually allotted a ballplayer. That makes it plain that we must make all the money we can during the short period we may be said to be star players."

And that's just what Willie Keeler was doing when, in the darkness, something went suddenly wrong on that November night as the horses pulled the surrey about 15 miles outside Sacramento. The carriage had drifted left and the wheels ran off the road, down an embankment. The vehicle rolled over, and big Jake Beckley, 100 pounds heavier, landed on top of Keeler, who wrenched his shoulder. The next day, Dr. Coffey, chief of surgeons at the Southern Pacific Railway in San Francisco, popped the dislocated collarbone back in place and said there was a fracture. Keeler's throwing arm, his self-proclaimed "money-making arm," was in a sling, and he sat out the rest of the trip, then made his way back home. His deal with the AL guaranteed his salary in case of injury, but he worried that his career might be over.

Reports of the seriousness of Keeler's injury varied wildly, and word of his deal to jump from Brooklyn to the American League had preceded him home. He exchanged letters with manager Ned Hanlon, who asked Keeler not to sign anything until they had a chance to speak again.

When Keeler got back home to Pulaski Street on January 3, he had added some pounds to his 5-foot-4 frame, and reporter Abe Yager, who covered the Superbas with intrepidity, arrived at the front door to ask if it was true, did he sign with the AL? In fact, both leagues had released rosters, and Keeler's name appeared on both.

"Sure," Keeler told him. "The people here can't give me the money the American League has promised me, I signed with them when I was in Chicago a couple of months ago. I've only got a few years longer to play ball and the money they offered me was enough for me to leave Brooklyn."

If Hanlon and owner Charles Ebbets could prove he was contractually bound for 1903, as they claimed, he would stay. What about the sentiment of the Brooklyn fans, Keeler was asked, many of whom had contributed to a fund to pay Keeler more money than the team could afford to stay in Brooklyn in 1901? In Keeler's mind, he had been playing at a hometown discount for a couple of years, but with the AL coming to New York, that would no longer be necessary.

"Sentiment don't go when the coin is to be considered," he said, "and I am telling you that I am getting a salary for two years that nobody could touch. Sentiment? Who remembers a ball player after he is through with the game? Charlie Ox, maybe, or somebody with long whiskers. I'm a philosopher, I am, and believe in the good old coin, as doled out by Uncle Sam."

Well, at least he didn't say, as so many future free agents, "it's not about the money." Keeler was honest to the bone, and the New York American League franchise had its first big star, its first certified *legend*, for "Wee Willie" Keeler's permanent place in baseball history was etched a couple of years earlier.

Brooklyn's game against the Giants at the Polo Grounds on August 6, 1901, was rained out, and Yager came down to chat with some of the ballplayers, who were needling one another about the pennant race and the batting race. Keeler began chortling about the fan letters he'd been receiving lately. "I'll have to hire a secretary if this keeps up," he said.

Then he pulled a piece of paper and unfolded it—a letter from Littleton, North Carolina, to "Mr. William Keeler," which Yager was allowed to peruse and reprint:

> *Dear Sir; Have you any treatise on the art of batting written by yourself? If so, please inform me where I can obtain such and the price thereof. I enclose stamp for reply. I have always considered you the best hitter in the country and from your work this year I am satisfied that you are. Hence, wishing to become a batter myself, you can readily see why I wish to obtain information from the country's best batter.*

Keeler put down the letter, looked at Yager, and said, "Wouldn't that make you chesty? I have already written that treatise and it reads like this: *Keep your eye clear and hit 'em where they ain't.*"

Has the science of hitting ever been stated more succinctly? One of the most famous quotes in baseball history ran near the end of Yager's rainy day column in the *Brooklyn Eagle* the next day. Three weeks later, Henry Chadwick, 77, who had invented the box score, batting average, and ERA and liked to consider himself "the father of baseball," was so moved as to write a long letter to the editor of the *Eagle*, gushing over Keeler's "treatise," which would one day be the top line of his plaque in Cooperstown.

"Now, here is a small volume on batting given in a few fitting words. Brief and to the point," Chadwick wrote, "this advice of Keeler, to 'hit 'em where they ain't' is never, or hardly ever taken by the chance batsman known as 'sluggers,' fellows who go in for homers and are practically ignorant of the true science of batting."

By then, the science that Keeler applied to baseball had broken records, winning the admiration of fans and the respect of his peers for a decade.

"Keeler could bunt any time he chose," Honus Wagner recalled. "If the third baseman came in for a tap, he invariably pushed the ball past the fielder. If he stayed back, he bunted. Also, he had a trick of hitting a high hopper to an infielder. The ball would bounce so high that he was across the bag before he could be stopped."

William Henry O'Kelleher was born on a snowy March day in 1872, the third and smallest of three brothers. His parents, Pat and Mary, had come over from Ireland with nothing a dozen years earlier, met in Brooklyn, and married. Willie's father dropped the *O* from O'Kelleher and worked on the DeKalb Ave. trolley line, first horse-drawn, and later as a switchman when the rails were in. They scrimped and saved and bought the house on Pulaski Street and some land to raise cows and goats on the other side of the borough.

Though Willie was tiny, he could thrash his brothers in front-yard boxing matches. His father put a baseball bat in his hand as a toddler, and later he would spend all day on the sandlots. But as the boys grew older, Pat expected them to work. Willie dropped out of school as a teenager and began working at various jobs, but making as much money to play for their industrial league teams.

His mind was always on baseball, and one day he left a job at a cheese factory to play for a semipro team on Staten Island, and that was it. His father was hip enough to know that money could be made in baseball, too, and was satisfied when a team in Plainfield, New Jersey, began paying Willie $60 a month in

1891. They preferred "Keeler" to Kelleher, and Willie went with that.

Willie Keeler choked up on a thick, 30-inch bat, nearly halfway up, and almost never swung and missed.

"About the first time a boy picks up a bat he acquired a style of batting," Keeler wrote, in a syndicated column in 1901, "and he'd hold it for the remainder of his life. You can't change a man's style and make him successful."

Keeler made it to the full professional ranks, signing with Binghamton for $90 a month in 1892 and leading the Eastern League in hitting. The Giants bought him, and he debuted at the Polo Grounds on September 30 with an infield single and two stolen bases. Oddly enough, he was playing third base and shortstop as a left-handed thrower, and it wasn't working out.

The next season, he fractured his leg sliding into third base and missed two months. When he returned, he was shipped to Brooklyn, to play before his hometown fans. But teams bunted on him relentlessly when he took the field, and he was sent back to Binghamton.

But during that season, Hanlon, managing the Baltimore Orioles, had seen enough to be convinced Keeler was perfect for the style of play he was creating. He acquired Keeler in a trade for 1894, and made him his right fielder, and leadoff hitter—perhaps the game's first great offensive catalyst.

Foxy Ned's Baltimore Orioles reinvented the game. The groundskeeper kept the patch in front of him plate-hard, for the chop-and-run. Once on base, Keeler would usually take off again, and John McGraw perfected the art of stroking the ball through the vacated spots on the infield. The team included Hughie Jennings and Wilbert Robinson, who, like McGraw, became successful managers in the 20th century, and Joe Kelly. Fifty years later, major leagues were still referring admiringly to a hard-nosed player as "an old Oriole," a reference to that team.

The team was known for brawling, but Keeler was more known for joking and laughing. But when there was a fight, they found, as his older brothers had, that "Wee Willie," just 5-foot-4 and 140 pounds, could hold his own. The Orioles finished first in the NL in 1894 but lost the Temple Cup series, forerunner of the World Series, to the second-place Giants. They won the Cup in 1896 and '97, after which the series was discontinued.

Over five seasons, from 1894 to 1898, Keeler hit .388. At his peak, he hit safely in 45 consecutive games, the last game of 1896 and the first 44 of 1897, a record that lasted until Joe DiMaggio shattered it in 1941. Keeler finished the '97 season with a .424 average and went on to get 200 or more hits in eight consecutive seasons, a mark matched a century later by Ichiro Suzuki, probably the closest resemblance to Keeler in modern times.

"He was really something," Sam Crawford, one of the great sluggers of the time, told writer Lawrence Ritter. "He choked up on the bat so far he only used about half of it, and then he'd just peck at the ball. Just a little snap swing, and he'd punch the ball all over the infield, and you couldn't strike him out. He'd always hit the ball somewhere."

Common sense suggests that Keeler's style could not have endured if he did not have enough power to keep teams from bringing the outfielders up behind the infield. Keeler could line the ball between, or over, drawn-up outfielders—he had 54 extra-base hits in 1894, and enough doubles, triples, and inside-the-park homers to keep them honest.

In those eight 200-hit seasons, Keeler had more than 600 at-bats each time and struck out only 5.8 times per season—only twice in 633 at bats in 1899. By then, the Orioles had broken up and Hanlon moved to Brooklyn, reassembling most of the club, including Keeler, there with the "Superbas," who finished first in 1899 and 1900, third in 1901, and second in 1902.

Keeler was playing before adoring fans at Washington Park, along the Gowanus Canal, an easy trolley ride up from Pulaski Street via the DeKalb line. When the American League began calling—perhaps for a return to Baltimore—Keeler favored the appeal of playing in Brooklyn. Still, when he asked for $4,000 for 1901, it took a community effort to pay him. Fifty fans raised about $1,000 of that money to help owner Charlie Ebbets keep Keeler in Brooklyn, though it bothered Keeler to be playing for a hometown discount.

In 1901, the Harvard baseball captain wrote Keeler to ask how much he would want to come and coach the hitters before spring training, as Cy Young would come and work with the pitchers. A new revenue stream was opened. For a kid who never cared much for school, Keeler proved to be an adept teacher, businessman, and, eventually, investor.

Then Keeler, the catalyst and capitalist, made the last big move of his career. After confirming to Yager that he had, indeed, signed with the AL to play wherever their ballpark would rise in 1903, he went to St. Mary's Hospital for another look at that shoulder. The X-rays showed no fracture, and Dr. Charles Wuerst told him he would be good as new by April.

"This is the greatest load ever lifted off my mind," Keeler said, "I got the impression it was all up with Willie as a ballplayer and I hadn't enough experience yet to pose as a bench manager.

I'll start practicing for the work of annexing my signature to fat checks on the first and fifteen of the month. Incidentally, too, I'll play some considerable baseball. Where? In New York, unless Hanlon can show me I had a two years' contract."

The owner of the Superbas, Charles Ebbets, had insisted all along he had a "unique" contract with Keeler that covered 1902 and '03 and probably had a case. But when NL owners voted to make peace in Cincinnati later that month, to get the raiding of players to end, Ebbets was persuaded to relent and allow the American League to keep Willie Keeler as part of the deal.

"I'll not cut loose until the middle of May," he told the *Eagle*, "in order to make sure my wing is OK. I hope to be there with the goods when it comes to the first quarter of the race."

It was not to be—he would never be quite the same player. Farrell and Devery would be paying Keeler $10,000 a year for what he had already done. He played tentatively on the hazardous field at Hilltop Park in 1903, and he hit .313, with 160 hits, 14 for extra bases. It was not Brooklyn, either. The 15-mile trip from Pulaski Street, over one of the bridges and nearly the full length of Manhattan Island took at least an hour, by carriage or trolley, and more when he took those "inconspicuous" roads.

But he would play more seasons, seven, with the Highlanders than anywhere else. He had a more Keeler-like season in 1904, hitting .343, with 186 hits in 143 games, as the Highlanders fought for the pennant to the final day of the season, but he never hit better than .304 again as age and injuries slowed him down.

After leaving the Highlanders, Willie was a pinch-hitter and coach for McGraw's Giants in 1910 and eventually became a coach and scout, mainly for Brooklyn. His golden touch faded;

he fell on hard times, investments went bad, and his health failed. A lifelong bachelor, he had to sell the house on Pulaski Street and take a room in Clara Moss's rooming house nearby. They became close, and Keeler willed her what was left of his fortune when he died, after long battles with tuberculosis and heart disease in 1922. He was only 50 years old and thus didn't live to wave at an Old Timer's Day and didn't wear a number to be retired. When he took his rightful place in the Hall of Fame, he was not around to enjoy it, to hobnob with his contemporaries.

But Wee Willie Keeler's legend was made for all time on that rainy day he uttered the phrase, "hit 'em where they ain't." Whenever that legend is retold, however, his years with the Yankees are but a footnote.

CHAPTER 4

THE TITLE THAT SLIPPED AWAY

It went down like a dipper-duck and whacked [the catcher] on the toe. I was so excited, I almost shook. [He] must have thought I'd a-found a gold mine, the way I was acting.

—Jack Chesbro

The who, where, and how of baseball's creation has been argued by scholars for a century and a half, but what set it apart from all other sports was apparent from the beginning. It would be a team game, yet at its core, its very core, stands one man, holding the ball and the destiny of that team in his hands—and losing much of that control whenever the ball leaves his grip.

The heartache felt for that pitcher who leaves his heart and soul on the mound and "deserved a better fate" plays on the heartstrings of fans to this day, right up to Matt Harvey in the 2015 World Series, and no other sport has anything quite like that.

And for that man in the center, the pitcher, there remains the never-ending search for the secret pitch that makes him the best, giving the ball a life of its own as it hurtles toward the batter and all but eliminates random results. Hollywood conceived of it in 1949, the wood-repellant substance chemist Ray Milland invented in *It Happens Every Spring*.

But 45 years before the film, on a spring day in 1904, the Highlanders' Jack Chesbro believed he had found the magic elixir. Arriving in New Orleans to join the team as it prepared for its second season, he watched a young pitcher named Elmer Stricklett throw for the hometown Pelicans. Chesbro, then thirty, was primed for a big second season with New York, weighing 20 to 30 pounds lighter than the year before and in the best shape of his life after spending two months coaching and working out with the collegiate pitchers in "the cage" at Harvard.

Now, he watched as Sticklett's pitches squirted out of his hand and darted this way and that, seeming to change speed and course in midflight.

"He'd let it go when he had two strikes on a player," Chesbro recalled, for a syndicated newspaper series in 1924, "and they'd miss it by a bat length. Wee Willie Keeler, who, as you know, could hit, was completely puzzled. He came to the bench after missing one so badly it was laughable and says, 'never saw anything like that. The ball just comes right up to you and dives.' That's what it did. Well, sir, I began to watch him, watched him a long time."

And so launched the most interesting, dramatic, best-remembered, and, despite the painful finish, successful season the franchise would have before Babe Ruth's arrival, still 16 years away. This also helped launch the chain of events that would ignite the sport's most enduring rivalry, the Yankees and Red Sox, though both went by different names at that time.

Jack Chesbro had discovered a potion—the art of applying saliva, maybe with a little tobacco juice, on the baseball. Such a potion would lead him to set still-unreachable records and a trip to the Hall of Fame, albeit 15 years after he died, still lamenting the spitball that slipped away and took the 1904 championship away with it.

"Happy Jack" Chesbro carried the regrets of his 1904 wild pitch for the rest of his days, but his larger error was insisting on pitching too much. *Bain News Service, courtesy of the Library of Congress*

No pitcher ever poured out more blood, sweat, and, finally, tears for his team than Chesbro did that year. Perhaps the passage of 11 decades should offer this much in the way of perspective: To simply say the 1904 Highlanders lost the American League pennant on Chesbro's wild pitch is wildly unfair. The pitch allowed the deciding run to score in the deciding game, but as things played out, there would be plenty of blame to go around, from the owners on down to the fielders, and Chesbro's greater error was demanding to pitch, running his right arm ragged in the final days of the season, until such a meltdown was inevitable.

But there is no denying that 1904 was The Season of Jack Chesbro, the good, the bad, and the slippery.

Chesbro had ventured from his family farm in North Adams, Massachusetts, in the Berkshires, to make his way as a ballplayer and by 1899 arrived in the National League with the Pirates. Through his natural conviviality, he earned the sobriquet "Happy Jack." Young, burly for the time at 5-foot-9 and close to 200 pounds, and powerful, he peaked at 28–6 for the remarkable Pittsburgh team of 1902, then jumped with six others to New York and the American League, getting a $1,000 bonus. In 1903, he was 21–15, starting 40 games, completing 36, and throwing 324 innings, about 40 more than ever before. He had been steady and solid, but, as of April 1904, unspectacular.

Stricklett, a youngster from Kansas by way of the University of Santa Clara, had picked up on the spitter during his minor league journey and was chatty when it came to the pitch, believing that while he didn't invent it, he had perfected it and was the first to feature it. He was on his way to the majors and would debut with the White Sox in 1904. It was by chance that he was in New Orleans that April.

Chesbro saw enough to tell himself, "this, you must learn," and tried it.

"I got the juice on it and let the ball go with lots of speed," he said. "The catcher put his glove where he thought it was coming. But it didn't, no sir. It went down like a dipper duck and whacked him on the toe. That was enough for me. I was so excited, I almost shook. The catcher, Jack Kleinow, must've thought I'd a-found a gold mine, the way I was acting."

The Highlanders, as they approached the opening game at American League Park (or Hilltop Park, as it was more commonly known at that point), were already full of exuberance. Their ballpark had fixed the problems that marred the play and fan experience in 1903, filling in that swampy ravine in right field, closing up the grandstand, and adding a fresh paint job. Keeler and center fielder Dave Fultz had the speed to cover the vast and now-smooth outfield. The roster had also been retooled. Griffith acquired a promising rookie catcher in Jack "Red" Kleinow, who would split time behind the plate with forty-year-old Deacon McGuire and pitchers Tom Hughes (from Boston) and Jack Powell (from St. Louis). Best of all, he would have a swift, solid infield with Kid Elberfeld at shortstop from day one. Outfielder John Anderson had come aboard, too, via a trade with the St. Louis Browns.

"Keep your eye on the New York American team this season," Professor Willie Keeler, who would hit .343 in a bounce-back season, had told reporters at Harvard, the day he and Chesbro arrived to coach on February 16. "It took some while for us to get to going last season, but this year the men know each other better and we will be ready for all comers and when the league starts playing. Frank Farrell is a brick. He wants a pennant-winning team, and Clark Griffith will not be hampered in getting such an aggregation together. We have the players and there is no reason we won't make a strong bid for the pennant."

Professor Chesbro, replacing Cy Young at Harvard, concurred in that analysis, with one caveat. "The hardest team we will have to beat out is Boston," he said. "If we can dispose of them, we will win the championship."

The defending champion Boston Pilgrims had given the American League the ultimate credibility, beating the Pirates in the first World Series. At Johnson's urging, they traded Long Tom Hughes to New York for Jesse Tannehill, who had been a Highlanders disappointment in '03.

The flags, the bunting, and the military band were all back for the second Opening Day on April 14. Chesbro, "he of the cotton top and the Harvard sweater," according to the *Evening World*, warmed up to face Boston's Cy Young. The Highlanders knocked the great one all over the yard and won, 8–2. On April 22, Chesbro nearly no-hit the Senators, settling for a one-hitter and a 2–0 victory.

For now, Chesbro was relying on his fastball and curve, for Kleinow was still learning how to handle the spitter, and they kept it quiet. He was on a seven-game winning streak when the Highlanders arrived in Cleveland for a game on June 9 and gave up two runs in the first inning. "I went to Clark Griffith and I told him I had a new ball," Chesbro said. "It was all right with him. . . . They simply couldn't touch it."

Cleveland, Nap Lajoie or not, managed only one hit over the final eight innings, including eight strikeouts, and the

Highlanders rallied to win, 3–2. Every team in the league had seen him once—the old Jack Chesbro. Now, the league faced something entirely different.

"The spitball is the most remarkable discovery made within the last decade," Griffith said, holding court during a photo shoot in the city. "This new addition in the pitching art has come to stay, and when it is gotten under control by pitchers other than Jack Chesbro, I believe it will be the downfall of several of the game's greatest hitters. While we all use the spitball occasionally, Jack Chesbro is the only man who has thoroughly mastered it."

By midsummer, the city's sports cartoonists were showing how much excitement Chesbro was creating with his "shoot" ball, or "corkscrew curve." On July 1, a cartoon in the New York *Evening World* showed Chesbro, who was going for his 13th consecutive win that afternoon, leaping over the No. 13. "Happy Jack expects to hurdle that unlucky number today."

He did, and then made it 14 with a 9–3 win at Philadelphia on July 4. Everyone wanted in on the secret, and Chesbro, relishing the role of ballplayer-as-scientist, happily explained. It was all in the thumb, he would say. The ball left the hand as if squirted like a watermelon seed and was guided by the thumb, not the first and second fingers.

"You moisten the first and second fingers of the pitching hand," professor Happy Jack said, "allowing the fingers to rest but slightly on the surface of the ball, which is held in a fairly firm clasp between the thumb and third finger doubled into the hand. The grasp, except for the fact the ball is not clasped firmly by the first and second fingers, is the same as used for throwing a fastball. The style of delivery is the same, too. But as the ball simply slides over the moistened fingers, instead of being guided by them, the ball does not revolve as it goes toward the batsman. On the contrary, it is about as motionless as a slow ball. There is no twirling motion to it. The ball is likely to take any kind of shoot when it reaches the batsman. I have seen a spitball drop off a foot and a half, making the batsman who struck at it look ridiculous."

Other Highlanders pitchers were beginning to throw it, including Al Orth, acquired from Washington for the disappointing Hughes in midseason. On June 17, more help arrived. Patsy Dougherty—a hero of Boston's victory over the Pirates in the first World Series, having hit two home runs in one game—was suddenly traded to New York for the unheralded Bob Unglaub and, perhaps, cash considerations.

They went crazy in Boston, and it was widely believed that this was Ban Johnson's latest intervention to prop up his pet New York project, with the Giants leading the National League race. In the AL, Boston was first, Chicago 3 ½ games back, and the Highlanders four back. Why in the world would Boston make such a trade?

Dougherty, who hit .342 in 1902 and .331 in '03, had a bitter salary dispute with ownership that strained relations, spilling over to his relationship with manager Jimmy Collins. He had contracted malaria, too, and his averaged dropped to .272, his play listless.

"It was not sentiment," Collins told a banquet audience in Buffalo after the season, "it was not friendship, it was not animosity. It was a pure business deal. New York wanted him, I wanted to sell him, and I did. And there you are."

New York was beset by injuries and badly needed a speedy outfielder, having had to send a pitcher out to the field on some occasions that June. Even at half speed, Dougherty would plug the hole, hitting .283, but would fail when his big moment came.

"Keep an eye on the Invaders," Griffith said, after a series in Boston in May, "we took two of three from the world champions and can do it again."

The furor over the trade subsided and the race resumed. Chesbro shut out the Senators again on June 21 to start New York off on a six-game winning streak that extended to 12 wins in 14 games—including two of three at Boston, making good on the manager's boast—to run the record to 40–23, just 1 ½ games behind. Then the champs arrived on the Hilltop July 7, stopped Chesbro's winning streak, and showed they were still the team to beat. Boston won three in a row, with the Highlanders salvaging the last game.

More controversy came when the Highlanders signed Harvard pitcher Walter Clarkson, who debuted July 2. It was supposed, with good reason, that Chesbro and Keeler were involved in recruiting him.

But Clarkson did not help much, throwing just over 66 innings, his ERA 5.02 by the end of the season. Nor could Griffith, whose own pitching skills were sunsetting, find enough pitchers to fill out anything resembling a "rotation" behind Chesbro and Powell, who would win 23. Orth was 11–6 with a 2.68 ERA after he arrived. They took flyers on Ned Garvin, a once-solid vet cut by Brooklyn despite a 1.68 ERA, who was battling the bottle, and a kid named Ambrose Puttman. Garvin made two ineffective starts, the last of his major league career on September 16, while Puttman won a couple of games late.

Throughout the summer, New York, Chicago, and Boston grappled. Chesbro took just two, maybe three days between starts, but sometimes only one day. As he continued to pile up wins, starts, and innings, the other pitchers held their own, winning a little more often than they lost.

On August 5, the Highlanders won in Cleveland behind Jack Powell to move 20 games over .500 and into first place for the first time in the franchise's two-year history. Five teams were within six games of first place at that point. The Yankees, as some newspapers were beginning to call them, and Boston Pilgrims would now separate themselves from the pack. In September, first place changed hands five times.

After Chesbro won his 40th game, a shutout in St. Louis on October 4, and Powell won the next day, his 23rd win, the Highlanders (90–56) were still a half-game out. The championship would be decided in the five-game series with Boston to finish the season. Meanwhile, Farrell, looking to make a buck wherever he could, had agreed to rent the ballpark on Saturday, the 8th, to Columbia for its big football game with Williams, never dreaming that, or perhaps not caring if, it might impact the pennant chase.

It was a blunder as big as anything that would happen on the field. Boston agreed to host the Saturday doubleheader but, pressing its advantage, would not agree to a last-minute proposal to play two in New York on Friday and one in Boston on Saturday. The Highlanders boarded their train for the 24-hour trip home from St. Louis, knowing when they detrained, they would have to play the Pilgrims on Friday afternoon, October

7, then travel overnight to Boston, a ferocious place for a visiting team in a big game, to play two Saturday. With no baseball allowed on Sundays then, the season would conclude with another doubleheader, back in New York, on Monday, October 10. The winner of three of the five would be the AL champs for 1904, and although the Giants' John McGraw and John T. Brush, still angry with Johnson and the concept of a competitor in Manhattan, said they would not play any such "World Series," there was no guarantee they could resist the public pressure and potential profits of an all-New York series.

The Highlanders were front-page news now and the air was electric, as Collins and the Bostons, with a contingent of "Royal Rooters" (the legendary flock of Boston fans that drove opponents to distraction), returned to begin the series. Chesbro faced Norwood Gibson, who had ended the 14-game winning streak three months earlier, and was both brilliant and gritty. As was becoming the norm, Chesbro had to pitch around mistakes made behind him, and he was tiring at the end. But he got the last out, won, 3–2, and vaulted the Highlanders back into first place. Chesbro now had the never-to-be-equaled 41 wins, and though he tried to stop them, delirious Highlanders fans—there now was such a thing, with attendance more than doubling from 212,000 to 439,000 in year two—hoisted him on their shoulders and carried him to the clubhouse.

"There's nothing like taking the starter," Griffith chortled, "we've got Boston on the run."

What happened next? Several accounts have survived, but a long, syndicated Sunday story that appeared in mid-December 1904 in the *Salt Lake City Tribune*, attributing Griffith and that, incidentally, may have been one of the first articles to refer to the team as "the Yankees" throughout, spelled out the drama in great detail.

In the postgame euphoria, Griffith pulled Chesbro aside and said, "You stay in New York, Jack, and be trim to win for us on Monday. We'll be sure to take one game tomorrow, and then we only need one more. You can win that for us on Monday."

Chesbro was incredulous: "You don't mean that, Griff, do you?"

Griffith: "Of course, I do. We can get along all right, and the journey might have a bad effect on you. I want you at your best on Monday . . ."

The questions that come to mind: Why would Griffith, who had relied so heavily on Chesbro, now take the cautious step of leaving him home? Even if he was not planning to start him in the doubleheader, it would not have been out of the ordinary in those times to use him in relief, as he had four previous times between starts. And what made Griffith so confident, the way the other pitchers had been performing, he could split without Chesbro?

Chesbro dressed and left the clubhouse without saying another word. But when the Highlanders met at Grand Central to board their 11 p.m. sleeper to Boston, Chesbro was there with his suitcases.

"Hell, Jack, what are you doing here? I thought you'd be in bed," Griffith said.

Chesbro: "I'm going to Boston. "You can't leave me behind. Besides, I'm as much interested in these games as you are. You might need me."

Griffith relented and bought Chesbro a ticket but assured him it would be Powell and the kid, Puttman, pitching on Saturday. The team arrived in Boston and breakfasted at the hotel, then retired to private rooms. Soon Griffith heard a knock on his door.

"I've come to tell you, Griff, that I've decided to pitch the first game today," Jack Chesbro announced.

Griffith: "Chase yourself, Jack. There's nothing doing. 'Powell and Puttman' is my program, and that's all there is to it."

Chesbro walked back to the door and said, "I'll pitch and I'll win. I never felt better in my life," and departed.

When players arrived at the Huntington Avenue Grounds, things got crazier. There was to be an overflow crowd of 30,000, most standing in roped-off areas on the field. Chesbro was met by 150 fans from East Douglas, Massachusetts, who presented him with diamond cufflinks and had come hoping to see him pitch. Chesbro went to warm up.

In the dugout, Farrell and Griffith were chatting when they saw the familiar figure of Chesbro throwing out in the outfield. "What's Chesbro doing out there?" Farrell asked. Griffith replied, "He thinks he's pitching, but he's mistaken."

The ace of the staff knew he had an ace to play. When he saw the key players gathered near the dugout, Chesbro stopped throwing and jogged in. "I'll pitch the first game, Griff, and I'll land it. You know I never asked you to let me go in and then lost for you. Come watch me warm up. I've got everything today and I feel like a winner."

That was all Keeler, Elberfeld, Wid Conroy, and Jimmy Williams—and the owner—needed to hear. The big man wanted the ball? What was the question? They let the manager know who they wanted on the mound.

Griffith told Chesbro to warm up, and the manager took a position behind Kleinow, who by now was trusted with nearly all the catching. "He had everything, all right," Griffith said. "His speed was wonderful, his control superb and his ball broke wherever he wanted it to break. I went back to the bench and talked with Farrell and finally agreed to let Chesbro pitch."

When the game began, Chesbro shut Boston down the first three innings and took a 1–0 lead into the fourth, then all fell apart. Williams tried, ill-advisedly, to get an out at home and the Red Sox scored, with the chance for more. Chesbro then allowed 5 hits in a row and was knocked out of the game. Boston scored six in the inning and went on to win, 13–2.

In Game Two, Powell pitched great, but Cy Young outdueled him, 1–0. The game was called due to darkness after seven innings, robbing the Highlanders of their last two licks. The Highlanders, having used their two best pitchers Saturday, now needed to win two on Monday.

"I'll trim 'em for you Monday, Griff," Chesbro said, sullenly, as they shared a carriage back to the station for yet another overnight train ride. "I'll trim 'em for you if it costs an arm."

The Boston fans were a disruptive force, and thousands of them boarded the train with the team and arrived in New York to annoy anyone in sight, usually by singing their theme song, "Tessie," a barbershop quartet kind of number that had about as much to do with baseball as "Sweet Caroline" does but was bellowed from the grandstand until opponents never wanted to hear a note of it again. The Royal Rooters had megaphones and cowbells, as well as Dockstader's Band (a local brass band). They were led by pol and barkeep Michael "Nuff Said" McGreevy, who frequently ended debates with that phrase.

And they marched two blocks from their hotel to Hilltop Park, settling in a block in the left field grandstand to claim the climactic game of the season, on October 10, regardless of the turf.

Boston fans, though, for much of the day were drowned out by the crowd, as more than 28,000, twice the seating capacity, overwhelmed the little ballpark.

Chesbro warmed up again and took the mound. It was his 51st start and 55th appearance of the season, his team's 150th game. After 445 innings, twice what the most durable pitcher of today would be asked to work, could he have nine more great ones left? Was he as sure of himself as he was two days earlier? Or had the potion stopped working when Jack Chesbro needed it most? The answers would be yes, no, and apparently.

Still scoreless when Chesbro came to bat in the fifth, the game was stopped. More Happy Jack fans, now from his native North Adams, stormed the field and presented him with a fur coat. When they were cleared, Chesbro, who had tripled earlier, now singled, and the Highlanders scored two runs off Bill Dineen, on singles by Dougherty and Elberfeld, but left the bases loaded.

In the seventh, Chesbro, with a one-hitter going, suffered as his second baseman, Williams again, muffed a slow grounder and then, with a chance to redeem, threw wildly when he had a runner dead at home. Boston was given the tying runs, and the last was drained from Jack's tank. In the eighth, he was hit hard, but Elberfeld threw a runner out at the plate to preserve the tie.

Now, Chesbro was straight with his skipper and told him he was finished. Griffith sounded out young Kleinow, who told him it was "50-50," Chesbro was clearly gassed but could baffle them one more inning, the catcher suggested.

Lou Criger reached on an error by Elberfeld. Dineen sacrificed and Kip Seelbach grounded out. With the go-ahead run on third and two out, Chesbro threw two quick strikes to Freddy Parent, then wet his fingers for the most important of the thousands of pitches he threw that year.

"I don't know whether I got a hunch," Elberfeld told the *Sporting News* in 1942, "but after he got those two strikes, I ran to him and said, 'Be careful, Jack, with this one. Don't let it get away.' He laughed and replied, 'Don't worry Kid, I'll take care of it.'"

The spitter left his hand and soared, sailed, over Parent and Kleinow and clear to the backstop, 75 feet behind home plate. Criger scored. When Chesbro finished the inning (not before Parent, history has forgotten, got yet another infield hit that could have scored the run anyway), he went back to the bench, and, witnesses, notably sportswriter Mark Roth, swore for years, put his head down and just sobbed. Griffith had fallen to his knees as the run scored, burying his head in his hands.

The Highlanders drew two walks in the ninth, but with the tying and winning runs on, Dineen struck out Dougherty to virtually end the season. Puttman won the meaningless second game, and New York finished 92–59.

Chesbro finished the season 41–12, with a 1.82 ERA through all those 454 2/3 innings. The wins, the 51 starts, and the 48 complete games are records never to be approached. Not until Whitey Ford in 1961 would another Yankees pitcher win 14 in a row, and not until Ron Guidry in 1978 would Chesbro's club mark of 239 strikeouts be exceeded.

"Well, no, it wasn't a wild pitch," Chesbro said, years later, "if I must be pinned down. I don't want to appear as trying to put the blame elsewhere, but I am speaking from my conviction. Kleinow, I thought, should have got the ball. It wasn't one he couldn't reach."

When asked, Elberfeld and Ganzel sided with the catcher in this meaningless debate. "That's silly," Elberfeld told the *Sporting News*, "that ball went so far over Jack's head, he couldn't have reached it with a crab net." Griffith, who remained close to Chesbro, agreed it was a passed ball, though newspaper accounts of the day had the pitch flying several feet above the batter's head. At the time, Chesbro blamed himself for trying to throw the pitch too hard, rather than applying too much lubricant.

He could have blamed the catcher who didn't reach high enough, or the fielders who failed him so often (40 of the 140 runs scored against Chesbro in 1904 were unearned). The owners' foolish decision to rent the ballpark out and force the team to play in Boston, the manager's reluctance to protect Chesbro from himself and stick to his "program," and Chesbro's own hard-headedness in insisting to pitch back-to-back days were all part of the heartbreak of October 10, 1904.

Never again would Chesbro be in as good a shape, or throw with the same power or effectiveness. He remained with the Highlanders until 1909, then after one game with Boston he was done, with a total of 198 wins, 132 losses, and a 2.68 ERA. He tried repeatedly to leave the chicken farm and lumber business he had in Conway, north of Springfield, Massachusetts, and get back in the game. He even had a few tryouts in 1912, pitched semipro ball into his 50s, and coached here and there, including a couple of months in Washington, 1924 (the year the Senators, now owned by Griffith, won the World Series). The spitball, by then, had been made illegal, with only a handful of pitchers grandfathered in to throw it; the last was Burleigh Grimes in 1934.

On November 6, 1931, Chesbro walked up to the top of a hill on his poultry farm and died of a heart attack. The headline, in part, in the *New York Times*: "Jack Chesbro Dies . . . Veteran, whose wild throw once cost The New York Americans Pennant, Expires at 56." His devoted wife, Mabel, lobbied until her death in 1940 that it was a passed ball. No vindication was necessary once the Old-Timers Committee voted Chesbro into the Hall of Fame in 1946.

But Chesbro had left his heart and soul back on that other hilltop in 1904, and he deserved a better fate. Two months after the pitch, a sportswriter from the *Boston Post*, Frederic P. O'Connell, rode out to Conway to interview no-longer-Happy Jack on his farm.

"I have thought it over and over," Chesbro told him, "I don't think I will ever forget it. In all of New York, I don't believe there was a more sorrowful individual. I would have given my entire year's salary back, but could I have had the ball back."

CHAPTER 5

THE PRINCE'S LAST STAND

Fielding? Are you kidding me? Prince Hal is the greatest first baseman who ever played. He was worth the price of admission just to watch him toe-dance around first base and pick those wild throws out of the dirt.

—Babe Ruth

A very pretty lady, a secretary in the Colusa Memorial Hospital's office in California, arrived to pay her daily visit. She cut the courses of his lunch for him to eat, and Hal Chase flashed that smile—that old, charming, lady's man smile that used to bring so many women to the ballpark that the sportswriters groused that they couldn't see over all the hats.

A photographer at the foot of the hospital bed popped the picture. Off to one side was Jessie Topham, his adoring sister, armed with newspaper clippings she claimed exculpated Hal Chase, that he was made a scapegoat. On the other side, taking notes, was J.W. Sehorn, longtime sportswriter and now managing editor of the local paper, the Woodland *Daily Democrat*.

It was April of 1947, and Chase's baseball career was three decades past. Though fans and aged scribes never forgot "Prince Hal," the game wanted nothing to do with him now. The gambling, the heavy drinking, the wrecked marriages and reputation, the estranged son, who had recently sent a telegram, were all weighing Hal Chase down now. And he had long ago run out of time to fix any of it.

The Prince was dying.

"I would give anything if I could start in all over again," Chase said. "What a change there would be in the life of Hal Chase . . ."

Hal Chase died lamenting that he "didn't have a good name," but his reputation as a spectacular fielder outlived him. *Bain News Service, courtesy of the Library of Congress*

For Chase, starting in all over again, and on the right foot, would've taken him back to March 1905, the day Clark Griffith and the Highlanders grouped to begin training in Montgomery, Alabama.

Chase? . . . Chase? . . . Where was the new first baseman?

John Ganzel had given back $3,000 in salary to gain his release, so that he could return home and play for a minor league team in Grand Rapids. Griffith "drafted" Chase for $2,700, the protocol of the time. But Chase and Jim Morley, the owner of the Los Angeles minor league team, believed there was war with the major leagues and announced Chase would stay—which meant that one, or both, really wanted more money. Chase, too, was dealing with the death of his brother in January, from a ruptured appendix, and had grown lukewarm about moving across the country.

Ban Johnson got involved in the dispute, and after 10 days, Frank Farrell received word that the rookie was on his way. The team sent train fare to New Orleans, but Chase was not there when the team arrived, and on March 22, Clark Griffith blew a gasket.

"Chase got our advance money and now it is the New York Americans or nothing for him," Griffith told reporters. "This nonsense has gone far enough and I'm tired of it, through and through. If Chase plays with Los Angeles, it shall be under open war conditions."

Of course, the AL had the bigger war chest, Griffith noted. Eventually, Chase relented and joined the Highlanders in Jackson, Mississippi, on the 28th. At the start of April, the Highlanders moved on to Atlanta, and by then Griffith had seen enough to be convinced Chase was worth the trouble.

"I certainly like the looks of my new man, Chase," Griff told the *Atlanta Journal* when the Highlanders arrived there on April 2. "He looks more like a comer than any man coming out of the minor leagues the last few years. He fields nicely, gets around the bases in a hurry, comes in on a bunt, is able to hit, and plays like a player born. That's the kind of man I want on my team."

Chase had just turned twenty-two. Writing about the Highlanders was another young phenom, the *Journal*'s twenty-five-year-old Grantland Rice, who wrote of that spring 37 years later, "one of the first plays he made proved his place. There was a runner on second with no one out, the next man bunted toward first. In place of taking the throw, Chase was on top of the ball in a flash for the out at third. And it wasn't a fast bunt."

The baseball scribes of 1905 had never seen a player like Hal Chase. The typical player was short and scrappy. Chase, sandy-haired and blue-eyed, was long, lean, and graceful. First base had been the position to hide a clumsy slugger; Chase, a left-handed thrower, changed the game by making one of its staple offensive weapons, the bunt, less effective. And he played the position with such panache. As the Highlanders worked their way north, the curiosity built.

"In the [exhibition] game at Jersey City Saturday, Chase was the most closely watched man on the team," wrote Bozeman Bulger in the *New York World*. "On his first putout, the ball was thrown very high, but with the runner nearly upon him he made a quick stab with his gloved hand, caught the ball, and cleverly ducked out of the way."

So began Hal Chase's eight stormy years with the Highlanders/Yankees. An Alex Rodriguez of his time, he embodied the best, and worst, of early-20th-century baseball; he gravitated toward controversy, and when he broke the rules, he seemed to want to be caught. A century after his final games, he remains an unfairly maligned figure to some, a reprehensible lout to others. He has inspired more than one book, and in many others it has been debated whether he was really as good a player, or really as corrupt, as he has been made out to be.

By the time Chase donned the Highlanders' new 1905 uniforms—all white at home, all gray on the road with a blue, interlocking *N-Y* on the left breast—on Opening Day, his reputation for controversy and stylishness had preceded him to the Big Apple. A century later, Derek Jeter would tell newcomers, "don't try to eat the whole Big Apple, just take a bite," advice that would have served Hal Chase well, if he wasn't already on his way to a Manhattan pool hall, or poker joint, where his "sleight-of-hand" was known to produce the right cards out of thin air.

Chase's first game was notable only because it was his first game, the 1905 season opener. Hitting seventh, he had a double in four at-bats and made six putouts without an error as the Highlanders won in Washington, 4–2. Chesbro threw a six-hitter, struck out seven, and conducted business in a tidy 1 hour, 35 minutes. If Chase's acrobatics could save throwing errors by the other infielders, who knows how good Happy Jack could be in 1905?

But the season soon turned disappointing. Keeler hit .302, and that was by far the best of any regular. Chase hit .249 with 22 steals. Neither Chesbro, who was 19–15 despite a 2.20 ERA in 303 innings, nor Powell, 8–13, 3.50, came anywhere near their 1904 production. Al Orth was 18–16. The team fell to sixth place, 71–78, attendance dropping to 309,000, also sixth in the American League. Now that the league and its eight teams were entrenched, Ban Johnson was content to let them stand, or fall, on their own acumen. With Farrell and Devery now on their own, the franchise was in for a rough decade.

Chase's second season was his breakthrough. He hit .323 in 1906, with 76 RBIs and 28 steals, and the Highlanders contended for the championship, to have everything fall apart in the final weeks. Chase made fast friends with the players in town, American and National Leaguers alike, including John McGraw and Christy Mathewson. He hobnobbed with the stars of vaudeville, like George M. Cohan.

It soon became fashionable to come up to the hilltop, with the subway now delivering fans nearly to the main entrance, just to see Chase work his magic at first base, fly in on a bunt so that he almost looked as if he intercepted the pitch, and hustle back to the bag just in time to catch the throw. The great writers of the day—Rice, Bulger, Damon Runyon, all of them—used some of their most elegant sentences to describe the way Hal Chase played first base.

He made errors at an alarming rate, but this was chalked up to the difficult plays he attempted, the hot-dogging of easy plays, and, in time, it would be wondered by more than one manager if he were making them on purpose.

"I know there is an errors column in the box score, so the errors must count in baseball," Chase said later in life. "But they never bothered me."

Very little did bother Chase, except the idea that baseball's hierarchy could dictate where he played, and when, and for how much money. He could get what he believed he deserved only by rebelling. The player, he believed, was the "exploited" party in the system.

He went home to California to play after the 1905 and 1906 seasons and threatened again to stay there in 1907 unless his salary was raised to $4,000. When the major leagues announced players could no longer play for the outlaw California League, Chase continued to play for San Jose under the name of "Schultz."

In 1908, the year Griffith was finally forced out by Farrell, Kid Elberfeld was named player-manager, which also made Chase angry. When he missed much of the summer with a sprained ankle, a story appeared in August that hinted the team believed he was not giving his best effort. On September 3, with the Highlanders having fallen deep into the AL basement, Chase announced he was quitting organized baseball. "I am not satisfied to play under a management that sees fit to give out a story detrimental to my character and honesty," he was quoted in papers across the country.

Chase signed with Stockton, precipitating a quarrel for his services even among two teams in an "outlaw league." Restless, he petitioned for reinstatement and signed with the Highlanders for $4,500 in 1909, and promptly came down with smallpox and was quarantined.

When, at last, he returned to the Highlanders on May 3, there was a great ceremony, and Chase was photographed grinning ear to ear as the teammates on whom he had quit the previous season presented him with a silver loving cup. Nothing Chase did, at this point in his life, was unforgivable.

Ty Cobb, who debuted with the Tigers in 1905 and got his first hit, a double, off Chesbro on August 30, was one of the many stars of the day who admired Chase's artistry. In a 1914 syndicated article, Cobb wrote of one battle of wits.

"If I reached first base, [Sam] Crawford, who followed me, was to bunt," Cobb explained, "Instead of stopping at second, the usual play, I was to whirl along to third. The first time we worked this play, it was successful. Hal Chase was caught napping. After the game, I looked around for a drink of water. 'Where's our cooler?', I asked the trainer. 'You'll have to go into the Yankees' coup,' he said.

"At the old American League grounds, the clubhouses were adjoined to each other. I walked into the Yankees' quarters and stopped at the cooler near the door. The New York players were hidden by a high row of lockers and I heard my name mentioned. Chase was talking.

"'Cobb made us look like chumps today on that bunt play,' he said. 'Tomorrow, we'll get him. You stick to third base and I'll play the ball there without paying any attention to the batter going to first.' . . . 'All right,' replied the man to whom Chase was talking, and from his squeaky, penetrating voice I recognized him to be [Jimmy] Austin, the New York third baseman."

Cobb then went back to his clubhouse and told Crawford to dig hard for first base the next time, and he would stop at second, and when Chase threw to third both would be safe.

"The next day, I got on base," Cobb wrote, "and Crawford bunted. Chase rushed in and pounced on the ball. After rounding second, I made a pretense of going to third, but pulled up sharp. Chase fell for it, he pounded the ball to Austin and we were both safe. That made Chase sore—he is always sore when one of his schemes goes wrong.

"'Why didn't you go to third on that last trip, Ty?' he asked. 'Because I got a drink of water in your clubhouse yesterday,' I replied. . . . But Chase thereafter perfected his play to such an extent that although we worked ours on other teams 19 out of 20 times that season, we did not dare work it against the Yankees."

In his short 1923 book, *How to Play First Base,* Chase defined his art: "First base is no longer a fielding sinecure for a heavy hitter. It is a position demanding speed, accuracy, a good pair of hands, quick judgment, fair throwing ability and plenty of nerve. There are never enough really high-class first basemen to supply the demand."

In 1909, Farrell abandoned the Elberfeld-as-manager experiment and brought in George T. Stallings, a disciplinarian who managed in civilian clothes. He, too, would clash with Chase, who was named captain and insisted he should direct in-game matters on the field. The club finished fifth in 1909 but drew more than half a million to the park, as Chase hit .283 in 118 games.

In 1910, the Highlanders were 88–63, good for second place. But Chase, in his role of manager-on-the-field, feuded with some players and favored others. When Jack Knight was on a hot streak, Chase asked to use his bat. When Knight demurred, saying it was the only one he had, Chase broke it, as Jimmy Austin later told Lawrence Ritter for the book, *The Glory of Their Times.* Said Austin, "That's the kind of guy [Chase] was."

Stallings was in no position to challenge Chase, now as big a star as any in the game. A year before, Stallings was involved in a sign-stealing gambit—which we will get to in Chapter 7—that had Ban Johnson, an old enemy, looking to run him out of the league. Chase missed time with malaria and sustained a minor neck injury in a train accident. He hit .290 with 28 errors, and late in the season Stallings went to Farrell and accused Chase of giving less than his best effort.

Though minds were made up, Farrell and AL vice president Charles Somers interviewed players individually, and, Farrell reported, Chase emerged exonerated. "Stallings had utterly failed in his accusations against Chase," Ban Johnson said. "He tried to besmirch the character of a sterling player. I am happy to say that the evidence given by New York players . . . showed Stallings up."

Stallings was out, and Chase became the manager. "God, what a way to run a ball club," Jimmy Austin later lamented to Ritter.

The Highlanders won 10 of 14 under Chase and finished second, then he got to match wits with McGraw in the postseason exhibition series that, in New York, overshadowed the World Series between the A's and Cubs. The Giants won, but the series was a commercial success.

Playing for himself, Chase put out a big season in 1911, hitting .315 with 32 doubles, 7 triples, and 36 steals, but the team finished 76–76, and he got fed up with managing and told Farrell to find someone else for 1912. That turned out to be Harry Wolverton, a nondescript baseball lifer, and the Yankees sank to the bottom of the league.

From playing and managing the Highlanders, barnstorming with the biggest stars of the game, and other opportunities, such as appearances on the vaudeville stage, Chase gathered enough money to buy an orange grove in California, which his sister and her husband ran. He got married and had a son, but his carousing turned the marriage sour and it ended quickly, an off-the-field scandal that received extraordinary coverage for the time.

On a September day in 1912, Chase was in the batting cage before a game with Boston and, between swings, invited backup catcher Gabby Street to come play poker at one of John McGraw's establishments downtown. The stakes were too high, but Street was convinced to come anyway, for the spectacle, and his version of events survive in an unpublished manuscript—as referenced in Jim Reisler's Before they were Bombers—by long-time scout Gib Bodet, bringing Chase vividly to life.

According to the account, when Street entered the venue, Chase beckoned to him, saying "Stand behind me, Gabby, and watch a master at work."

And so it was, as Street recounted, that Hal Chase "turned that pair of kings into four of a kind right before my eyes!" As for his opponent, Guy Zinn, he was now out six months' salary. But as the story goes, Chase gave Zinn back $1,000 . . . without admitting to any kind of cheating.

According to Street, "[Hal] wanted to show he could palm a pair out of his sleeve in that tough company and not get caught. But it's like he also wanted somebody to know it."

In what became the last, desperate stab by the Farrell-Devery regime to produce a winner, Frank Chance was lured from the Cubs to manage in 1913. Best remembered as the first baseman in "Tinker to Evers to Chance," he managed the Cubs to the World Series in 1906, 1907, 1908, and 1910 and earned the moniker "the peerless leader."

The team was moving into the Polo Grounds, a sign of the new friendship with the Giants, and would officially be known ever after as the Yankees. But the Yankees got off to a disastrous start, and Chance's temper flare-ups came to be mocked by Chase. Frank Graham later recounted that Chase would sit next to Chance, who was deaf in one ear, and mock him right in the dugout.

At last, Chase's act was growing tired in New York. He was hitting only .212, with 10 errors in 39 games, no longer digging bad throws out of the dirt. After one game, Chance exploded to a pair of reporters, "Did you notice some of the balls that got away from Chase today? They weren't wild throws, they were made to look that way. He has been doing that right along. He's throwing games on me."

On June 1, the day Chase married his second wife, he was traded to the White Sox for mediocre first baseman Babe Borton and utilityman Rollie Zeider, who was known to have chronic foot problems, inspiring Mark Roth to write that the Yankees had traded their biggest star for "a bunion and an onion."

Chase didn't stay in Chicago long. When the Federal League started up and offered a place to which to jump, Chase characteristically jumped for the money and actually came into his own as a hitter. When the league disbanded, he signed with Cincinnati and won the NL batting crown with a .339 average in 1916. But when Christy Mathewson, who had been a friend in New York, came to manage Cincinnati, he also suspected Chase was laying down. Chase ended up with McGraw and the Giants in 1919 but was suspended in August, again suspected of letting balls go by on purpose, and never played in the major leagues again.

Hal Chase (left) and John McGraw were rival managers when the Yankees and Giants fought for the heart of New York in a 1910 exhibition series that was played for keeps. *Bain News Service, courtesy of the Library of Congress*

In 1920, Hugh S. Fullerton, the Chicago sportswriter who began unraveling the World Series fixing scandal, wrote in *The New Republic* that Chase had fixed games in 1919 but was cleared because teammates would not speak up.

"As usual, the players who were in possession of the facts evaded giving testimony," Fullerton wrote, "and Chase was cleared of the charge and promoted from Cincinnati to New York. The Chase case gave many players the idea they could play dishonestly and not be discovered, or if discovered or suspected would be cleared. They believed the club owners feared publicity so much, they would be safe."

It can never be known for sure if Hal Chase threw games for money during his time in the major leagues. The obsession with making money on the side, the brazen willingness to cheat at cards and his keeping of fast company, and all the managers who called him out for one degree or another of indifference all suggest it would not have been out of character. He said he could have made a million dollars if he had been as corrupt as all that, but he admitted only to betting on his own team in games in which he played. He was caught trying to bribe a teammate to fix minor league games in the west later on.

What Chase did admit: after the 1919 season, he heard from a former teammate, "Sleepy Bill" Burns, that the World Series was to be fixed but kept this information to himself. "I never had any use for a stool pigeon or a squealer," he would say. Not telling the proper baseball officials, he said, was his "greatest error." He insisted he was not involved in the plot and never made a cent from it.

Through the 1920s, Chase played minor league ball on the West Coast, and later semipro ball in Arizona. He became a desert drifter and an alcoholic. In December 1933, the Columbia football team checked into a grand hotel in Tucson for a week of training for the Rose Bowl. The Lions trainer, Charlie Barrett, had worked for the Highlanders 25 years earlier.

"A disheveled and broken figure stumbled into the gorgeous lobby of the Hotel El Conquistador," wrote the *New York World-Telegram*. "I'd like to see Doc Barrett," the man said, "tell Doc it's Hal Chase."

New York writers gathered to jump on the story as Chase and Barrett hugged and shed tears. Chase was working in copper mines, picking up C.W.A. jobs, washing cars, and drinking. Someone asked his age as he left the lobby, and Chase said, "forty-six." Barrett said, "I happen to know he's fifty-one. Even though he is down and out, he's still Hal."

Chase ended up on a ranch in California owned by his sister and brother-in-law, who built a cottage to keep him out of the main house. He contracted beriberi, a kidney disease related to his drinking, and, photographed on his front porch, gave an interview to Oakland sportswriter Lester Grant in 1941. In the long, two-part series in the *Sporting News*, Chase gave his thoughts on baseball, past and present, lavishly praising commissioner Kenesaw Mountain Landis for cleaning up the game and upholding players' rights, and agonized over ruining two marriages, losing touch with his son, and destroying his name. "Baseball was very good to me," he said. "But I'm afraid I wasn't very good to baseball. Most of the grief I had during my career as a player was my own doing."

He avoided testifying at the Black Sox's trials. Later, he exchanged letters with Landis, but his status remained unclear. Yet he remained a sympathetic figure to some, and he received some Hall of Fame votes, 11 in 1936 and 18 in 1937. When in 1941 the Oakland Oaks young first baseman, Ferris Fain, was heralded by the team as the greatest fielder since Hal Chase, Art Cohn, columnist for the *Oakland Tribune*, exploded: "Organized baseball has never forgotten Prince Hal, as long as it could commercialize his name. It kept the name and killed the man . . . broke the man and shattered his spirit."

Finally, in 1947, Chase, having suffered a stroke and his liver, kidney, and heart all failing, wrote his own epitaph for J.W. Sehorn.

"You note that I am not in the Hall of Fame," he said. "When I die, movie magnates will make no picture like *Pride of the Yankees*, which honored that great player, Lou Gehrig. I guess that's the answer, isn't it? Gehrig had a good name, one of the best a man could have. I am an outcast, I haven't a good name. I am the loser, just like all gamblers are. I lived to make great plays. What did I gain? Nothing. . . . I was all wrong, at least in most things, and my best proof is that I am flat on my back, without a dime."

On May 18, three weeks later after Sehorn's story was published, Hal Chase, just 64, died in that hospital bed, leaving generation after generation of baseball lovers to ponder what might have been, if only he could have gone back to the beginning and started over.

CHAPTER 6

FIGHTING MAD

Elberfeld is the gamest ballplayer in the business. They can talk about their Wagners and other great players around shortstop, but Elberfeld makes a big hit with me every time I see him in action . . .

—Tom Connolly, Hall of Fame umpire, who ejected Elberfeld
on five occasions, as told to *Sporting Life* in 1908

The short-lived history of baseball played up on the hilltop was nothing like New York's other ballparks. Yankee Stadium was the cathedral, and Shea Stadium, Ebbets Field, and the Polo Grounds all had moments of magic and majesty.

Not Hilltop Park. There was never a World Series staged there, and only a handful of truly meaningful games between 1903 and 1912, but it was often home to the theater of the absurd, from the early games played on the unfinished field, to Chesbro's wild pitch, the 13 stolen bases against a young catcher named Branch Rickey, Ty Cobb running up into the stands to beat up a disabled fan, and much more. Oh, there was a lot of absurdity for one decade.

The Labor Day doubleheader between the Yankees and A's, on September 3, 1906, was what the sober *New York Times* described as "one of the most disgraceful exhibitions of rowdyism ever witnessed on a baseball field."

And, 11 decades later, it may still be near the top of that list of such exhibitions. The raging central figure in all of it was Norman Arthur "Kid" Elberfeld, whose well-known nickname, "the Tabasco Kid" did not even hint of his on-field demeanor. He wasn't fiery, he was combustible—more fittingly the nitroglycerin kid.

Kid Elberfeld was a gentle man and a loving father away from the diamond, but his temper between the lines was uncontrollable, especially when directed at umpires. *Bain News Service, courtesy of the Library of Congress*

Elberfeld, who was 5-foot-7 and about 145 pounds, had very definite ideas on how the game should be played, based on the old Orioles of the 1890s, his boyhood heroes, and he expected everyone around him to be as . . . well, today it would be euphemized as "passionate" as he was.

Elberfeld lamented to the *Sports News'* J.G. Taylor Spink in 1942, three decades after he left the early Yankees:

> Maybe we weren't a great club. It was a crime how we threw away at least two of them, 1904 and 1906. But do you know what was really wrong with that club? We didn't have enough fight on it. We didn't have many fighters on that club, players who fought for everything, the way the old Orioles used to fight and the way the Giants then were fighting and scrapping in the National League. Jack Kleinow, our first-string catcher, would flare up once in a while, but the rest of the club was pretty quiet. Willie Keeler was a great player, but he didn't have the fight of the old Orioles. . . . Why, it used to burn me up, when we were hustling and fighting for games, to hear Willie singing to himself in the outfield.

If his teammates were too nice, and perhaps didn't care enough, Elberfeld cared too much. As he may or may not have figured out later in life, when he became a wonderful father and instructor of young players, the element of self-control can be just as important to winning baseball. After all, passion, without poise, can be rather counterproductive. Elberfeld wanted to win so badly, he often hurt his team's chances—and never more so than in 1906.

The Yankees acquired Elberfeld in the controversial deal with Detroit in 1903. The Giants had signed him the previous summer—he was John McGraw's kind of player for sure—but when peace was made between the leagues, Elberfeld was returned to Detroit and the AL as part of the deal. Unhappy, and at loggerheads with manager Ed Barrow, Elberfeld, one of the game's most gifted shortstops, was practically given to the Highlanders. Right under the irate McGraw's nose, he immediately made Clark Griffith's team better.

Already a veteran of five major league seasons, Elberfeld was known for vicious spiking, opponents returning the favor, and for "sterilizing" his spike wounds with whiskey. Some of his spike wounds were severe enough to be career-threatening. "The old leg has gotten so many spikes shoved into it, it won't heal," he said in 1908. "I'll have to give it a rest. One doctor said I'll never play again, but they've said that before. I'll give it a year's rest, and it'll be all right." He played six more years.

Shortly after he arrived in New York, in 1903, he was arrested at a hotel near Hilltop Park. Apparently short-changed, he called waiter Albert Becker a thief and flung a bottle, hitting him in the jaw. There would be similar instances. At the ballpark, Elberfeld was annoyed by photographers creeping too close to the action and was known to fire baseballs at their cameras.

Once, John Ganzel was spiked at first base, and, though he maintained it was an accident, Elberfeld took it upon himself to retaliate. On a double-play ball, he waited until the runner was point-blank and fired the ball off his head, so hard the ball ricocheted into right field.

There was a rookie umpire, Billy Evans, in a story he repeated the rest of his life, who followed Elberfeld to the dugout after one altercation and challenged him to fight, successfully calling The Kid's bluff. But most umpires, some subjected to kicking, others subjected to handfuls of mud flung in their face, could do little more than eject the Tabasco Kid, and restore order until the next flare-up. Umpire Silk O'Loughlin would be Elberfield's most consistent foil.

When rookie Ty Cobb slid headfirst into second base in 1905, Elberfeld came down to make the tag with one knee on the back of Cobb's neck, scraping his face in the dirt. Cobb slid feet first after that, and when he later knocked Elberfeld into left field, Cobb told his biographer, Al Stump, "The Kid got up, shot a stream of tobacco juice, and looked me over reflectively. 'Son, that's how it's done. You've got it,' he said. 'More power to you.'"

That was the Tabasco Kid. And in 1906, though he missed significant time with injuries, Elberfeld was at his zenith. "Norman Elberfeld is playing the grandest ball of his career," *Sporting Life* rhapsodized as September began, "and despite his bad habit of umpire fighting, candor compels even his severest critics to pay him high compliment. The dash and energy of this brilliant little performer are excelled only by his fearlessness. Elberfeld is in the game heart, head, and soul from beginning to end, and his work is an inspiration to the entire team."

Indeed, the Kid was fielding well by the standards of the day, though he made 42 errors, and was hitting over .330 at the start of September. Elberfeld's motto was "hit or be hit"; he had perfected the art of turning into the path of the pitch, taking a relatively painless glancing blow, and being awarded first base. On August 8 in St. Louis, O'Loughlin refused to award him the base, and Elberfeld went after him with his bat and was ejected, one of six times he was tossed that season. It certainly didn't help his team, which went on to lose, 2–1, in 10 innings.

On August 23, after Al Orth beat Cleveland 3–1, New York was in third place, seven games behind the first-place White Sox. But that victory started the Yankees off on a run of 19 victories in 20 games that vaulted them to the top. This was an era of long road trips and homestands, and the Yankees were playing at home for all but three games between August 15 and September 12, then went on the road for the final 25 games. They were to finish the season 53–23 at home, 37–38 on the road.

The heat of another race was getting to manager Clark Griffith, who was said to be limiting his diet to olive oil and raw eggs to alleviate stress-related digestive trouble. But pitchers Chesbro, Orth, and Walter Clarkson, who was beginning to realize his potential, were holding up, even during a brutal stretch of *five doubleheaders in six days* that began on August 30.

They were on an eight-game winning streak when the defending league champs, Connie Mack's A's, arrived for the doubleheader on September 3. In the ninth inning, with the game tied, Philadelphia's Danny Murphy took off on an attempt to steal third base. It was a close play, but the consensus was O'Loughlin was correct in calling him safe. Third baseman George Moriarty began to argue, and the New York players surrounded the umpire, who made a dismissive wave in Elberfeld's direction.

The Tabasco Kid detonated, rushed at O'Loughlin, and tried to kick him, according to the *New York Times'* detailed account. The umpire backed away but ejected Elberfeld, who "again rushed at the umpire and made six deliberate attempts to spike him. He waved his hands threateningly in the face of O'Loughlin, and made repeated attempts to step on the umpire's feet with his spiked shoes. He then jerked savagely at O'Loughlin's arm and endeavored to push him back."

The umpire controlled himself, and the fans, over 20,000 spilling over onto the field that day, began to jeer—at Elberfield, their own team's leader—as the scene went from ugly to juvenile. O'Loughlin appealed to nearby police, and captain John W. Cottrell with two of his patrolmen hurried to the scene, leading Elberfeld by the arm back to the Yankees bench.

As an aside, Cottrell, three years earlier, was defending himself for failing to prevent a disturbed man, Arthur Deming, from approaching President Teddy Roosevelt, Bill Devery's old nemesis, during a visit to New York. At least Deming only handed Roosevelt a letter.

Once again, Cottrell and his men were ineffective offering protection. Kid Elberbeld charged again when O'Loughlin made it clear he wouldn't allow the game to go on until Elberfeld was out of sight. The pitcher, Orth, tried to stop Elberfeld, who was so out of control, he nearly knocked out his teammate. Now, the police escorted Elberfeld to the gate, where he turned, folded his arms, and refused to leave. Finally, Griffith, fearing this critical game would be called a forfeit, went out and got his shortstop under control. Play resumed, and O'Loughlin, according to the press, was cheered for his restraint. The Yankees scored in the bottom of the ninth to win the game, 4–3.

Remarkably, even for 1906 baseball, Elberfeld was allowed to play in the second game of the doubleheader, though he was booed and hissed when he walked out to shortstop and each time he came to bat. The A's were winning the game in the ninth when New York's Jimmy Williams grounded to short. Keeler, running from second, collided with fielder Lave Cross, and the ball rolled into left field. Two runs scored to tie the game, as O'Loughlin did not call interference on the runner. The Philadelphia players surrounded the umpire. Mack, who managed in civilian clothes, was thus not allowed on the field. The argument was long and threatening enough for O'Loughlin to forfeit the game to New York.

What a day! With the White Sox losing twice to Cleveland, the Yankees were in first place with a record of 71–48, two percentage points better than Chicago, at 72–49.

The next day, the Yankees were in Boston for yet another doubleheader and won both in shutouts to run their winning streak to 12, but between games, Ban Johnson sent word that Elberfeld was suspended indefinitely for his actions from the day before. With the championship so close at hand, Elberfeld would have to sit some of the most important games of the year.

Johnson, with his league now established, was past tilting his decisions toward helping his New York franchise. But perhaps because he saw the importance of keeping popular players on the field, the AL president suspended Elberfeld just eight games. The Yankees won six of the eight, their winning streak ending at 15 with a loss against Boston on September 10, but their momentum was disrupted.

On September 11, the day before Elberfeld was to return, there was more mayhem at Hilltop Park. Boston second baseman Hobe Ferris accused right fielder Jack Hayden of loafing on a ball, and when the team returned to the dugout, Ferris reached up to grab the roof and kicked Hayden in the mouth. Cottrell's men arrested him after the game. Baseball circa 1906.

The Yankees, who outdrew the Giants for the first time with 434,000 customers, finished their home season the next day. Elberfeld returned to play shortstop and hit third, with his replacement, Joe Yeager, back to the bench. Elberfeld got 2 hits, but the game was lost, 4–2, to last-place Boston. New York was 78–50, one game ahead of Chicago, and off to Washington to start their 24-day, seven-city road trip.

They split four in D.C.; took two of three, with a tie game, at St. Louis; and reached Chicago for a showdown series against the White Sox, who were known as the "hitless wonders." They hit .230 as a team but rode fabulous pitching, especially from Ed Walsh, who had learned the spitball, like Chesbro, from Elmer Stricklett.

Chesbro and Walsh matched up on September 21, and New York scored three in the ninth to win the first game of the doubleheader, 6–3. Bill Hogg pitched a three-hitter in Game Two to win, 4–1, a game shortened to six innings by darkness, and vault the Yankees back into first place.

Orth was hit hard the next day, losing 7–1, and for the series finale Griffith went back to Hogg on one day's rest. Before the largest crowd the White Sox had drawn to that time, Walsh again started for Chicago. In the first inning, Elberfeld walked and kept running as Chase singled and the ball was fumbled in the outfield by former teammate Patsy Dougherty. Elberfeld subsequently scored from third on a double play. In the eighth, Keeler took off from first on a hit-and-run, and Elberfeld, lunging at a wide pitch, lost the bat and it went hurtling toward the mound. The crowd, believing Elberfeld purposely threw the bat at Walsh, nearly rioted before things were cooled down and the game played to a finish. Hogg allowed only 2 hits, striking out 8, to win, 1–0.

The emotional series win was to be the high-water mark, and Elberfeld later offered that the Yankees thought they had the pennant and suffered a letdown after leaving Chicago in first place.

"In all my experience in baseball," Elberfeld recalled to Spink, "I don't remember a week in which so many things went wrong on a club [such as the one after the Chicago games]. Grounders were taking bad hops, poor hitters were hitting balls they never hit before, we were misjudging flies, running into each other until the club was almost off its head."

They lost three in a row at Detroit. Elberfeld made a key error during the Tigers' 6-run rally in the eighth that changed the first game. The Tigers scored two in the ninth to beat Orth the next day. Then Chase made a critical error, and Cobb singled home two runs, as the Tigers beat Hogg in the third game, 2–0. John Ewbank, a thirty-four-year-old rookie, allowed 10 hits but kept New York off the scoreboard for one of his eight career wins. The Tigers of Cobb and Sam Crawford were no fluke, though. They went on to win the AL pennant in 1907, '08, and '09.

The Yankees, now two games behind, were pummeled, 10–1, in Cleveland on September 27 in the first game of a double-header. The second game was another tie, stopped due to darkness despite helpful Cleveland fans' attempts to illuminate the field by building bonfires.

That was it, the pennant was gone. New York finished 90–61, salvaging second place with two wins in Boston to finish the season. Elberfeld lost his temper one more time and was ejected from the second-to-last game by umpire Tom Connolly. Limited by injuries and suspensions to 99 games, he hit .306. Yeager, his usual backup, hit .301 in 57 games. The White Sox defeated the heavily favored Cubs in the World Series.

Elberfeld couldn't will the Yankees to the championship he had predicted.

"Still," he moaned decades later, "we should have won two early American League pennants. The other clubs didn't beat us, we beat ourselves."

In 1907, the team fell back under .500 and to fifth place, as Elberfeld hit .271, his career average, for the season. He also began feuding with Griffith about his performance. Elberfeld had a string of error-filled games in June, and Farrell suspended him on July 29 citing, of all things, "indifference."

The dissension carried into the next season, and Griffith's relationship with the owners deteriorated.

As his time in New York was drawing to a close, on May 5, 1908, after a game with the Senators was rained out, Griffith had the distinction of bringing the Highlanders to the White House. Theodore Roosevelt had never been a fan of the game but was warming up to it as his young son, Quentin, became a fan and played at school with Charlie Taft, son of Roosevelt's successor.

"Here is a good, husky bunch of voters," Griffith told the president, "who would get out and work for you. If you'll only run again, every one of the boys will root for you to beat the band."

Roosevelt, who had decided not to run for reelection in 1908, laughed, talked about Quentin's love for baseball, and offered his hand to the Highlanders. "I would have felt insulted if you had not called on me," he said.

As T.R. left office, Grantland Rice wrote a poem, whimsically theorizing that, despite eight years of fighting presidential battles and his famous hunting exploits, Roosevelt could never last as an umpire. "Choking angry wolves to death as sport would stack up raw . . . When you see Elberfeld swinging for your under-jaw."

On June 24, 1908, Griffith, saying he was "disheartened," resigned in Philadelphia. Farrell, unable to get Keeler, that rock of stability, to take over, turned to Elberfeld on what was termed a "temporary" basis.

Elberfeld, who suffered the aforementioned ghastly spike wound on May 1, did not play much during his time as manager and was ejected four times in a little over three months, three times by Silk O'Loughlin. Worse, the team, especially Chase, resented Farrell's choice. Elberfeld's temper drove Chase and Keeler—two of the players he long believed were too laid-back—to leave the team before the end of the season. The Highlanders lost 15 of the first 18 games and 12 of 13 during another stretch, and players groused in anonymous quotes to writers about their manager (yes, that happened in 1908, too). The Yankees finished 27–71 under Elberfeld, still one of the worst records ever compiled in a big league managerial career of any length.

He remained with the Yankees as a player when George Stallings was hired to be the nonplaying manager in 1909, and a young infielder named Jimmy Austin, nicknamed "Pepper" (and obviously a kindred spirit of Elberfeld), joined the team. When Elberfeld got hurt again and Austin took over, the scarred-up old Kid insisted on dispensing with the tradition of rookies and non-regulars getting the uncomfortable upper berths on the trains. "Put the youngster down in the lower booth," Elberfeld told the traveling secretary, emphasizing the important of rest for Austin. That, too, was Kid Elberfeld—away from the ballpark.

After he left the Yankees, Elberfeld played in 1912 with Montgomery in the Southern Association, and he tutored the young outfielder Casey Stengel. Once, Stengel recalled, Elberfeld instructed him to take off from second base for a hit-and-run. Stengel did, and the catcher called for a pitchout. Elberfeld intercepted the pitch with his bare hand. A long argument ensued, and when it was over, Stengel, who would have been out by a mile, was returned to second base. Later that season, Stengel was called to the majors, and Elberfeld told him, "you won't be coming back, forget about dental school," and had the youngster buy a new suitcase.

Elberfeld returned to the major leagues briefly with Brooklyn in 1914, and when it was time to finally hang up his sharpened spikes, he expressed interest in (wait for it . . .) umpiring. Never happened.

In a long career as a minor league manager, Elberfeld remained a victim of his own temperament. In 1921, with Little Rock, he was suspended 30 days and threatened with expulsion after attacking an umpire. "The truth of the matter is The Kid is anything but a roughneck," wrote the *Brooklyn Eagle*. "He is the most concrete example of a dual personality the game has ever furnished. His willingness to fight with anything under the sun that interfered with winning a ballgame, whether it is played for money or marbles, has given the public a totally erroneous impression of his real character. Off the field, he is a soul of good nature. . . . He is simply an aggressive, scrappy leader who lets his temper get the better of him too frequently for his own good."

He mellowed some after that. Along the way, he influenced the careers of a number of future major league stars, such as Stengel, Travis Jackson, and Bill Terry. Elberfeld, who lived in Chattanooga, ran a series of successful baseball schools in the south in the 1930s and would playfully call a youngster a "hardhead" after a mistake. And he raised five daughters, The Elberfeld Sisters, pioneers of women's athletics who played basketball together in exhibitions and competed successfully in a variety of sports.

The Tabasco Kid died at age sixty-nine following a bout with pneumonia on January 14, 1944. Griffith, who by then was the beloved owner of the Senators, told the *Washington Post*: "He couldn't lick Cobb, he weighed only 150 pounds, but he never stopped trying. When Cobb came into the bag and Elberfeld was covering, we'd just stand around with our arms folded for the next few minutes and watch the goings-on, until one or both of 'em were thrown out of the game. They didn't call him Tabasco Kid because he was shy."

CHAPTER 7

SPYGATE, 1909

Give me a ballclub of only medium ability and, if I can get the players in the right frame of mind, they will beat the world champions . . .

—George T. Stallings, for *Collier's*, November 28, 1914

The Clark Griffith era of Yankees history was over, and Kid Elberfeld was obviously not managerial timber. So Frank Farrell searched for a new manager as the 1908 season closed.

As the club was foundering in the summer, Farrell had his eye on Mike Kelly, a brawny first baseman who was finishing his playing career with Toronto in the Eastern League and was considered a bright, young leader of men. And again, Farrell floated the idea of recycling old "Foxy Ned" Hanlon, who was out of baseball.

But he soon settled on George T. Stallings, son of a Confederate general. It was widely reported that he was a graduate of Virginia Military Institute and had attended medical school, though

George T. Stallings managed in civilian clothes and was certain he had the game all figured out, but got himself in hot water in the American League. After leaving the Yankees, he made his name synonymous with a baseball miracle. *Bain News Service, courtesy of the Library of Congress*

records securitized later do not support those claims. Always stylishly dressed, bow tie and all, he managed in street clothes and brought an impressive, urbane bearing to the game.

Oh, Stallings could spray curse words to match even the most roguish of players during the games and was at that time being sued by a minor league umpire who was charged with assault in a fight in Rochester, but he was quite affable once the last out was recorded, flashing the wide grin that lives forever, under a straw boater hat, on the cover of the highly collectible 1914 World Series program.

Stallings, an undistinguished catcher in the 1890s, was the manager in Detroit in 1901, and Johnson suspected he was scheming to move the franchise over to the NL. Johnson never trusted Stallings, and it's fair to say he wasn't thrilled to have him back in the American League. Stallings, forty-one, had spent the decade as a successful minor league manager in Buffalo, selling his interests in the club at a nice profit, and he did the same at Newark in 1908, where he and Farrell did business, and the latter was impressed. The agreement was consummated in July of 1908, and rumored during the summer, but not announced until after the season, on October 12.

The hire was lauded in the press. Stallings had innovative ideas and enjoyed expanding on them, charming the writers. Today, he would be called the kind of manager who thinks he invented the game, and soon Stallings's creativity would enmesh the franchise in a Patriots-like cheating scandal that wouldn't go away until he did.

Stallings's first task was to talk Chase, who had declared he was finished with New York, back onto the team. Beyond that, Farrell made it clear the new manager was given a free hand to remake the club, now that the window for winning a title had all but closed on the original core of Willie Keeler, Kid Elberfeld, Jack Chesbro, Wid Conroy, et al.

"One of the toughest jobs a manager faces is housecleaning," Stallings would write for *Collier's* in 1914, "because it must be done gradually. No one can afford to tear a team to pieces all at once, but he must work with what he has and fill in when he has a chance."

Stallings took a room at the Hotel Wolcott in New York and would work with top scout Arthur Irwin out of the Flatiron

Building, spending the winter wheeling and dealing for new players. He took occasional trips home to Georgia on business. The family had lost its plantation, The Meadows in Haddock, outside Macon, during the late 19th century. George Stallings had been saving his baseball earnings to buy it back, piece by piece, and closed the deal shortly after signing with Farrell. It was big enough to serve as the Yankees spring headquarters.

"We will start south about the usual time," Stallings told reporters, "and go direct to my place in Haddock, [Georgia]. I have a big athletic field there, and an old Colonial dwelling big enough to accommodate a good-size squad of ballplayers. I have absolutely no idea how my batting order will read for the opening game, but every good man will get a chance."

As would soon become apparent, Stallings was a man who *always* had an angle. The press reported that Stallings planned to feed his players the freshest, healthiest meals at his farm, and put them to work. "The Yanks manager thinks there is nothing so beneficial as good, old-fashioned farming to develop the strong man," read a story in the *Hartford Courant* in November, "and it may be that the Yanks will be put to work hoeing potatoes and shucking corn when they reach the Georgia plantation. Of course, if they don't know anything about farming, Stallings will teach them. He has already purchased copies of 'Every Man His Own Crops' and players will read up on the subject."

Hal Chase hoeing potatoes and shucking corn? Stallings ordered the older players, including Keeler (who had been talked out of retirement by Farrell), Chesbro, Elberfeld, Conroy, and Kleinow, to Hot Springs, Arkansas, at the start of February for treatment in the hot baths. The younger players, he called to the farm where he would drill and instruct them personally.

Pete Wilson, who played for the minor league Hartford Senators three seasons and pitched a handful of games for the Yankees in 1908, provided the *Courant* with dispatches on this bizarre spring training. On March 2, the paper printed parts of a letter from the strapping, twenty-four-year-old Wilson, enthusiastically describing the 4,000-acre farm, its horses and cattle, the after-dinner snipe shooting and possum hunting, and the large number of African-American workers, to which he referred as "smokes," a racial slur of the time.

"They call me 'Massa Pete,'" Wilson wrote. "Some of them can play ball, too. There is one nine in the Connecticut League that might use a few." As the group headed to Macon for its first games, Wilson said he "felt like a peacock." Wilson made the club and went 6–5 in 13 starts before drifting back to the minors and returning to Hartford.

By early March, the team had moved the 23 miles to Macon for exhibition games. Stallings, who often used a chalkboard in his lengthy lectures, recalled looking at all the veterans on the first full squad meeting, including Elberfeld, Chesbro, Keeler, "and others who had big reputations and a large newspaper following, and I knew it devolved on me to let every one of them go sooner or later and stand the certain criticism for it, because they were all getting old and useless. I had come to take charge of the team, a busher who had handled only bush league clubs. And they had put this job of releasing them up to me."

Chase had agreed to return from California and was on his way to complete the club. When he arrived, he shook hands and made peace with Elberfeld.

All was going well, until Chase started showing signs of illness. It turned out to be smallpox, and while he was quarantined in Augusta, the team was vaccinated and began its northward barnstorming, having to be stopped, checked, and in some cases revaccinated.

By the time the 1909 season began in Washington, the lineup bore little resemblance to the old Highlanders. Elberfeld moved to third base, with youngsters Jack Knight and Jimmy Austin joining the infield. Joe Ward kept first base warm until Chase recovered. Ray Demmit, Clyde Engle, and Birdie Cree were taking over in the outfield as Keeler faded further. A group of young pitchers fought for innings as the old guard, Chesbro and Orth, were on their way out.

Stallings radically changed his lineup if a rare left-hander started against the Yankees; "platooning" hitters later became common practice. And the manager's many eccentricities and superstitions—keeping the dugout free of trash and seeds, removing or painting over anything the color yellow in the ballpark, sliding up and down the bench until the seats of his trousers wore out—became head-scratchers. The *T*, by the way, stood for "Tweedy."

He agonized over every pitch and, on his deathbed, quipped that "those damn bases on balls" were the cause of his heart disease.

"He cussed something awful," Jimmy Austin recalled. "Once, in a game, he gave me a real going over. Later that night he called me in and said, 'Jim, I'm sorry about this afternoon. Don't pay any attention to me when I say those things. Just forget it. It's only because I get so excited and want to win so bad.'"

The Yankees were improving, 7–9 in April, 11–9 in May, and played a little better at home, though not unusually so. On April 25, with the team on its way to Boston, Farrell and Devery again found a way to monetize the ballpark. That spring, a group of the greatest marathon runners in the world gathered in New York and ran a 26-mile race inside the Polo Grounds on April 4. Henry St. Ives won, but the event was popular enough to justify a rematch of sorts just three weeks later.

So American League Park would be rented as the site of a 15-mile match race between St. Ives and Alfred Shrubb of England. The race was run at night, so temporary gas lighting was installed, using holes cut in the outfield fence, and Shrubb won the shorter distance by a wide margin.

Stallings's mind was always churning in search of an angle. A decade earlier, when he was with the Phillies, a backup catcher named Morgan Murphy used to position himself outside the outfield walls, steal signs with binoculars, and relay them to hitters, first through the hole in an OFC Whiskey sign, then by signaling the third-base coach with a wire, run underground to a buzzer buried beneath the coaching box. The plan was exposed, the story goes, when an opposing runner tripped over the wire while running the bases.

The story that Stallings rented an upper-floor apartment in a new building just outside the ballpark and had his chief scout, Irwin, watch games and relay signals to the dugout using a mirror is one of several versions of Stallings's sign-stealing that has been oft-reported through the years. The plan didn't work in cloudy weather, so Stallings looked for some other means.

Perhaps those holes left in the outfield fence could be of use? The Yankees were 11–17 in June, 14–19 in July, and 11–16 in August and entered September with a lackluster 54–66 record, 28–29 at home, scoring 4.2 runs per game on their own turf. On the road, the Yankees were 26–37, averaging 3.0 runs per game. So if there was a "signal-tipping bureau," as baseball folk called it in those days, it was only marginally impactful for the Yankees. Nevertheless, there was an OFC whiskey ad in right-center, and some thought they saw the *O* opening and closing, just like in Philadelphia.

Then in September, things picked up. Considerably.

The Yankees were 17–10 that month, outscoring opponents 82–55 in 18 home games, 55–51 in 10 road games—so, despite the whispers of cheating going on, they actually were more productive hitting on the road. Back in June, they won four in a row from Washington on the Hilltop, outscoring the Senators, 20–6. Washington manager Joe Cantillon saw something he didn't like and sent his trainer out to investigate. Jerry Ettinger recognized a former pitcher, Gene McCann, out beyond the outfield fences with binoculars.

Nothing more came of it, but when the Tigers came to New York in late September, they were fighting for the pennant and Cantillon had tipped them off to possible sign stealing. They won the first game of a doubleheader, 2–1, and the nightcap 10–4, but Detroit manager Hughie Jennings got suspicious, even though things were going fine. Ed Summers, who won the first game, allowed opposing hitters a .106 batting average in

1909, but the Tigers thought the Yankees were swinging too well against him.

Here, Tigers trainer Harry Tuthill, who believed he saw the crossbar in the capital *H* of a sign advertising Young's Hats rotating between pitches, picks up the story, as he explained it to *Sporting Life* after the season:

> Jenning sent Bill Donovan out to examine the fence, but he came back and reported that he could not find anything out of the way. I was positive that Summers was being hit harder than he should have been in the first three innings, so I quietly walked out to the center field fence and looked over. I thought I saw something that was wrong and jumped on top of the fence, but could not get over because of the barbed wire that had been stretched. I went to a point near the clubhouse [which was located beyond the outfield] and discovered that there was an opening, and finally got over.
>
> A man ran out of the coop as I came in. I think I know who it was, but I would not be positive. I found a perfectly equipped arrangement in the coop. There was a handle which moved the crossbar in the H, which I tore off, and the glasses I picked up and have turned it over to Jennings. It was none of my affair after I protected the Tigers, so I refrained from saying anything but when Mr. Johnson wired me I wrote him the truth and that ends my part on the affair.

In other reports, Tuthill claimed to have found a half-eaten sandwich and freshly opened bottle of beer in the "coop." In his long interview with *The Sporting News* in 1941, Hal Chase described what he called the "Black Hand" scheme and revealed the code. When the crossbar of the *H* was slanted at a right angle to the left, the pitcher was going to throw a curve. When the bar was slanted at a right angle to the right, the pitch was to be a spitter. Pointed straight up, a fastball was coming. And if the sign "wiggled in all directions," there would be a change-up.

The Tigers won the pennant. The Yankees finished 74–77, good for fifth place, though an improvement of 23 games over 1908. The "Deflategate" of its day, the sign-tipping scandal continued to dominate baseball coverage throughout the offseason. Stealing signs from the dugout or the field was considered good, head's-up baseball, then as now. Field glasses and revolving crossbars in the letter *H* was a different story. Clark Griffith, who had resurfaced as manager in Cincinnati, piled on. "Nothing of that sort was ever pulled off while I was in charge of the club there," he told reporters. "I would never have stood for such a thing. When it comes to using a lot of tricky paraphernalia, there is no sportsmanship in it and I would never allow anything of the kind."

(Of course, this still goes on in modern times, using "tricky paraphernalia" like Apple Watches to steal signs.)

There were no specific rules against sign tipping. Stallings denied the fact that they tipped signs at all, and though Johnson did not like Stallings, he thought the public disclosure of cheating would be damaging to the league. On December 15 and 16, the league owners met at the Hotel Wolcott, Stallings's offseason home the winter before, to examine the evidence. They determined, according to *Sporting Life*, "the iron lever attached to a post was part of an appliance used to string acetylene gas lamps around the outfield on the occasion of the 15-mile match race between St. Ives and Shrubb, which was held at night."

The official verdict: "The board of directors has considered carefully all of the evidence. Resolved, that in the opinion of the board the New York club is free from all complicity in such a tipping affair and it is further resolved that any manager found guilty of operating a sign tipping bureau should be barred from baseball for all time."

To state the obvious, the lights installed for the race would explain the hole in the fence, and perhaps the levers and barbed wire, but would not account for both the Washington and Detroit trainers actually *seeing* someone back there with binoculars.

Essentially, the AL owners told Stallings and the Yankees, "We know you did it. Don't do it again," and hoped the issue would go away. Stallings stayed on the job, and the Yankees, with Farrell mindful of the smallpox outbreak of 1909, stayed away from the plantation and Macon and ran a more conventional spring training in 1910.

The youth movement continued apace. Keeler, Elberfeld, and Chesbro were dispatched during or after the 1909 season. All the starters were under thirty and were threats to steal bases. Rookie Bert Daniels stole 41, a mark that stood for Yankees freshmen until Alfonso Soriano broke it in 2001. Another rookie, Russ Ford, was 26–6 with a 1.65 ERA across 299 innings. Chase was now the veteran and captain and claimed credit as the Yankees were 23–10 by the end of May (see Chapter 5).

At Stallings's urging, Yankees hitters peered out to the outfield fences as they came to bat at Hilltop Park. He knew he was in opponents' heads, and the White Sox took the bait. Manager Hugh Duffy, a brilliant hitter in the 1890s, sent pitcher Irv Young (who was nicknamed "Young Cy") and catcher Fred Payne out to investigate during a series in July, and Ed Walsh thought he saw the field glasses. The Yankees took three of four, winning the first game, 13–4, and the last, over Fred Olmstead, 8–4, on July 9.

Soon, "Spygate," a.k.a. The George T. Stallings Signal-Tipping Bureau, was reported in the Chicago papers as being back in business. Hugh Fullerton, the writer who would later help unravel the Black Sox Scandal, wrote in the *Chicago Examiner* in early August that he had affidavits from Chicago players, and one from a New York player, attesting to its existence, and his paper was offering $500 to match a standing offer from Ban Johnson to anyone who would offer conclusive proof. "There is not a player on the Sox club who is not confident the catchers' signs are being tipped off," said the *Chicago Tribune*.

Now, Farrell came to the defense of his franchise and his manager. "Those lies have gone far enough and I propose to make this man, Fullerton, toe the mark. I will add another $1000 to the $500 promise made by Johnson and I have written Mr. Johnson asking that an investigating committee be appointed."

Stallings, too, offered not only a public denial, but a very expansive—and archetypal—defense.

He told reporters:

This is official and you can make it as strong as you like. There was never any attempt to learn the signals of players via a telescope through a hole in the outfield fence. But we have learned other clubs' signals in other ways, entirely legal ways.

. . . What are you going to do when Olmstead of the White Sox puts his right foot in the box for every out-shoot and his left foot in for every in-shoot all season long? What are you going to do when practically every Chicago pitcher insists on giving his own signals from the box and the signals get familiar, they are repeated so often? What are you going to do when one Cleveland pitcher holds his hands over his right breast when he serves one ball and over his left when he serves another? We've learned the childish signals employed by some clubs that way, and that is the only reason any of our batsmen can know what to expect. We made such huge jokes of the White Sox when they visited us that Duffy had to do something to square himself with the fans at home. But I am surprised that a man of Duffy's intelligence should have fallen for such a lot of rot as he appears to have believed. Is it reasonable to believe that I, as a manager, liable to release a half a dozen players a season, some of whom may consider they have a grievance against me, am going to put myself in their hands by installing sign tipping at my park when they can give me away just as soon as they leave the club?

True, Stallings had gotten rid of a number of players in 1909 and 1910, none of whom publicly blew the whistle, though players of that period frowned on "squealing" and instead tried to police the game themselves. The Yankees were 49–25 at home,

39–38 on the road in 1910, not an unusual differential. They averaged 4.45 runs per game at home, about a run per game more than on the road.

"I am still convinced there is nothing to this yarn about the signals," Ban Johnson responded, "but the charges said to have been whispered around the league must be probed. I am for clean baseball first, last, and all the time and the person who have set up such claims must prove their assertions."

Before any such second investigation was complete, Stallings picked his fight with Hal Chase, accusing him of laying down. "Stallings has always shown a tendency to go behind a man's back," Chase told reporters on September 22.

After the series of meetings referred to in Chapter 5, Farrell fired Stallings on September 27 and made Chase the player-manager. Stallings went away mad.

"Johnson has had it in for me for years," he told reporters before leaving town, "Later on, I may tell the true story of our falling out. . . . Farrell may be able to find a better manager, but not one who worked harder to make the team a success. I will have something to say which will throw light on this matter very soon. For the present, I can only say I have received a check in full for my services for the year and my connection with the New York Americans was terminated."

Once again, everyone else was happy. Farrell was rid of a troublesome manager who believed himself to be the smartest guy in the room and was able to make his most popular and marketable player the undisputed face of the franchise. Chase got a promotion and a raise. And Ban Johnson was able to get Stallings out of the American League without throwing a shadow on the cleanliness of its on-field operations.

Who can say whether Stallings had cooked up the case against Chase to deflect attention from the "signal-tipping bureau, part II," or whether he knew the end was coming and looked to get himself fired? Irritated by the owners' meddling and second-guessing—Devery was anything but a "silent partner" behind the scenes—Stallings may have been looking for a way out. He was not the first or last manager to have the issue with Chase, and he was never technically charged by baseball officials with doing anything illegal, though there is ample reason to believe that, if exaggerated, it was true that he had someone out behind the fence at some point, twirling the *H* in Young's Hats to signal his hitters.

What is certain is that he was in the process of successfully rebuilding the Yankees in 1910, and after his departure he would have the last laugh. The Yankees sank right back to the bottom.

The Boston Braves, after a 52–101 1912 season, were desperate enough to hire Stallings. Two years later, he orchestrated one of the great comebacks in baseball history, leading the "Miracle Braves" from last place on July 4 to the 1914 World Series, where they shocked and swept the heavily favored A's, who had won the Series in 1910, '11, and '13. The turnaround, Stallings explained, was facilitated when he and his players began to tear the upper right corners off $2 bills, "to kill their jinx."

The signal-tipping bureau was long forgotten, and George Tweedy Stallings was celebrated as the "Miracle Man" the rest of his life, which ended at sixty-one due to heart failure on his beloved plantation in 1929.

CHAPTER 8

FOR THE HEART OF NEW YORK

Every pitcher of an inventive turn of mind indulges in dreams of what he would like to do with the baseball. If any of these dreams ever came true, it would be good night and curtains for .300 batting averages . . .

—Pitcher Ernie Shore, for *Baseball Magazine*, 1917

Russell Ford was like so many other young pitchers, struggling in the minor leagues and looking for a way up to the majors. He was a wiry right-hander, 5-foot-11 and 175 pounds, born in far-off Manitoba before his family moved to Minnesota. He had made his way through the low minors with better-than-average stuff—fastball, spitter, and curve—and was pitching for Atlanta in the Southern League in 1907.

He was already twenty-seven, and the clock was ticking.

On a rainy day, Ford and catcher Ed Sweeney went back under the stands to warm up. One pitch got away, hitting a wood pillar, and then Ford's pitches were swerving every which way.

"I noticed the ball breaking a peculiar way," Sweeney remembered, a few years later. Nothing more was said of it.

The wood had scuffed the ball, and by accident Ford noticed that the ball would take a vicious swerve, right or left, depending on what side the scuffed spot was on. He began experimenting. Later that season, Sweeney joined the Yankees, and Frank Farrell asked him to identify the best pitcher in the Southern League. He mentioned Russ Ford, who had won 31 games in two seasons in Atlanta, and the Yankees drafted him.

For one magical season, with one magical pitch, Russell Ford was the equal of any pitcher in baseball—even the lordly Christy Mathewson. *Bain News Service, courtesy of the Library of Congress*

"The next spring, Ford and I went south together to join the Yankees and on the train he told me he had a ball no catcher in the world could receive," Sweeney said. "I laughed at him, but he persisted and told me he would explain it when we reached training camp. Once there, he took me into his confidence about the emery ball. He said he experimented with it the previous season, but had not mentioned it [then]. He was telling me because he wanted me to catch him, and he knew he couldn't get away with it unless I knew it was coming."

Dutifully, Sweeney kept his batterymate's secret, not even telling the Yankees' other pitchers and catchers. Russ Ford was sewing a piece of emery paper into his glove and scuffing the ball— inventing what would be the first pitch to be banned by Major League Baseball.

"When I cut it loose, the ball would go up to the plate with a fast hop and then sail," Ford told Reese Hart of the Associated Press in 1958. "I have been called a cheater, but I wasn't. A lot of pitchers roughed up the ball more than I did. There was no rule against doing it."

Ford started with the Yankees in 1909, but after one ineffective outing in cold weather, he was farmed out to Jersey City, where he went 13–13 with a 2.41 ERA, allowing only 172 hits in 276 innings pitched. Veteran hitters were missing his pitches by a foot. "The success gave me the biggest problem of my young life," Ford recalled. "I had come across a delivery that without doubt would make me the greatest pitcher in big league baseball—if I kept it to myself!"

Ford never did discuss the emery ball, until writing a piece for the *Sporting News* in 1935. First, he cut emery cloth into three-quarter inch squares, sewed the patches into his glove, and, in the era when players left their gloves on the field, he took his with him to the dugout after each inning. Then he attached a one-inch piece onto a ring on his glove hand, and cut a hole in the glove to expose it only to him.

With Chesbro and Orth gone, Ford made the rotation in 1910. He started the fifth game of the season and beat the A's, the best team in the league, 1–0, at Shibe Park, allowing 5 hits, no walks, and striking out 9.

What came next was a pitcher's magic carpet ride, à la Jack Chesbro's 1904 magic or Ron Guidry's 1978 magic. Russ Ford's emery ball, which everyone but he and his catcher thought was a spitter, was unhittable. He shut out Ty Cobb and the Tigers on May 11, Shoeless Joe Jackson and the White Sox on May 25 and June 5, and Nap Lajoie and the Indians on June 15. On July 14, he outdueled Cy Young, who was going for his 500th career win, 4–1. He then shut out the Browns twice in August, eight shutouts in all. He finished 26–6, the most wins ever for a rookie, and still the most by a Yankees pitcher named Ford, one better than Whitey in 1961.

"He kept his secret a long time by pretending it was a spitter," Cobb remembered. "He would deliberately show his finger to the batter and wet it with saliva."

What was unhittable was also uncatchable. Later that season, when Sweeney had to leave a game, Red Kleinow, who had also kept Chesbro's spitter a secret, came in to catch, and the ball kept sailing to the backstop. "If I can't catch a fastball, I'm washed up," Kleinow grumbled, in a story told for years by legendary Yankees scout Paul Krichell.

Russ Ford's secret wouldn't hold forever, and he would be gone from baseball before his time. But in 1910, he was the equal of any pitcher in the game. He wanted to lead the league in winning percentage and lobbied Chase to pitch him against the

A's during the last week of the season. The A's, who had clinched the pennant, did not want to pitch their ace, Chief Bender, and Ford believed that Chase had made an agreement with Connie Mack not to pitch Ford. So Bender finished 23–5 (.821) and Ford 26–6 (.813). "I implored acting manager Chase to let me pitch," Ford wrote.

But when the Yankees and Giants finally agreed to play the postseason showdown that had been on the table for years, Ford would be called upon to battle the great Christy Mathewson, an epic pitching duel that packed the Polo Grounds on October 13.

The Giants boycotted the World Series in 1904, when an all-Manhattan match was possible to the last day. Farrell spurned the Giants overtures for a postseason series in 1906.

But the teams now saw the mutual benefits of better relations and agreed to meet in 1910, a year in which the Yankees reportedly cleared $80,000 profit. In the first "Subway Series," there was nothing on the line except pride, the hearts of New Yorkers, and money. The players would share in the proceeds of the first four games, the winners getting 60 percent of the kitty. While the A's and Cubs were getting ready for the World Series, fans in New York were consumed by the Yankees-Giants showdown, as were fans in Ohio to an Indians-Reds series. Elsewhere, a team of AL All-Stars that included Cobb and Walter Johnson, was playing the A's to keep them sharp during the offweek. All of this was under the auspices of the National Commission, forerunner of the MLB commissioner's office, and two of the best umpires in the game, Bill Klem and Billy Evans, were assigned to the

Yankees-Giants series. With the Tigers out of the World Series after three consecutive appearances, their manager, Hughie Jennings, was hired to write about the series for a New York paper.

Hal Chase, who had replaced George Stallings with 14 games left in the season, would have to match wits with John McGraw, the most famous manager in the game. Leading up to the game, it was assumed the managers would avoid pitting their best pitchers against each other, but when reporters asked Chase who would pitch, "he smiled slyly when Russell Ford's name was mentioned," according to the *New-York Tribune*.

"Fans are hoping that Mighty Matty will be the man for the Giants," the *Tribune* continued. "But in all probability McGraw will save 'the Big Six' unless perchance Chase picks out [Hippo] Vaughn or [Jack] Warhop to do the twirling."

The Giants were installed as 10-to-8 betting favorites, as money was plunked down all over the city on the long-awaited matchup of Manhattan rivals. The official paid attendance was 24,398, but writers were convinced there were far more than that in the stands. After all, the Polo Grounds held well over 30,000, and in a surviving panoramic of the day, it appears nearly every seat had an occupant. Most wore heavy overcoats and wool caps as the temperature dropped below 40 when the sun disappeared.

As fans arrived for the scheduled 2:45 p.m. first pitch on a Thursday, they were there to see McGraw shake hands with a Yankees manager, Chase—awkwardly, but amicably, behind home plate and more delighted to see both "The Big Six," Christy Mathewson warming for the Giants, and Russ Ford, "The New Matty," warming for the Yankees. Like the poker players they were, Chase and McGraw decided to go all in for Game One.

Mathewson, far taller than the average player of his day, had just turned thirty yet had already been the ace of the Giants and the idol of New York fans for a decade, amassing 273 wins. In 1910, he had a typical season, by his standards, finishing 27–9 with a 1.89 ERA across 318 ⅓ innings, leading the NL with 27 complete games. He relied on no "tricks," nothing to deface or discolor the baseball. He simply threw a fastball with impeccable command, a curve, and the "fadeaway," the signature pitch he invented that drifted down-and-away from left-handed hitters, comparable to the "screwball" or perhaps the "circle change" of later generations. Hitters seeing it for the first time, as most of the Yankees were on this day, usually had no chance.

Where Mathewson seemed to be playing catch, Ford was what today would be called a "maximum effort guy." McGraw, scouting him late in the season, determined that a pitcher who expended so much on each delivery could be tired out.

As Mathewson related in his 1912 book, *Pitching in a Pinch*, McGraw gathered his players in the clubhouse before Game 1 and told them, "If Ford pitches today, wait everything out to the last minutes. Make him pitch every ball you can."

In the 1905 World Series, Mathewson pitched three complete-game shutouts, establishing himself for all time as a big-game pitcher. He began by striking out Daniels, the Yankees' rookie speedster, who was frozen and staring at the fadeaway, and the crowd roared. Charlie Hemphill reached on an error but was thrown out stealing by Chief Myers, Matty's reliable catcher, and Chase fouled out.

Then Ford took the mound and walked the leadoff batter, Josh Devore, who stole second. But Ford retired the next two, striking out Fred Snodgrass, and picked Devore off second to end the inning.

Mathewson struck out three more batters in the second, but the Yankees scratched out a run. Jack Knight singled, but when Mathewson had him picked off first, the first baseman, Fred Merkle (he of the famous 1908 muff) threw the ball into left field. Knight reached third and scored when Merkle dropped a two-out pop-up.

As Ford and Mathewson settled in, the crowd bundling up and huddling together, the pitching duel moved into the late innings. Merkle again messed up in the fifth, when he led off with a double but was out after over-sliding the bag.

It was still 1–0 when the Giants batted in the sixth. Devore beat out an infield hit and stole second, moving up on a bunt. When Larry Doyle, who had bunted, was called out at first, McGraw got himself ejected by Billy Evans. Ford struck out Snodgrass again, but Red Murray's bloop hit, which just eluded Birdie Cree, scored the tying run.

Cree doubled to start the seventh, and the Yankees put runners at the corners with no outs. Mathewson struck out Ford and Jimmy Austin, and Daniels popped up to end the inning. "It was no wonder that the fans, once more, almost lost their reason," wrote the *Tribune*.

Chase doubled, narrowly missing a home run, in the eighth, and after an error, the Yankees again had runners at the corners. Mathewson struck out Cree "in the coolest and most deliberate fashion, and once again the crowd rose as one man to applaud the wonderful work of a remarkable pitcher." It was strikeout No. 14, but Matthewson knew he was in a battle.

"Ford was pitching perfectly," Mathewson wrote, "with all the art of a master craftsman."

In the bottom of the eighth, Mathewson singled, and Devore, reaching base for the fourth time, beat out a bunt. Then Doyle bunted to first, giving Chase a chance to make the play for which he was most famous. He charged, scooped, and fired to third on the dead run, but Austin bobbled the throw and Mathewson was safe, loading the bases.

Ford struck out Snodgrass for the fourth time, then got Murray on a fly ball. Nearly out of the wilderness, he faced shortstop Al Bridwell. Now, McGraw called time, jogged out from the dugout, and whispered something into Bridwell's ear, and Bridwell nodded. "The whole thing was a pantomime," Mathewson said, "a wordless play."

When Bridwell got back in the box, Ford, his rhythm lost, hit him on the leg to force in the go-ahead run. Art Devlin stroked a clean single to left to score two, and another scored on an infield hit, when the lumbering Chief Myers beat Chase to first base. Ford finished the inning and trudged back to the dugout to watch his teammates go down meekly in the ninth. The Giants had won the first game, 5–1, which generated $19,262 in receipts, $10,489 to be shared by the players.

What did McGraw whisper? According to Matty, it was "How many quail did you say you shot when you went hunting last fall, Al?"

The Polo Grounds and American League Park were actually located just one subway stop apart on the IRT line, but the lines for the elevator at the 168th Street stop made it easier for fans to get off at 157th, the Polo Grounds, and walk the rest of the way. Mathewson and Ford would not duel again in the series, which moved further uptown, the city still transfixed as the Giants set foot on the Yankees' turf.

"At every season's end since the American League established a team on the Hilltop, the fans of Gotham have begged and prayed for the Giants and the Yanks to clash," the *New York Times* gushed after Game One. "The collision didn't arrive until yesterday, and the explosion which followed went thundering over Manhattan Island from one end to the other."

Every seat was filled, the weather considerably warmer, though there was no overflow of spectators in the outfield or in foul territory for Game Two. About 10,000 came to the Hilltop and saw a sloppy, rowdy game so typical of the times, a "sand-lot exhibition," the *Brooklyn Eagle* called it. "The lowliest fan of Yaphank would refuse to recognize it as a championship battle. Yet most of the 10,000 Manhattan 'educated' baseball bugs yelled themselves into a state of near imbecility."

In the eighth inning, as Chase rounded third and headed home with the tying run, the Giants' Art Devlin deliberately got in his way. Evans called obstruction and Chase was awarded home. In the ninth, the Yankees' Fred Mitchell deliberately stuck out his leg and was hit by a pitch from Hooks Wiltse, igniting the game-winning rally.

The Giants scored two in the second inning and one in the third off Jack Warhop, and Wiltse held a 3–1 lead into the eighth. Hemphill walked with 2 out and scored when Snodgrass, most famous for his error in the 1912 World Series, muffed Chase's single to center. Chase scored from second, despite the obstruction, on Knight's single.

The Giants regained the lead against Warhop in the eighth on an RBI double by Devlin, who had become the villain to the Yankees crowd. In the bottom of the inning, Mitchell was awarded first on the disputed hit-by-pitch, putting two runners on. Austin subsequently tied the game with a hit, and Wiltse, still furious over the umpiring, walked two batters to force in the go-ahead run. Warhop closed it out.

In Game 3, back at the Polo Grounds, the Giants nicked up Vaughn and took a 5–1 lead, but pitcher Louis Drucke weakened in the seventh. With the bases loaded and no outs, McGraw brought in Mathewson. Mathewson got two out, but Hemphill singled to score two runs and Chase beat out an infield hit to score another, and suddenly it was 5–4. But Mathewson, striking out four in three innings, got the "save."

There was no baseball on Sundays. The series resumed at the Yankees' home on Monday, October 17, the day the World Series began. Now the Hilltop swelled with 13,000 fans, and Ford was back on the mound for Chase but did not have his stuff, allowing 10 hits and 5 runs.

The Yankees scored three in the eighth to take the lead, but Devore's single tied the game against Warhop with two out in the ninth. The potential winning run was thrown out at the plate by Cree, and the game went to extra innings. With the 2:45 p.m. start, time was of the essence, and this one was called a 5–5 tie after 10 innings. With four games in the books, the series had drawn nearly 76,000 fans and the players now had $32,000 to divvy up.

"Christy Mathewson once more proved too strong, clever and resourceful for the Yankees, and he held them like babes in his arms," wrote the *New-York Tribune* after Game Five. Josh Devore, the sharpest thorn in the Yankees' side in the series, began the game with a home run, a poke into the short Polo Grounds porch in left. In the second inning, with a run in and two on, Larry Doyle hit one over the head of center fielder Roach, and, as the ball rolled out to the clubhouses, 500 feet away, Doyle circled the bases to give the Giants a 5–0 lead. Mathewson pitched a five-hitter with 9 more strikeouts, so he now had 28 strikeouts and 1 walk in 21 innings in the series.

Back at American League Park, where only 7,642 paid their way in, the great "event town" was clearly just about over this one. Chase, 10-for-29 in the series, decided to have his team bat first (interestingly, teams had a choice in those days). The home team often batted first to get first whacks at the new baseball. The Yankees whacked it around for eight runs in the second inning and won, 10–2, as Quinn pitched 6 ⅓ scoreless innings in relief.

Rain put off Game Seven, giving Mathewson an extra day. McGraw had a chance to wrap it up at the Polo Grounds, so there was no doubt who would get the ball on October 21. Doyle hit another three-run homer, this one into the over-hanging upper deck in right field, as the Giants pounded Warhop and built a 6–1 lead. Ford relieved and pitched four decent innings, but the Yankees did nothing with Mathewson, except for a couple of meaningless runs in the eighth.

Mathewson and the Giants clinched the series with a 6–3 victory. Devore hit .414 and Doyle .378, but the star, as could only be considered fitting, was Mathewson, who had 3 wins and a save in eight days, striking out 35 in 30 innings, with 1 walk.

"Matty smiled as he ran off the field," the *Tribune* recorded. "Calling for the ball, he tossed it to the crowd in the right-field bleachers. A fortunate fan caught the sphere, a souvenir from the king of pitchers to be cherished for years, and the big series was over."

Ford, by contrast, allowed 26 hits in 19 innings, and what would be his one moment on the big stage was over.

"Either the Giants sluggers had come to Hilltop Park to watch me pitch on their nonscheduled days," Ford later lamented, "or else they were hitting at their top of the season form. They hit the emery ball—and how!"

The unmistakable response to New Yorkers was crazed excitement, followed by boredom—only 4,439 paid their way into the Polo Grounds for the final game, bringing the series total to 103,033. The Giants' winning shares were estimated at $1,166 per man, the Yankees' $706. In an era where few players made more than a few thousand, it was a nice chuck of change.

The Giants reached the World Series in 1911, '12, and '13, losing them all. The idea of a New York series was renewed in 1914, and it was no contest, the Giants winning 4 games to 1. Mathewson, who was 24–13, had his last great season, and in the opener he struggled through 10 innings to win, 6–5, and did not pitch again in the series. He had 351 career wins and would get only 12 more before retiring in 1916.

Russ Ford would never again be what he was in 1910. He went 22–11 with a 2.65 ERA in 1911, then 13–21 and 12–18 the next two years. By then, he claimed, he was no longer using emery but doctoring the ball using his fingernails, soaking them in alum water to toughen them. The National Commission, at the urging of many managers, outlawed the use of emery, or other materials, to doctor the baseball in 1914, six years before the spitter was abolished.

"Baseball can get along without these freaks," said "Wild Bill" Donovan, just after he became the Yankees manager in the spring of 1915. "A good pitcher doesn't have to use such tricks. Look down the list of great pitchers; how many of them were spitball or emery ball pitchers? Not many."

With scuffed balls illegal, the umpires began putting brand new balls in play far more frequently, costing the owners more money, as I.E. Sanborn reported for the *Chicago Tribune* in 1917, when horsehide was getting hard to acquire due to World War I.

Ford, after a contract squabble with Farrell, joined Chase and many others in a jump to the outlaw Federal League in 1914, but after two years in Buffalo, the league folded. In the spring of 1916, Ford said, he wrote the new Yankees owner, Jacob Ruppert, telling him he didn't think he could win without the emery ball and asked for his release. He pitched in the minors at Denver and on May 26, 1917, told reporters, "I cannot get into form," and retired at once, resuming his career as a draftsman, and he eventually settled in North Carolina.

But the art of scuffing the ball, and making it do tricks, lived on long after Russ Ford. With the Gas House Gang Cardinals of the 1940s, Leo Durocher used to go to the mound from shortstop, cut the ball on his belt buckle, and hand it back to the pitcher, saying, "it's on the bottom, buddy." Mike Scott of the Astros made great use of the "does-he-or-doesn't-he?" head game in the 1980s. Whitey Ford was known to cut the ball with his sharpened wedding ring, and as Jim Bouton related in *Ball Four*, an umpire once went out to the mound and told him, "Whitey, go into the clubhouse. Your jock strap needs fixing. And when you come back, it better be without that ring."

The "regional series" concept didn't have quite the same staying power. It took hold only in Chicago, where Cubs and White Sox met in Octobers until 1942. In New York, the Yankees would meet the Giants (who turned down a Yankees challenge in 1920) or the Dodgers in a dozen future Octobers, but in the World Series. New York fans would come out for nothing less.

CHAPTER 9

STRANGE DAYS, INDEED

Up at The Hilltop, things change strangely. For the American League team has no local following or particular allies . . . not a trace of a special clientele that is all its own.

—*Baseball Magazine*, 1911

The early Yankees were often disappointing on the field and played in a ballpark without amenities. The prevailing perception was that they had few fans, only customers who got their baseball fix when the Giants were out of town, who came to see the visiting stars like Ty Cobb, Tris Speaker, Nap Lajoie, Walter Johnson, and Smokey Joe Wood.

William A. Phelon wrote of the Hilltop experience for *Baseball Magazine* in 1911: "They cheer good plays with absolute indifference as to the player, and visiting athletes get as much approval as the Highland crew. Strange reversal of form: the New York rooter is the most partisan on earth when he is

117

at the Polo Grounds, and the most impartial when he is at the other ballyard in his home city!"

When the Giants were out of town, though, some high-profile baseball fans came to American League Park, and in New York at that time, that meant vaudevillians, like George M. Cohan, who helped arrange a charity game for victims of the Titanic, and George "Honey Boy" Evans, who often set up New York's baseball players to appear on stage as "monologists" telling funny baseball anecdotes.

Born in Wales, Evans—a minstrel singer, comedian, and entertainer—became so fascinated with baseball after settling in New York, he commissioned beautiful silver "loving cups" five years in a row, to present to the "world's champion batsman." Honus Wagner got the first, Ty Cobb the next four.

When fans made the trip uptown and filed in to the American League Grounds, they never knew what would transpire— especially in 1912, the ballpark's last season in existence. *Bain News Service, courtesy of the Library of Congress*

On Saturday May 11, 1912, when the Tigers came to American League Park for the start of a wild and vicious four-game series, Honey Boy made his usual trip up to the Hilltop to present Cobb with his latest sterling silver work of art, a large platform with figurines of pitcher, batter, and catcher on the top.

Cobb accepted the trophy graciously before the game as the crowd applauded, recognizing the brilliance of the man who hit .420 in 1911 and was starting out on a .409 season.

Then things got crazy, as they so often did at Hilltop Park. When it closed on October 5, 1912, there would be no great ceremony, no tears, no one scooping up dirt to save as a memento. The team's lease on the land expired; The Institute for the Blind did not want to extend, even for a short term. The park was shuttered and razed by 1914 to make room for the hospital, and the Highlanders moved in to share the Polo Grounds and officially became the Yankees.

When the old Yankee Stadium closed in 2008, the Yankees liked to talk of "bringing the ghosts across the street" to the new place. If there are ghosts remaining on 168th and Broadway, where the spot on which home plate stood is marked inside the courtyard of Columbia Presbyterian, they are giggling ghosts.

Such was the short, but colorful history of the park. And when the last fans walked out on October 5, 1912, they were, indeed, laughing.

The Yankees of that season, the worst in franchise history, were managed by "Fighting Harry" Wolverton, a longtime baseball man, as a bit player in the majors and player-manager in the minors. Farrell brought him east from the Oakland Oaks, the same franchise from which the Yankees would recycle Casey Stengel in 1949. But Wolverton, who pinch-hit occasionally and off the field wore a sombrero and smoked the biggest cigars he could find, was no Stengel, and the 1912 Yankees bore no resemblance to the turnkey dynasty Stengel inherited. They were 5–13 when the Tigers came to town, so it was little wonder that Ty Cobb was the main attraction.

But on May 11, it was the umpire, Silk O'Loughlin, who was in the center of a maelstrom. The Tigers broke up a pitching duel with five runs off Russ Ford in the seventh inning, and four Highlanders were ejected. Pitcher John Quinn walked Donnie Bush and was so enraged by the call, he heaved his glove to the bench. O'Loughlin tossed him immediately, and then Bert Daniels, on the bench, flung a baleful of bats in the air. He was gone, too. After another walk, catcher Gabby Street got a little too gabby, and O'Loughlin, who was cheered by fans for his tolerance of Kid Elberfeld in the 1906 melee, had by now ejected Wolverton and was dodging soda bottles thrown from the grand-stand. The Tigers won, 9–5, and O'Loughlin once more required police protection to get off the field and safely out of the ballpark.

Into his trunk, Cobb packed away what would be the last of the Evans loving cups—all of which are now in Cooperstown. Before Honey Boy died of stomach cancer in 1915, he was named honorary president of the Baseball Players Fraternity, announced in a letter from Dave Fultz, the original Highlanders' center fielder.

The next day was a Sunday, a much-needed day for everyone to cool off. New York won on Monday, Detroit on Tuesday,

Ty Cobb never felt remorse—in fact, he took immense satisfaction—from beating up a crippled fan in the stands at Hilltop Park. *Bain News Service, courtesy of the Library of Congress*

and through it all the combustible Cobb, 5-for-12 so far in the series, was jawing with the rowdy group of fans along the left-field line, just past the visitors' dugout.

One of those fans was Claude Lucker—or Lueker, as some papers spelled the name. A pressman at one of the morning papers, Lucker lost all of one hand, and three fingers of another, in a terrible accident on the presses about a year before. He then became a page in the Tammany Hall office of sheriff Tom Foley—an old patron of Farrell and Devery, who owned 10 percent of the Yankees. Lucker made the long trip from his home on James Slip, near the southern tip of Manhattan, up to Washington Heights for nearly every game. Having come from Georgia, born near Cobb's hometown of Royston, Lucker took particular interest in ribbing "The Georgia Peach," and vice versa, as Lucker would later tell the *New York Sun*, and it had always been taken in fun. He was with a group of friends and Lower East Side rowdies in the third row of bleachers that included Henry Zahn, warden of the grand jury, and neighbors Louis Linden, John Flynn, and John Jordan.

On the pretty spring afternoon of May 15, Farrell, Devery, and Ban Johnson were all in box seats for the last day of the series. That's when things got out of control.

"I did not get to the game until after the first inning," Lucker told the *Evening World* a few days later. "When the Detroits came on the field, there was a good deal of kidding and booing of Cobb. Still, there was no harm in what was said. I had on an Alpaca coat, and he seemed to single me out, for he yelled, 'Go back to your waiter's job,' but that was no harm. Then someone near me hollered out to Cobb, 'Oh, you're dopey anyway.' Cobb turned and yelled, 'Yeah, I'm dopey because I was out with a member of your family last night.' He followed this up with some vile talk."

Keeping in mind, this is Lucker's version. This being New York in 1912, each of the several papers had its own set of details. Lucker said he joined in the booing as the jawing continued while Cobb, hitless in two at-bats, took the field for the fourth. "In the middle of it, a man near me called out, 'Oh, go out and play ball, you half-coon.' I forget just what Cobb said back at this, but he quieted down before the inning was through."

It was likely another racial epithet that was used.

Rather than go directly to the dugout, which was on the third-base side, Cobb ran across the outfield and up the first-base side. He confronted Farrell and Devery in their box seats and the police detail on hand.

For his 1961 memoirs, Cobb recalled the events a little differently. "In the third-base bleacher was a man who had ridden me hard in past New York appearances. He wore an alpaca coat and was rude beyond belief. Right at the start of this day he began braying at me. I made as if I didn't hear him, which only increased his foul abuse. . . . In the [fourth] inning, he was cursing and reflecting on my mother's color and morals."

Cobb came from a troubled background, his mother killing his father with a shot gun, claiming she thought he was an intruder, so any mention of his parents was bound to enrage him. In 1912, a white southerner was also sure to become enraged if it was suggested he was biracial. Cobb said he stopped by the Yankees dugout and warned Wolverton, "There is going to be trouble if this fellow isn't stopped. . . . I repeated the warning at a box occupied by New York club officials. All I got was shrugs. We players were fed up with the unconcern—the stupidity—of owners. You were supposed to take obscenities and never lay a hand on your attacker. Well . . . Polonius didn't figure that way. Nor did I."

When he got back to the bench, Cobb said, Sam Crawford and Jim Delahanty told him, "If you don't do something about that, you're gutless, no good . . ."

That was another thing one did not say to Ty Cobb. He lost his head, claiming in 1961 that he doesn't remember how he scaled the high barrier and made it up through the fans to reach Claude Lucker. But reach him, he did.

Back to Lucker's conversation with the *World*:

"He let out with his fist and he caught me in the forehead, over the left eye," Lucker said. "I was knocked over, and then he jumped me. He spiked me in the left leg, and kicked me in the left side. Then he booted me behind the ear. While I was down and Cobb was kicking me, someone in the crowd yelled 'Don't kick him. He's a cripple and he has no hands.' Then I heard Cobb say, 'I don't care if the [obscenity deleted] has no feet.' I

123

was pretty well bruised up and covered with blood when Cobb was through with me."

When Cobb pulled out a scrapbook nearly 50 years later and read the list of Lucker's injuries—forehead, ribs, leg, ear— he wrote, "I'm pleased to note I didn't overlook any punitive measures."

Several of Cobb's teammates had followed him with bats, and eventually players, spectators, and police pulled Cobb away and took Lucker to safety. The *New York Herald* reported Lucker, with "extensive alterations to his face," was hollering as he was helped out of the park, "He hit the wrong man this time. I'll get Cobb yet." Lucker's friends, with their political connections, made similar, cryptic statements and corroborated his side of the story, for what that is worth.

Ban Johnson, the AL's "czar" sitting in the stands, was not pleased, and he suspended Cobb indefinitely, pending further investigation, as he collected affidavits from all involved. Cobb learned of the suspension when the Tigers got to Philadelphia the next day, and he doubled down when the writers asked for reaction:

> No man with a right to the title would stand for the things I was called. If President Johnson would allow them to be used to him without knocking down the man who said them, then he is not a man.
>
> . . . I should have at least had a chance to state my case. I feel that a great injustice has been done. I was only kidding that fellow, and I frightened him to death, but

I would not take from the United States Army what he said to me. The fans in New York cheered me to the echo when I left the field. I don't look for applause, but I'm glad the fans were with me this time. This fellow is one of those men who go to a game and make it bad for everybody near him by roasting. I stood it for a long time, but I am only human. I warned him once, and when he started again I went after him. He yelled before I could get ahold of him, he was the worst scared man I ever saw. They got between us before I started good and he was pleading for mercy.

Amazingly, 1912 or not, support for Cobb was almost universal, even as the man's disabilities became known. The Georgia congressional delegation sent an official letter of support, and Tigers manager Hugh Jennings, as well as players and managers everywhere, expressed, one way or another, that something had to be done about the abuse players were taking from fans. The *New-York Tribune* noted that police stood within earshot of the goings-on and did nothing until "the outraged player was provoked into administering a well-deserved beating."

Johnson had none of it. "No player has any right to strike a spectator," he said. Cobb could have gone to umpires and complained and had the fan removed, he reasoned, rather than "take the law into his own hands." The suspension stood, and the Tigers called a "work stoppage" that would bring far more outrage than the incident. The players refused to play without Cobb, and, despite Johnson's threats of major fines, perhaps even revoking the franchise, they sat out a game in Philadelphia. The Tigers fielded a team of local amateurs and lost to the A's 24–4 on May 18. Cobb asked the players to return, out of respect to owner Frank Navin, and they did so on the 21st.

"The boys are doing this because they are in no condition to fight," Cobb said. "The fight was altogether against Johnson, and not against the Detroit club. As the club appeared to be the chief sufferer, the boys decided to call off the strike."

Navin paid the 18 players' fines of $100 each for the game they skipped. When Johnson completed his interviews, he fined Cobb $50 and set the suspension at 10 days, to end May 26. He determined that Cobb was responsible, as "the first to employ vicious language in replying to a taunting remark of a spectator." Johnson promised to beef up security at all parks, but also to punish players "who assume to act as judge and avenger of real or fancied wrongs while on duty," according to *Sporting Life*.

There was a report in the *Sun* that friends and neighbors of Lucker's on the Lower East Side would cause more trouble for Cobb when the Tigers returned, and with Lucker having retained a lawyer, that an arrest warrant would be waiting.

But by August, when the Tigers were to return to New York, things had pretty much blown over. Then Cobb was lured out of his car and attacked by a gang at a stoplight in Detroit, sustaining a superficial knife wound, and there was talk of a connection. John McGraw heard rumors and asked a writer to alert Cobb when he got to New York. But he was in the Tigers' lineup on August 13 when they returned, and because their baggage was left behind by the railroad—yes, that also happened on trains in 1912—they had to wear New York's road gray uniforms. It appeared Cobb was wearing Ed Sweeney's gear, the pants too big, the shoes much too tight. More good-naturedly, fans hollered that the great Cobb would look good in that uniform all the time. Cobb, playfully, reached base and kept wandering off second base and evading shortstop Bill Stumpf's attempts to tag him. Everybody toyed with the Highlanders in 1912.

"I guess I can take care of myself," Cobb joked after the game, "that is, if I can get these shoes off."

Fans making their way to The Hilltop never knew what they might see. When the Yankees acquired a little-known catcher from St. Louis, a smart, rugged-looking kid named Wesley Branch Rickey, who knew the history they would see?

For religious reasons, Rickey would not play on Sunday. He coached baseball and football at Ohio Wesleyan University, all three successfully, during the offseason. Proud of his throwing arm—"that's what got me to the major leagues," he later wrote—Rickey injured his shoulder while demonstrating throwing technique to his college players in 1906. He had promised his new bride, Jane, that 1907 would be his last season of baseball; he would settle down and study law.

Early in the 1907 season, Rickey reported to manager Clark Griffith that his shoulder was hurting badly, and he was sent for two weeks to that favored healing spot, Hot Springs, Arkansas, which did not help. When Rickey returned, he played sparingly, mostly in the outfield. "I couldn't throw accurately and at a time when my arm would be cold, I could not throw the ball hard and it was painful up under the shoulder," Rickey recalled many years later.

On June 28, with Red Kleinow hurt and forty-four-year-old Deacon McGuire the only other option, Griffith asked Rickey to get behind the plate. "I'll try," Rickey responded.

". . . I tried to catch and the first three or four men who tried to steal, I tried to throw them out."

This game, too, became a vaudeville skit, but unintentionally. "They played rings, circles and orbits around the New Yorks," the *Tribune* reported. "The Washingtons went on a base-running spree—waxed merry over a jag of pilfering sacks." (Translation: They stole a lot of bases.)

"Rickey threw so poorly that all a man had to do to put through a steal was start. The Washingtons soon discovered that as a thrower Rickey was many chips shy and they paused in their travels only long enough to get breath."

Rickey's first throw to second was lofted high and wide and landed in right field. The second bounced in the dirt several feet in front of the bag. He appeared to throw a runner out at third, reporters conceded, but the umpire, perhaps by force of habit, called the runner safe.

"First he would apparently try to carry away Elberfeld's leg, and next he would throw a fly out to center field," chortled the *Washington Evening Star.*

"Rickey could not gauge the distance to the second station," wrote the *Washington Evening Star*, "having an idea that it was either just behind the pitcher's box, or out near Danny Hoffman [in center field]."

Since the Senators got 20 hits and 9 walks off Highlanders pitching, the carousel kept turning, and those fans remaining at Hilltop Park took to whistling popular songs in unison during the late innings.

Humiliated, Rickey just stopped throwing and later recalled the last six or eight bases were stolen without a throw from him. The Senators finished with 13 steals, a record that still stands, in a 16–5 rout.

Rickey never caught again, and after hitting .185 in a handful of games played in left field and first base, he retired as a player and returned to his job at Ohio Wesleyan in September. But he would return to baseball, as a manager and executive, where he made his everlasting mark in 1947, signing Jackie Robinson to break down baseball's racial barriers. Rickey's journey ended in the Hall of Fame.

Postscript: When Rickey signed Robinson in 1945, Griffith was one of the loudest in opposing integration of baseball. As Senators owner, he kept his franchise out of the red by renting his ballpark to the Homestead Grays and did not want the major leagues to wipe out the Negro Leagues.

The 1908 Highlanders were a dispirited bunch, and as the season wore on they didn't put up much of a struggle at bat. Two of the greatest pitchers of all time, one on his way out, the other just beginning, took advantage of the lackluster at-bats.

On June 30, Cy Young came in with Boston, three months past his forty-first birthday, tall and portly, his best fastball a decade behind him. He was having his last 20-win season, on his way to 21 wins and 299 innings pitched, but he was doing it with guile, as the *Sun* reported the following morning.

"Old, ancient, antediluvian Cy Young, relic of antiquity and the youngest man in baseball—for he gets better with the

Hilltop Park was known for its beautiful vistas, overlooking the Hudson River. It never hosted a championship event, but its ghosts would have some funny stories to tell. *Bain News Service, courtesy of the Library of Congress*

years—pitched a no-hitter against the New Yorks at American League Park."

The 1908 Highlanders, as previously noted, lost 100 games and, with Griffith gone and Kid Elberfeld an unpopular choice to replace him, weren't offering much resistance. The Red Sox pounded rookie Rube Manning to take an 8–0 lead, and old Cy went to work. He walked the first batter of the game, Harry Niles, who was thrown out stealing, and then he retired the last 26 batters in a row, striking out only two.

"The performance required exceptional fielding, for several of Young's offerings were sent back with wicked force," wrote the *Sun*. Young, who had 2 hits and 4 RBIs, also saved his no-hitter with a deft fielding play, when Neal Ball tried to bunt for a hit.

"Even aside from his pitching proclivities," said W.W. Aulick in the *New York Times*, "this gay old blade was the life of the party, galloping around the bases like he was out for the Swift Stakes."

Will Wroth Aulick offered colorful, cutting-edge prose to readers of the sad sack Highlanders throughout 1908. On September 4, with little left to cheer or cry about for either team, the seventh-place Senators came to The Hilltop for a four-game series. New York was in last place to stay, 14 games behind Washington, but manager Joe Cantillon, perhaps, held out hope of finishing sixth, or fifth. In any event, he had some reason for risking the future of the franchise.

In contrast to Young, Walter Johnson was still a teenager— two months shy of his twentieth birthday—and his record since debuting 13 months before was under .500, though his ERA was well below 2.00. He pitched the first game of the series, on a Friday, and breezed through the Highlanders, winning 6–0, a 6-hitter, with 1 walk, 4 strikeouts. Time of game, 1:33.

Aulick: "If we could arouse ourselves to sufficient loyalty, we would chide that pitcher for holding us down as he did. But we can't arouse."

The next day, Cantillon handed Johnson the ball again. Another shutout occurred: 3–0, 4 hits, 1 walk, 9 strikeouts. Time of game, 1:28.

Aulick: "Here, all along, a lot of the sympathetic set have been sobbing aloud because of the alleged fact the New York Nationals have only two pitchers. How about a one-pitcher team? . . . When you asked those in authority why Johnson pitched twice in a row, they said it was because Washington didn't have any other pitcher. The four other names on the programme were just printed to give the page balance."

Johnson may have been saved a career-ending arm injury the next day, because Sunday baseball was still outlawed in New York. But before leaving the park, Cantillon told the writers Johnson was going to pitch *both* games of the doubleheader on Monday, September 7.

He started game one and threw another shutout, winning 4–0, a 2-hitter with no walks and 5 strikeouts. Time of game, 1:40.

The umpire for those games, Billy Evans, in a syndicated column 20 years later, called it the greatest pitching feat of his time.

When Johnson came to bat in the seventh inning, Chesbro hit him on the pitching arm. Perhaps the veteran was doing the kid a favor. "The game was held up at least five minutes as the trainer gave Walter first aid," Evans recalled. "It was evident he was in great pain the rest of the game. During the 15-minute rest between games, Johnson's arm became stiff and badly swollen. Had it not been for that, Cantillon would have sent him back to get four straight shutouts."

The Senators pitched Long Tom Hughes, the ex-Highlander, out instead, and he lost, 9–3.

Aulick: "We are grievously disappointed in this man, Johnson, of Washington. Did Johnson pitch the fourth game and shut us out? He did not. What a quitter!"

In a space of about 10 weeks, the smattering of fans showing up at the Hilltop saw Cy Young's last great moment and Walter Johnson's breakthrough. Young retired in 1911 with 511 wins, a record that cannot ever be touched. Johnson went on to pitch until 1927, winning 417 games.

It didn't appear to occur to anyone that the ballpark would be shutting down with the close of the dismal 1912 season and the Yankees moving to share the Polo Grounds in 1913. Farrell had already bought a piece of land farther north, on Marble Hill, and had ambitious plans to build a stadium there, and perhaps a short-term renewal could be reached with the Institute for the Blind?

It was a warm day, low 70s with a little breeze off the Hudson, when the Senators came to American League Park on October 5, 1912. The worst season in franchise history was mercifully coming to an end, the Yankees having already lost 101 games. Fittingly, the last opponent was the Senators, the opponent for the first game on April 30, 1903, and more fittingly Clark Griffith, the original Highlanders manager, was now running Washington, with a chance to clinch second place.

Griff was carrying a couple of clowns on his roster. Nick Altrock had been a promising young pitcher and a World Series hero with the White Sox in 1906, before an arm injury wrecked his career. Now, he was "coaching" and developing a baseball comedy act that was getting laughs at the ballpark, and on the vaudeville stage. Altrock would wear his hat on backwards, a giant glove, lots of juggling and sleight of hand, and once a year Griffith would put him in a game as a pinch-hitter, or a pitcher. This went on until Altrock was well over 50 and kept him in the game, a forerunner of future "Clown Princes of Baseball," Al Schacht and Max Patkin, the rest of his life.

And there was Herman A. "Germany" Schaefer, infielder and popular cut-up who once stole first base (of course, he had been on second and ran back to first to distract the pitcher). A .257 hitter over 15 seasons, he had hit an outlying .334 for

Washington in 1911 but was back to normal, .247 in 60 games in 1912.

After the sixth inning, the Senators were leading, 6–5, when Griffith walked over to the press area behind home plate and asked his old friends, the New York scribes, for the score in Philadelphia. He was told Boston had won, 3–0.

"Good," Griffith said, according to The *Herald*. "That gives me second place in the race."

Griffith yelled to the mound, "get out of there," and Carl Cashion went to the bench. In came Altrock, who had been entertaining the few thousand fans the first six innings from the coaching box. Altrock took the mound, puffed out his chest, and pitched slow balls with a big, exaggerated motion. As the umpire was announcing the changes with his megaphone, Schaefer, who went in at third base, lay down in the outfield to hide. The Yankees were so bad, Altrock got them out without a run in the seventh.

Two batters reached the next inning, and Griffith, at forty-two, put himself in to pitch—for the first time all season. Chase hit one over the right-field fence, the last home run hit at Hilltop Park. Chase, with 14, hit more than any other player there. The three-run shot gave the Yankees the lead, and Schaefer came in from his position and "fired" his manager, taking over the pitching himself, getting the final two outs.

"It was advertised as a baseball game and developed into vaudeville entertainment," the *Herald* said.

When Schaefer came to bat, he motioned the New York outfielders to move back and he dropped a hit in front of them, but the Highlanders won, 8–6, and, the following day, newspapers would struggle to fit that name in headlines for the last time.

"When the game was over, everybody was happy," reported the *New York Sun*. "The crowd because of the harmless fun and rare comedy provided by prize jesters, the Washington men because second place was theirs, and the Yankees because they wound up with a victory."

Such was the end of baseball on 168th and Broadway. Two who were not happy were Frank Farrell and Big Bill Devery. The frustrating seasons, piled one upon the last, were fraying their famous friendship, as their extravagant lifestyles and poor business sense were draining their ill-gotten fortunes. They were looking for yet another new manager, and, as far as the dream of celebrating a championship, time had just about run out.

CHAPTER 10
THE LAST CHANCE

I have always wanted to work for the American League, and have long considered New York the best town to work in. I shall give my players a fair and equal opportunity and the good people of New York can count to the full upon my giving them the best I have in me . . .

—Frank Chance, for *Baseball Magazine*, January 1913

In the early morning hours of April 14, 1911, officer James McCann of the West 152nd Street Station was patrolling Harlem and saw something wrong—flames flickering, smoke billowing.

The Polo Grounds was on fire.

He called two fellow officers, Thomas Moran and Edward Heffernan, and the three policemen made futile efforts to extinguish the wooden left-field grandstand as the fire department raced to the scene.

The three policemen could do nothing, and it would take nearly two full days before the firemen, who heroically contained the blaze, could finally extinguish the flames. It consumed the entire grandstand, roof and seats lying in a smoldering heap. The distant bleachers were scorched, but intact. A trestle of the nearby elevated railway, along with 14 cars sitting on it, were destroyed.

Baseball was changing, outgrowing small, wooden grandstands like in the Polo Grounds and nearby American League Park. The A's opened palatial Shibe Park, which was double-decked and made of concrete and steel, with spires, in 1909. Comiskey Park, new home of the White Sox, was opened in 1910. Fenway Park in Boston was a year from its grand opening. Forbes Field in Pittsburgh (1909), Crosley in Cincinnati (1912), and Ebbets in Brooklyn (1913), all were breaking ground, if not open already. In Washington, the stands had also burned down, and the new park, which would come to be known as Griffith Stadium, opened in 1911.

So why not the Giants and Yankees? As the debris was cleared, the Giants activated plans that had been on the table for a while, to keep the usable bleachers, offices, and clubhouses in center field and ring the playing field with a double-decked steel and concrete structure. The new Polo Grounds, which would stand until 1964 and come to house the baseball and football Giants, the Yankees, Mets, and Jets, among other big-ticket events, would emerge in a matter of weeks.

In the meantime, the Giants needed a place to play. "While flames were raging fiercest and embers glowing," Giants owner John T. Brush would write for *Baseball Magazine*, "dismay, despondency and regret depicted upon the multitude of fans that had hastened to the park when it became known that it was being destroyed, that baseball philanthropist, Frank Farrell, phoned from Atlantic City—for that he deserves a monument—tendering use of his American League Park to the Giants as long as they might need it."

The Giants postponed just one game, then moved up to The Hilltop.

"It was a sad-faced and sorrowful lot of athletes that gathered in the smoke-covered clubhouse of the Giants this morning to empty their lockers, bundle up their bats and uniforms and move to the quarters of the American League club, where they will do battle for a month," wrote Bozeman Bulger of the *Evening World*.

John McGraw was most uneasy. American League Park, he knew, had about two inches of soil sitting on hard rock, which is why it was so expensive and complicated to lay out a field there in 1903. It was known to be hard on players' legs. "The Polo Grounds is of soft and spongy sod," Bulger noted.

The Giants survived their time at Hilltop Park rather nicely, winning their first seven games there, and 20 of 28, before reopening the Polo Grounds on June 28, where they went on to win the first of three consecutive NL championships in 1911. In 2 ½ months, workers had finished the 15,000-seat lower tier and, working during Giants road trips, had the upper tier ready for the World Series against Philadelphia. Brush was interested in exploring the Yankees and Giants splitting the costs and sharing the rebuilt Polo Grounds permanently, but neither Farrell nor Ban Johnson liked that idea.

But the Giants now owed Frank Farrell a favor.

Farrell had acquired a massive plot of land a mile or so to the north, at 225th Street and Kingsbridge, just off the tip of Manhattan in the Bronx. Marble Hill, the neighborhood was called, and it lay on soft ground, dampened by the Spuyten Duyvil Creek, which would have to be stanched, and piles would have to be driven to build on the land. In September 1910, Farrell announced his new park would be ready for Opening Day 1911, Memorial Day the latest.

At the close of the 1912 season, with the lease on The Hilltop expiring, nothing had been done at Farrell's site, and he called in his marker. John T. Brush died on November 16, 1912, but as he wished, the Giants and Yankees reached a one-year agreement to share the Polo Grounds. Harry Hempstead, new president of the Giants, issued a statement on January 22, 1913.

> Mr. Brush, before his demise, learned that by reason of a series of "vexatious delays," it would be impossible for the new grounds Farrell was building at 225th Street to be available for the use of his club at the beginning of the season of 1913. It later developed that the former grounds of the American League club at 168th Street could not be had for another season under any circumstances. Bearing in mind the generous and timely offer that was made by Mr. Farrell, who extended the use of the American League Park when the stands at the Polo Grounds were burned to ashes, Mr. Brush profered [sic] to Mr. Farrell the use of the Polo Grounds in 1913 for such dates as would be needed.

A FRANCHISE ON THE RISE

The foundation was laid to build a separate clubhouse for the Yankees, but both teams insisted this would be a one-year deal. Three years later, those "vexatious delays," the creek, the neighborhood resistance, were still preventing the start of any serious construction. For the Giants, it would be like allowing a ne'er-do-well brother-in-law to stay until he got on his feet. The Yankees, as they were now officially called, would share the Polo Grounds for 10 years.

Farrell and Devery now had twice as many seats to fill for each game and in baseball operations, with the Yankees coming off the 50–102 season of 1912, had to start all over again. Harry Wolverton was fired in November and went back to minor league ball for the rest of his career. The Yankees needed a big name, a proven winner, and one of the most successful, respected managers of the era had become available—Frank Chance.

Surely, Chance could change the culture and succeed where Clark Griffith and George T. Stallings had failed. As the first baseman, manager, and dean of discipline, Chance had earned the nickname "The Peerless Leader" and guided the Cubs to the NL championship in 1906, '07, '08, and '10. In 15 seasons as a Cub, Chance hit .297, with an on-base percentage of .394 and 402 stolen bases. After becoming the playing manager in 1905, Chance compiled an unfathomable .664 winning percentage in eight seasons, including the landmark 116–36 record in 1906.

His name was engraved permanently into history in July 1910, when New York sportswriter Franklin P. Adams, after the Cubs won a critical game at the Polo Grounds with help of a

Frank Chance and his wife, Edythe, made an elegant couple when they arrived in New York, at the brand new Grand Central Terminal. They expected to take the city by storm, but Chance was done in by the chaos of the Yankees' ownership. *Bain News Service, courtesy of the Library of Congress*

double play, penned a poem. "These are the saddest of possible words: Tinker to Evers to Chance. Trio of bear-cubs and fleeter than birds, Tinker and Evers and Chance." The Cubs' infield never did turn a remarkable volume of double plays, but the trio entered Cooperstown together in 1946.

Chance was bigger than most players, and fierce. He bowled them over on the basepaths, and crowded the plate. In the offseason, he also dabbled in boxing—all in all, an intimidating presence that kept the hard-to-control players of that period in line in Chicago. But a series of concussions, the result of beanings, put Chance's health in jeopardy; he needed emergency surgery to relieve blood clots in his brain after the 1912 season and would lose the hearing in one ear. Fighting with owner Charles Murphy, who wanted to break up the high-salaried Cubs—Chance, himself, was believed to be making $25,000 a year—the Peerless Leader was removed as manager and announced he would retire to the serenity of his orange grove in Glendora, California.

Farrell, perhaps at the suggestion of his old friend among the scribes, Joe Vila, who was close to Chance, reached out, though it took weeks of negotiation before Murphy granted Chase his release as a player—getting $1,500 from the Yankees. Farrell and Chance met in Chicago, and Farrell offered a three-year contract, with attendance clauses that could run the total to $120,000, or $2.9 million in 2016 dollars. "I honestly did not expect to sign," Chance told reporters when the news broke on January 9, "Mr. Farrell, however, offered inducements much better than I had dreamed of, and even excluding my love to the game as a factor, I could not decline them."

The deal rocked the baseball world. Frank Chance, who had broken the Giants' hearts so often, especially in a one-game show-down for the pennant in 1908, would now be sharing the Polo Grounds with John McGraw, a friend and rival. "The greatest deal in baseball history has been brought to a triumphant close," wrote *Baseball Magazine*. "By a series of masterly maneuvers . . . one of the ablest managers the game has ever known has been adroitly railroaded out of one major league into another."

Farrell had already named Arthur Irwin, who had been a hard-working, loyal scout, to the position of business manager; essentially GM. Irwin had largely assembled the team Chance was inheriting.

"I intend to assist him in every way to develop a first-class ball team," Farrell said. "He wanted to come here and hold his own with other American League managers. Chance does not claim he will win the pennant this year, but he does believe he will give New York a ballclub worthy of the name."

In fact, Chance didn't care for "Yankees," or any of the other nicknames, and in a letter to Farrell shortly after the contract was signed, he suggested the team should be called simply "New York" until it won something. "McGraw's men have a copyright on the nickname Giants and they deserve it for they have accomplished big things in the national league. The nicknames Highlanders, Yankees, and the others are meaningless. In cities outside of New York they attract no attention."

It was the first of many disagreements. They were the Yankees now.

On February 11, nine days after the monumental Grand Central Terminal had opened, Chance arrived via the Lake Shore Limited, Chance and his wife stepping off the train and out into the brand, spanking new main concourse to a raucous welcome.

"You know, this is quite different from 1908 when we came here to play that famous game," Edythe Chance told the newsmen, "there were no flashlights, or no loud cries of welcome. It shows, though, that New Yorkers do not hold to old dislikes. The people here are broad-minded and generous. I would not have been satisfied for Frank to have gone back into baseball anywhere else."

Chance, like Stallings in 1909, had secured a room at The Wolcott and was on board for plans for the New Yorks to train in Bermuda, an idyllic setting diametrically opposed to his hard-nosed ways. Going no-nickname wasn't the most radical experiment he had in mind. Chance had played only two games in 1912 but was planning to return to full-time duty at first base and move Hal Chase to second. Chase, a lefty thrower, did occasionally play other infield positions in a pinch, but, really? A full-time left-handed second baseman?

"I don't believe that I, or anybody else, can play first base as well as Hal Chase," Chance told Bozeman Bulger at Grand Central, "but I think it would strengthen the team if both of us were in the game, and the experiment will be tried."

Chase, characteristically, embraced the challenge when others scoffed. "I have a way of getting the ball away on any kind of play just as well as the fellow who throws the ball with his right hand. Second base is my hobby. I want to prove I can play it. It will be something new in baseball."

But Chase sprained his ankle falling off a bicycle in spring training, and Chance soon learned he, himself, could just no longer play, and he appeared in only 13 games, 33 plate appearances, as a Yankee. Chase did play five games at second, and 10 in the outfield before, as was inevitable, his relationship with the new manager became untenable.

Irwin and trainer Doc Barrett had scouted Bermuda, loved it, and sold the idea to ownership. The Yankees would be the first major league team to train outside the United States, making two diamonds on the sprawling Hamilton cricket grounds and quartering in two luxurious hotels nearby. This wasn't Montgomery, Alabama, or George Stallings's plantation. In this paradise, the players would be able to cut loose without fear of stiffening up, and be in tip-top shape for the season.

"All well," Chance cabled back to team secretary Tom Davis when he arrived at Hamilton, Bermuda, on February 17. "Looks like a good place to train. Turf in fine condition for a diamond."

Chance told Barrett to make sure the players were in bed by 11:30 p.m. each night, and after practices they would jog several laps around the grounds and then keep on jogging back to their hotels. A minor league team from Jersey joined the Yankees as sparring partners. The new manager would begin to get to know his new players, sure to impart that if the New York American League club was a country club in the past, it would no longer be the case. Utopian surroundings aside, the Yankees were in for a culture shock.

It was not only Chase, but promising young pitcher Ray Caldwell who ran afoul of the hot-tempered new manager. Caldwell, a spitballer, was 14–14 as a rookie in 1911 and 8–16 in 1912 for the abysmal teams managed by Chase and Wolverton. "It's hard to understand why Caldwell has not had better luck," Chance told Bulger, as he watched his pitchers get loose one day, "he appears to have everything that is needed for a big league pitcher. As yet, I have failed to find the trouble, but I'll keep putting him through the paces until I locate it."

As Chance was to learn, Ray Caldwell's daily paces included lots of whiskey, rye, and partying. Meanwhile, Chase's sprained ankle sidelined him for much of the camp. Yet, on March 20, Chance gave out his plans for a lineup, and he had himself penciled in at first, Chase at second.

Six days later, the Royal Mail steamer *Arcadian* docked in New York, and Frank J. Farrell, after three weeks in Bermuda, walked down the gangplank "brown as a berry," reported the *Sun*, tanned and exuberant. "Bermuda is the only place in the world for training a ballclub," Farrell said.

The players were in prime condition, the owner reported, and Chance "was a real manager . . . he has the respect of every man in harness. He is playing no favorites and insists upon the rules of discipline." Farrell shot down a report that Chance wanted to fine Chase $200 for missing curfew. "Chase is with his manager heart and soul and doesn't deserve to be pictured as a trouble maker."

He was so satisfied with camp that the Yankees management began work at securing Bermuda as a permanent home and convincing Charles Ebbets to bring the Dodgers there in 1914. But Chance, a man unaccustomed to failure, looked for someone or something to blame when he did fail, and when the Yankees got off to a poor start, he decided it was Bermuda. Players had gotten too used to the warm weather and were not able to perform in the chilly springtime in the Northeast.

Caldwell and Smokey Joe Wood hooked up in a pitchers' duel in Boston on April 14. Wood, who won 34 games and three more in the World Series in 1912, prevailed 2–1 on a cold, raw day that began with Chance asking, to no avail, for a postponement. Neither pitcher was the same after that—Caldwell did not win his first game until August 1. The Yankees lost seven of their first eight games and after a 14-game losing streak were sitting at 9–34 on June 6, and Chance had already announced they would not return to the islands.

By then, Chase was finally gone. From his catcher, Ed Sweeney, Chance learned that Chase had been sidling up to the manager's deaf side in the dugout and mocking him to the amusement of others, destroying the relationship most needed to make the team click. On June 1, Chance, after screaming his charges to a group of writers at the Polo Grounds, accusing Chase of purposely letting throws get by him, traded his first baseman to Chicago, the aforementioned "bunion and onion" deal. Prince Hal would become someone else's problem, but the Yankees had lost their best and most popular player, and Farrell and Devery thought he was given away in the manager's fit of rage.

As the Yankees languished in the cellar, rumors began to mount that Chance would resign at season's end. "I am not a quitter under fire," Chance told the reporters on August 1, "and this yarn is too serious to be ignored. I had my eyes wide open when I assumed this task. New York fans have been very patient and fair with me and in return I am anxious to repay them with better results."

In other words, Chance had a three-year plan, concurrent with his contract, and it would take that long to fix the mess he inherited. The Yankees won the last two games of the season, beating the A's, who had already clinched the AL championship, to escape last place with a 57–94 mark, a seven-game improvement over 1912.

"Frank was fit for work when he took hold of the Yankees," Christy Mathewson wrote, in a syndicated column in 1916, "but he did not have a good chance. Neither did the players, used to milder and more lenient managers, understand his methods. For example, he left Sweeney, the big catcher, back in New York as the

Yankees were starting a road trip, to watch the Cubs, who came to the Polo Grounds to play a series with the Giants. 'What I want you to do,' Chance told Sweeney, 'is stay here in New York and watch the Cubs play. Keep a particular eye on [Jimmy] Archer and how he catches, for I am here to tell you he can catch with his mouth and both eyes shut better than you can normally.' Sweeney was not used to this kind of talk. It hurt his feelings."

The schedules of the Yankees and Giants suggest that took place in July of 1913, when Sweeney did not catch between the 4th and 26th. Chance, still revered among National Leaguers like Mathewson, apparently unburdened himself to the Giants when both teams were in town. "I had deal after deal framed, and every deal I would fix up, somebody next to the owners would copper me. They would give back the money I fined players."

One player disappeared during spring training for three days, Chance told Matty, and when he tracked him down at a bar, he sent a writer in with a message. "Tell that bum if he ain't out in five minutes I am going in to get him and break up the joint. I only fined that bird $100 when I should have pasted him his full season's salary. And they gave the money back to him."

In a year when the outlaw Federal League was enticing players to jump—Hal Chase and Russ Ford were already with Buffalo—the owners wanted to keep players happy.

By the spring of 1914, when the Yankees trained in Houston, it was painfully clear this was just not going to work. In July, when Irwin was trying to acquire Clarence Kraft to play first base, Chance angrily announced to reporters he was staying with young Charlie Mullen. "Whoever made the announcement that Kraft would play for my club in the final game in Detroit certainly exceeded his authority. So long as Mullen continues to play good ball there is no danger of anyone taking his job from him."

Caldwell, who even played the outfield and pinch-hit when he was healthy and sober, had his best year, going 18–9 with a 1.94 ERA, and early on Chance was telling him, if he kept it up, he could be mentioned with the greats in the game, but manager and young ace had one run-in after another over Caldwell's lifestyle. In early August, Chance fined him $300 and warned him he would be dealt with more harshly if he didn't straighten out. On August 16, Caldwell, who didn't pay the fine, disappeared from the team, which was in Boston, and was reported to be bound for the outlaw league. Chance vowed that Caldwell would not pitch for the Yankees until he paid the fine. "Long ago I found that the only effective way of punishing a player for breaches of conduct was to take money out of his envelope," Chance said. "Now that I have fined Caldwell, if I remitted it any other player could feel free to do the same things that Caldwell did and get away with them. Unless Caldwell can pitch in his regular turn and obey my instructions, I don't want him at all. Since he voluntarily went away without giving us any notice, I have not bothered as to his whereabouts. I don't care."

Farrell did care. He was paying Caldwell and did not want to lose his best young pitcher to Buffalo of the Federal League. The Yankees had gone 6–20 in June to fall out of contention for 1914, doing a little better in July and August, but another season was down the drain and the manager seemed hardly indispensable to owners. The blow-up had been coming for some time, since the Chase trade. Chance wanted the Yankees to pay minor league people to tip them off on players, rather than rely on Irwin's scouting; Farrell thought it was too expensive.

Ray Caldwell was an immense young pitching talent, but his lifestyle drove more than one Yankees manager to distraction. *Bain News Service, courtesy of the Library of Congress*

And Chance kept complaining about the talent Irwin had provided, the *New York Times* quoting him as saying he "didn't believe it was possible to collect so many mediocre players on one big league ballclub."

The old Highlanders' pattern was about to repeat itself a third time. The strong, established manager promised carte blanche to do it his way, butted heads with the owners and the star players, and would eventually be replaced by an interim manager from the ranks of the players, sending the franchise back to square one.

In September, as George T. Stallings was being hailed for his leadership in Boston with the Braves surging to the championship, newspapers began reporting that the Yankees owners were trying to get Caldwell back and were refunding players for Chance's fines. The Peerless Leader decided he could lead the Yankees nowhere. On the 12th, Ed Sweeney's ninth-inning homer lifted the Yankees to a 2–1 win over the Athletics, but no one was celebrating. Chance sent word to writers to come down to the clubhouse.

"I can't do any better with the present material," Chance began. "Anybody at all can manage a sixth or seventh place team, but it is ridiculous to pay a man a high salary and then not give him proper material to work with. Mr. Farrell will not spend the money that should be spent."

Chance said he wanted Irwin out, and Farrell was willing to get a new scout, but not fire Irwin. The manager revealed that he had sent a letter to Farrell, proposing to resign on September 15, but expected to be paid for the remainder of the season. He showed the writers Farrell's return letter, in which he accepted the resignation, but not the terms. "I know you do not want to take money you do not earn," the letter concluded.

Farrell and Devery were outside the clubhouse, where Farrell defended his position. "I have never interfered with Chance in any way," Farrell said. "If he wants to quit of his own volition, I don't see why I should have to pay him for the rest of the season."

When the owners walked into the clubhouse, Chance and Devery, who had been a background character for years, got into it. Chance called the rotund old police chief a "second-guesser," and Devery called Chance a "quitter." Reported the *Herald*, "The manager resented this and aimed a blow at the former Chief of Police. The punch was wild and before the fight could resume the men were pulled apart."

Chance walked off to change out of his uniform, saying, "I'll be here next year managing," and Farrell hollered back, "Well, no one is trying to get rid of you."

Later, the two sides met and agreed to separate. Chance got his money for the rest of 1914, in exchange for walking away from his 1915 salary. "Chance and I parted the very best of friends," Farrell said.

The Peerless Leader, before starting the long trip back to California, said he was through with baseball, unless he could be a team president. "Farrell won over my resolution with the highest salary ever paid up until that time. I can now sincerely say it will take more than this, even, to wean me again from my orange grove."

Frank Chance made a sullen exit from New York, went home to his California orange grove, and did not return to baseball for 10 years. *Bain News Service, courtesy of the Library of Congress*

On September 15, shortstop and captain Roger Peckinpaugh, one of the few bright spots of the Chance era, managed the Yankees to a 3–1 loss to Philadelphia, which was going to its fourth World Series in five years, in the final home game. Chance, in a gray tweed suit, sat in the crowd and chatted with those who recognized him, talking baseball and remembering past glories with A's pitcher Chief Bender. In the sixth inning, the *Sun* recorded, "the tweed-clad man rose, shook hands with his friends, squared his shoulders and walked to the exit. . . . Ushered in two years ago with the greatest acclaim that ever greeted a diamond hero, he passed out without one in a hundred knowing he was gone."

Peckinpaugh, twenty-three, who will probably hold for all time the distinction of being the youngest manager in major league history, led the Yankees to a 10–9 record over the season-ending western road trip. Chance did return, to manage the Red Sox in 1923 with no better results. Irwin left the organization that winter, but later as owner of the Hartford Senators, he helped pave Lou Gehrig's way to the Yankees.

As the Yankees' 12th season closed miserably, they were in no better shape than 1903. Attendance was awful, 359,477 in 1914, less than in three different seasons at The Hilltop. The franchise and the new ballpark project were hemorrhaging money, and there was no identity and no talent.

A new manager could not change the culture; only new owners could do that.

CHAPTER 11
COLONEL RUPPERT IN COMMAND

My only regret is that I have quit baseball before I realized the ambition to provide New York with an American
League champion. I sincerely hope that Mssrs. Rupert
and Huston do not experience such hard luck and disappointments as I have suffered while the executive.

—Frank S. Farrell, January 30, 1915,
upon closing of the sale of the Yankees

Long before Larry Bird became its most famous son, the
town of French Lick, Indiana, was a most famous place. Around
its mineral springs a luxurious hotel resort was built, and rebuilt
even more lavishly after a fire in 1897. Through the early
decades of the twentieth century, the rich, the famous, and the
infamous—Irving Berlin, John Barrymore, Howard Hughes,
Al Capone, Louis Armstrong, the Vanderbilts, the Kennedys,
and the Roosevelts, to name a few—ventured there to drink and
bathe in the water, which contained sodium, magnesium sulfate,

and lithium, and were said to cure ills from arthritis to gout to cancer.

In its heyday, upwards of 150 people checked into the buff-colored, brick-faced French Lick Springs Hotel every day; the Monon Railroad laid tracks to deliver riders from Chicago right to the front steps, the spa town's population growing from 260 to 1,830 between the censuses of 1900 and 1910.

It's doubtful anyone was ever cured of anything there, though "Pluto Water" from French Lick's springs was an effective and big-selling laxative, before the classification of lithium as a controlled substance halted its bottling in 1971.

Maybe it was no fountain of youth, but for a high-rolling, lifelong bachelor and bon vivant like Col. Jacob Ruppert Jr., it was a place to go with his entourage each autumn for several weeks of relaxation and gambling in the illegal casinos that were a poorly kept secret.

When he wasn't in the soothing salt baths, kicking back in one of the bathhouses, or blowing off steam during his annual retreat in late 1914, Ruppert was receiving visitors, and working the messengers, candlestick telephones, and Western Union wires to communicate with associates back in New York who were haggling each day with Frank Farrell and Ban Johnson on the life-changing deal that would make Ruppert the icon he remains over a century later. For how many famous brewers are there?

Born in New York in 1867, Jacob Ruppert Jr. was the grandson of Franz Ruppert, a brewer who came to the US from Bavaria in the 1840s. His father built the brewery, producing Knickerbocker brand on the Upper East Side of Manhattan, and a mansion next to it at Lexington and 93rd Street. Jacob Jr. had a chance to go to Columbia to study to be a mining engineer but instead chose to learn the beer business from the ground up, starting as keg washer and, as he was ready, bumped up to vice president.

He enlisted in the state's national guard in 1886, rising to the rank of colonel, and was aide-de-camp to two governors, developing an itch for politics. Elected as a Democrat, he served in congress from 1898 to 1907, but his heart remained with his business and personal interests in New York; he missed 335 of 555, or 60.7 percent, of roll calls during that time, twice the median for his contemporaries. He was not a candidate for reelection in 1906 and thereafter concentrated on business and pleasure. Ruppert was a stern perfectionist, and when needed, he could be, well, ruthless.

"When I was thirty and perhaps forty," Ruppert once told writer Fred Lieb quite candidly, "I did not want a wife. It was too much fun being single. Then when I really wanted a wife, I was afraid to get married. I was afraid of what would eventually happen. I was afraid that I would kill her. I would be certain that she had married me for my money and that sooner or later she would take on a young lover. And then I would have no alternative but to kill her."

A "sportsman," in the parlance of the times, Ruppert loved horse racing, yachting, and baseball, since he "managed" a neighborhood sandlot team as a boy. Like nearly all of the City's elite, he was an avid Giants fan and loved hanging out with John McGraw. He considered buying the Giants as a young man, when Andrew Freedman sold to John T. Brush. After Brush's death, Ruppert began asking McGraw if there was any chance the Giants could be bought. He passed on a chance to buy the Cubs—after all, he was a New Yorker, through and through. As the 1914 season drew to a close, McGraw suggested the Yankees might be for sale.

McGraw's hunch, typically, was correct. Though the New York papers periodically carried Farrell's optimistic, bordering-on-delusional stories about the progress being made on the 225th Street/Kingsbridge site, the Yankees were available. In March 1914, Farrell unveiled impressive artists' renderings of a 40,000-seat, "fire-proof" park of concrete and terra-cotta, with subway and New York Central Railroad stations within walking distance, but nothing was done that year.

Even the brilliant, young Heywood Broun was sucked in, writing for the *Tribune* on December 2, 1914, that Farrell was no longer thinking about a baseball park to rival the Polo Grounds, but an 80,000-seat coliseum that could be used for big-time college football. "If the plans of Frank Farrell go through, New York will have a stadium next year which will make the Yale Bowl look like a drinking cup," Broun wrote. "Construction work will be begun in the spring, and the park will be ready in the fall, unless it seems likely that the Yankees will get in the World Series in which case it may be possible to finish the job a little more quickly."

In fact, the site was a boondoggle, and Farrell had just about lost his shirt on it. The Frank Chance disaster of 1913–14 shed bright light on the turmoil, and ineptitude, of the Farrell-Devery ownership. Since Gordon's lawsuit was settled in 1909, Devery owned 42 of 100 shares in the franchise, Farrell 38, and Tom Foley and attorney Abram I. Elkus 10 each. Farrell and Devery, once close as brothers, now quarreled over the running of the franchise and barely spoke.

As the National League meetings got underway at the Waldorf-Astoria the first week of December 1914, word was out that Devery was considering selling his share to a Cincinnati businessman, Rudolph Hynicka, and Hynicka wanted to buy star second baseman Eddie Collins from the A's and install him as manager.

"Mr. Farrell holds controlling interest in the New York American League Baseball club," said Tom Davis, the Yankees secretary, in a terse statement, "and as long as he does, he will do all appointing of managers."

On December 8, the A's sold Collins to the White Sox for $50,000, twice what the Yankees were said to be offering, and on that day came the first newspaper reports that linked Jacob Ruppert to the Yankees. Bozeman Bulger wrote in the *Evening World* that there was a rumor that Ruppert had purchased controlling interest. Neither Farrell nor Ruppert were in town to comment, but Bulger concluded, "the rumor is as well-founded as any floated at baseball meetings; in fact, a well-known National League manager is responsible for it."

Who had spilled the story? Smart money would be on George T. Stallings, smarter money on John J. McGraw, who seemed to relish in playing a manipulative role with regard to his cotenants.

Actually, the turmoil was widespread in baseball during the winter of 1914–15, far beyond the Yankees' mess, and in the chaos lay Ruppert's opportunity to get in, and get in on his terms, so it's understandable that he was willing to play it cool and take his usual sabbatical at French Lick. Baseball needed him, more than the other way around, in that December of 1914.

The Federal League, having declared itself a major league, was raiding both the American and National League for players, creating new escalation of salaries and operating costs. In Philadelphia, the A's had steamrolled to their fourth pennant in five years, but attendance fell—it seemed, Connie Mack would theorize, that fans were more interested in watching a team make its way to the top than fight to stay there. They played terribly in the World Series, the air rife with talk of players jumping, and were swept by Stallings's "Miracle Braves." Star pitchers Chief Bender and Eddie Plank jumped to the Feds immediately after.

"There was only one way to get out from under the catastrophe," wrote Mack, in his memoirs, "I decided to sell out and start over again. When it became known that my players were for sale, the offers rolled into me. If the players were going to 'cash in' and leave me holding the bag, there was nothing for me to do but cash in, too."

A century ahead of its time, the A's fixed on a strategy of not overpaying aging star players for what they'd already done. Mack, who owned a big piece of the team, and principal owner Ben Shibe collected as much cash as possible and used it to gather young players.

"I had intended Collins for New York," Ban Johnson told reporters, "but unforeseen happenings altered the original plans." Collins would have finally given the Yankees a player in the same elite category as Cobb, Lajoie, Wagner, and Joe Jackson. But Chicago's Federal League team had made a strong play for Walter Johnson, and White Sox owner Charles Comiskey was spooked. Johnson then arranged for the Collins sale to the White Sox, and the A's continued to break up their legendary team, including the "$100,000 Infield."

What the established leagues now needed was deeper-pocketed, more respected owners, and a boost to the value of their franchises. In New York, the Farrell-Devery ownership group, with its political ties, had served the purpose in 1903 but had proven to be woefully in over its head in the baseball business. Farrell's big talk about building the stadium at 225th Street, with no results, had worn thin.

Now, Jacob Ruppert and his partner were more the type of owners Johnson always had in mind for New York. Ruppert was astute, successful, and reserved in public, his clothes impeccably tailored and pressed. He was free of scandal despite the fling with politics and sophisticated—a lover of art, the opera, a collector of Chinese porcelain, a breeder of St. Bernards, and a keeper of exotic pets at a country estate in Garrison, New York.

He was also a civic leader in the truest sense. Random example: in those days, the *Herald* ran an "ice fund" to get ice to needy families in the summer. At the brewery, Ruppert read in the morning paper on August 13, 1912, that the fund was running low. He called the editor. "Well, I'd like to double my contribution," he said. "Make it 10 tons a day instead of five, that'll help some, won't it? You'll keep it open til about Labor Day, I suppose?"

His partner was considered a war hero. Ruppert got to know Captain Tillinghast L'Hommedieu Huston, known as "Til," or "Cap," through mutual acquaintances, including John McGraw. Both forty-seven in 1914, they frequented the Polo Grounds and hatched their dreams of getting into baseball, deciding to do it together. Huston was a Cincinnatian who made his name

organizing Company C, 2nd U.S. Volunteer Engineers, when
the Spanish American War broke out. The company was sent
to San Lazaro, a leprosy hospital, with orders to make it sani-
tary, and they performed courageously and effectively. After the
war, Huston stayed in Cuba and used his engineering skills to
make harbors navigable at Havana, Santiago, Cienfuegos, and
Matanzas, accumulating his fortune. He spent his free time in
New York, enjoying the life. McGraw vacationed in Havana,
where he met Captain Huston. McGraw, who was worried
about the Federal League's emergence, convinced Ruppert and
Huston that they were the ones who could make the American
League franchise a commercial and sporting success.

With Ruppert lounging in French Lick, Huston, husky,
bespectacled, and gregarious, was doing the talking with Johnson
and Farrell in New York. However, he said too much to reporters on December 8, when a deal was not nearly done. Everybody
had staked out forward bargaining positions, Farrell setting his
asking price at $500,000 and Ruppert offering $400,000 with
a list of conditions, and it would take weeks to bridge the gulf.
Huston later noted that he and Ruppert were "green" when it
came to baseball and had to rely on the advice of friends. Plus, as
he noted, "talks take time."

Ruppert wanted assurances that top-line players would be
made available, and he wanted an established manager hired
first. Convince John McGraw to manage the Yankees, Ruppert
reportedly told them, and he would buy the club.

This wasn't happening, so Johnson and Comiskey, who was,
like all AL owners, anxious to have Ruppert buy the Yankees, set
out on a breathtaking scheme. They found an investor willing to
purchase Connie Mack's shares in the A's and then journeyed to

Philadelphia hoping to convince Mack to come to New York as manager, and perhaps part owner. Mack agreed only to consider it. He, Johnson, and Comiskey traveled together to Oz to see The Wizard, or rather French Lick to talk to Ruppert, and when that became known, speculation ran amuck.

"You can bet all you like," George Stallings told the *Evening Telegram*, "that Mack will manage New York next year."

But it never got further than discussion. Mack's roots in Philadelphia were too deep, where he remained another 40 years. "Philadelphia is good enough for me and I expect to be right here on the job piloting the Athletics," the *Philadelphia Inquirer* quoted Mack on December 10. "And you might as well spike the canard now hard and fast."

The drama continued. Ruppert and Huston were said to be up to $450,000, Farrell holding out for $500,000. A story floated that William Smith and James McGill, nephews and heirs to the fortune of the late handicapper "Pittsburgh Phil," whom Ruppert had known from racing circles in the 1890s, wanted to make a bid for the Yankees. Smith and McGill owned the Indianapolis franchise of the American Association, right up the road from French Lick. Had they been enlisted to put pressure on the Colonel? Ruppert had his own leverage. The Federal League president, James A. Gilmore, and its Chicago franchise owner, Charles Weeghman, made a pilgrimage to French Lick to try to convince Ruppert to buy the Kansas City franchise. "Colonel Ruppert may not know much about baseball, but he is a good baseball man," John McGraw scoffed to Bozeman

Bulger. "You've got to hand it to that Gilmore for getting his league advertised."

Johnson was growing frustrated. "Nothing definite can be done, or has been done, until the present owners recede somewhat from the price asked," he reported.

Ruppert's attorney, Frank Grant, was going over Farrell's rather poorly kept books. As Ruppert insisted, Johnson and Farrell were trying to hammer out another lease agreement with the Giants, who wanted to raise the rent at the Polo Grounds, where the Yankees, as was obvious, would have to play several more years. And everybody was looking to line up a manager to Ruppert's liking. "We tried our best to get Hughie Jennings," Huston told reporters. "But Mr. Navin wouldn't hear of it." Tigers owner Frank Navin would not release Jennings, winner of three AL titles, so another big name was off the table.

Near the end of December, the sides remained $50,000 apart. "So the American League would like to have us very badly?" Huston asked Johnson at one point. When Johnson nodded, according to the *Sun*, Huston responded, "well, then, if they want us that bad, why don't the American League pay the difference?"

On December 17, Johnson, Comiskey, Huston, and staffers met again with Ruppert at the French Lick Springs Hotel, and talks broke down. John McGraw had been in town and had Ruppert's ear, to the vast annoyance of his old enemy, Johnson. If they were going to risk half a million, Ruppert told Johnson, he and Huston wanted guarantees of a "competent manager" and at least five veteran players who would impact the team. After two days of talks, Ruppert and Huston withdrew their bid.

The next day, talks were back on. They all met again in Chicago—Ruppert at last donning his business clothes and

Jacob Ruppert (left) and Til Huston (center) in their finest hour as coowners of the Yankees, the day the great stadium opened. Commissioner Kennesaw Mountain Landis is between them on Opening Day. *Bain News Service, courtesy of the Library of Congress*

moving from the resort. Word leaked from that meeting that "Wild Bill" Donovan, a successful Tigers pitcher and well regarded as an up-and-coming manager, had been lined up to manage the Yankees in 1915. Joe Lannin, owner of the Boston franchise, was employing Donovan as a minor league manager in Providence and agreed to let him go. Other AL owners, however, were not willing to let star players go to make Ruppert an instant success in New York.

On December 23, Heywood Broun wrote, "until further notice, the club will be sold on Tuesdays, Thursdays and Saturdays, while Mondays, Wednesdays, and Fridays will be reserved for denials." Ruppert arrived in New York to talk serious business that day. "There are still some points to be agreed upon," he said, "and those will have to be settled before we take over the stock."

Farrell, now infuriated by Johnson's all-too-obvious urgency to get him out of baseball, and by Huston's almost daily comments about a deal being just about complete, weighed in that afternoon. At last, he was going to meet the Colonel face-to-face. "From now on I am going to look after this thing myself," Farrell said. "I'll tell Mr. Ruppert he can have the club if he wants to pay $500,000, and that price goes, too."

By December 29, a two-year lease done with the Giants, Donovan agreed upon as manager, and a handful of serviceable, but unspectacular players shifted to New York, all that remained to settle was the final selling price, but Farrell remained intransigent. Johnson was fed up. "The deal will be closed by sundown tomorrow or not at all," Johnson said. "At least by that time I shall wash my hands of it. Naturally a transaction embracing so much money calls for time and consideration, but I believe the interested parties have had ample time for reflection."

At last on New Year's Day 1915, all the parties were ready to announce a done deal. The final terms were not revealed but believed to be $460,000 to $480,000, with the franchise's debts assumed by the new owners. "I gained my point, for I got my price," Farrell said. "Certainly, I am sorry to retire from the game I love. But I feel I have been repaid for all the efforts and disappointments. I will confess that my luck as a promoter was not such as I had hoped."

Ruppert told Johnson he would meet with the city's sportswriters over dinner at a later date, rather than appear at a press conference that day. "I cannot face them after all the procrastination of the last few weeks," he said, sheepishly. Huston exuberantly retorted, "No, that won't do. *I'll* give the dinner and introduce you to my newspaper friends."

So the managerial search that included John McGraw, Connie Mack, and Hughie Jennings ended with "Wild Bill" Donovan, winner of a minor league championship at Providence. The players coming to the Yankees were not to be Eddie Collins or Eddie Plank but included minor leaguer Wally Pipp (yes, *that* Wally Pipp) and Hugh High from Detroit, outfielder Wally Rehg from Boston, shortstop Joe Berger from Chicago, and utility player Ed Miller from St. Louis.

But everyone was satisfied. Johnson and the AL owners had new, well-heeled, and respected owners for the New York franchise; the Federal League threat was receding, as Washington proved able to hold Walter Johnson to his contract; sportsmen Ruppert and Huston had a team; and Farrell and Devery, who had paid $18,000 for the franchise, plus the costs of building the ballpark in 1903, retired with a nice profit, which they split and went their separate ways, never to reunite. They disappeared from the limelight for good and died nearly broke.

"Really, I have never thought of a club as a big money-making proposition," Huston told the *Evening World* during the long process. "If we could get a winning ballclub that did no better than break even financially, I would be tickled with the investment. Neither Col. Ruppert nor myself intends to let the ballclub and its troubles weigh heavily on us. We expect it to be a lot of good sport. If we have a loser, I expect we will be able to stand it."

Huston, who would hold the title of vice president, didn't know the president, Ruppert, as well as he thought. And he talked a bit too much in public for the reserved beer baron's tastes, planting the seeds for future problems. In the early years, Ruppert would spend most of his time running the brewery—his father's death in 1915 left him as president and heir to a fortune of over $6 million—and trying to find a place to build a new ballpark. Huston would be ubiquitous at the Polo Grounds, and on the team's train rides, hanging with players during the day, drinking with the writers at night, infatuated with the trappings of sports moguldom.

The entire Farrell-Devery crowd resigned, including Arthur Irwin, who would resurface in Yankees history as owner of the Hartford Senators, the minor league team that facilitated Lou Gehrig's early career. A business manager, or GM, would have to be found, and that would be Harry Sparrow, a solid, veteran executive and a longtime friend of McGraw. Mark Roth, who had covered the franchise from its first game for the *New York Globe*, was hired as a traveling secretary.

The first era was over, and the second era of Yankees history officially began when the deal formally closed on January 30, 1915, at the law offices of Elkus, Gleason and Proskauer at 170 Broadway. "I was not anxious to sell at any price," Farrell told reporters, sadly, after all the papers were signed, "but I cannot resist the fine offer made me, especially in these unsettled times."

That night, Huston, who put off plans to travel back to Havana, threw his promised dinner for Ruppert and the writers at the New York Athletic Club, where they raised glasses to toast "the sale of the New Yorks," and also to Ban Johnson, for his patience and fairness, and John McGraw, who was already in Havana, for his "advice," which Huston and Ruppert insisted had only come when they asked for it. The scribes' first impression of Col. Ruppert: "He strikes one as being all business, all of the time," wrote W. J. McBeth for *Sporting Life*.

"Manager Donovan will be judged by results," Ruppert said in his first speech as the owner of the Yankees, "and I am sure he will have nothing with which to complain in our treatment of him. Naturally, we hope to see improvement this very year, but I am sure myself and The Captain will be patient, too. We realize that a pennant winner cannot be made to order."

CHAPTER 12

WILD BILL AND HOME RUN BAKER

Baker will make the Yankees win many games. He'll play as well as he ever did for me. He will hit well over .300 and be Donovan's clean-up man. As a drawing card, Baker will be a success not only in New York, but all over the circuit.

—Connie Mack, February 19, 1916

The usual large crowd of sportswriters and sports luminaries gathered for the annual banquet in Philadelphia on the night of February 16, 1915, and had settled in their seats for a pleasant dinner when Connie Mack, the celebrated, angular A's manager and majordomo, dropped a bombshell:

"I can't say I've had as good a time this year as years gone by at this banquet for I have news on my mind," Mack told the gasping audience. "Frank Baker wrote me tonight that he will not play with the Athletics the coming year. I got this letter as I sat down to this banquet table. Frank has decided to quit the game for good. He's just plumb sick of traveling and wants to settle down for good on his Maryland farm."

As Mack told the crowd, Frank Baker was not angry and not fighting for more money. He just wanted to retire . . . at age twenty-nine. Despite how Mack explained it, the truth was that Baker wanted more money.

Among those with Mack on the dais was Wild Bill Donovan, who had played on Philly's sandlots and was the new manager of the Yankees, and he appeared to have recognized the opportunity immediately. He did not return to New York, as expected, and two days later there was talk Donovan had headed south, to visit Baker on his beloved farm in Trappe, Maryland, to see if he would be interested in playing for the Yankees. Mack's permission would have been needed and likely granted.

"Of course, I would like to have a player of Baker's worth upon my team," Cap Huston told the *New York Sun* on February 19, "and would go far to get him. If it is a case of dissatisfaction with his present berth, New York would be prepared to bid as high as anyone to save him to the game."

Given the times, the circumstances of both teams, and the American League, the transfer of Baker to the Yankees was a no-brainer, but nothing came easily for the Yankees of the 1910s. It took more than a year.

John Franklin "Home Run" Baker was the first player to make such a name for himself, the first to gain fame and, if he had his way, fortune by smacking baseballs into the stands—and his most famous wallops were at the Polo Grounds. He had led the American League four years running, with totals between 8 and 12, and in the 1911 World Series, he hit homers off Rube Marquard to win Game Two and Christy Mathewson to tie

Game 3 in the ninth inning. Fans began to chant "home-run . . . home-run" when he came to bat.

"Thousands of fans on their feet, hands waving, hats in the air and shouting as you round second base," Baker said, late in his life, "is something a man never forgets."

Baker hit another home run against Marquard in Game One of the 1913 World Series, setting the tone for another A's championship, the third in four seasons. With a wary eye on the marauding Federal League, Mack signed Baker to a three-year contract at $4,500 per year after that Series. But as good as Baker was, and as much as he loved baseball, he didn't need

Frank "Home Run" Baker was the first in a long line of sluggers the Yankees would acquire from the A's. But his glory days were behind him when he got to New York. *Bain News Service, courtesy of the Library of Congress*

it—and thus he had leverage. He had the farm on which he was born and raised, and each season Mack had to go down there and convince him to keep playing. Though it was only about 100 miles away, it took several connections to catch the train into Trappe, a tiny community on the Eastern Shore, near the Delaware state line, and as Mack related at the writers dinner, "I told him, 'Frank, I can't keep coming down here, sign up for three years.' And he did. He has two more seasons contracted for, and he wants to quit. I shall say 'Okay' and wish him luck."

171

What the shrewd "Tall Tactician," as Mack was called, was doing was painting Baker into a corner, knowing Baker would look greedy, and like a liar, if he now jumped to the Federals, or made public his recent demands to tear up that contract and renegotiate a new one, since the outlaw league had driven salaries beyond what he was to make in 1915 and '16. And if Mack had designs on selling him, as he had just sold Eddie Collins to Chicago for $50,000, Baker wanted a big chunk of that. There were other factors, too. Baker's wife had given birth to twin girls in January 1914, and they died less than two weeks old, so staying on the farm was not a bad thing for him.

When Baker talked of retiring, Mack called the bluff, and soon the reality of a summer out of baseball began to sink in. Indeed, the Federal League had come calling with an offer, president James Gilmore meeting Baker at the Wilmington, Delaware, depot and pressing a check into his hands. But Baker rejected it—he was proud, but principled, bristled at being called a "contract jumper," and was waiting on Mack to meet his demands, or sell him to another East Coast American League Club.

In March of 2015, a reporter made his way down to Trappe to interview Baker, who was "spattered in blood from head to foot" from the four hogs he had just slaughtered as he spoke. Gilmore's offer of "$15,000 is almost enough to make a man jump, but I couldn't jump far enough," Baker said. . . . "Understand, I don't believe a man should be paid a cent more than he is worth. He should be able to earn a great deal more for his team than his salary, but he should be paid according to his value."

With all the plow-pushing, axe-swinging, and chores that Baker was doing, he remained in playing shape, tall and lean, with a bushy "unibrow" above the eyes and an upper body powerful enough to wield his massive, 52-ounce Louisville Slugger, as thick at the handle as the barrel. If Mack didn't "come across" with $10,000 or so, he would stay on the farm.

While J. Franklin Baker was looking to be the object of one of the most lucrative deals in baseball history to that time, "Wild Bill" Donovan was nearly sold for one penny twenty years before. After one of Donovan's maddening, erratic performances on the mound, while pitching for Waterbury of the Connecticut State League in 1896, the manager, Roger Connor (the famed 19th-century slugger), was drinking at a local bar and offered Donovan to Meriden for one penny, before other members of the team stepped in and prevented the deal from taking place. The next day, Donovan pitched 14 scoreless innings and won the game with a home run, and all was forgiven.

Wild Bill Donovan was a well-liked and well-respected baseball man, but a star-crossed manager while with the Yankees. *Bain News Service, courtesy of the Library of Congress*

He was in the major leagues with Brooklyn by 1898 but spent the 1900 season in Hartford, winning 25 games and frequenting the "Chowder Parties" that were big in the city that year. The Hartford papers began calling him "Chowder Bill," or "Willing Willie."

Back in the majors, he became a star pitcher for the Tigers and a money pitcher on their pennant-winning teams of 1907–09. He was a player's player, and he had become a player's manager—gregarious, encouraging, always with a big, wide, toothy smile—and some New York writers took to calling him "Smiling Bill."

"He is unlike Stallings or McGraw in that he believes in leading rather than driving," wrote Grantland Rice from spring training in 1915. "In this respect he is more like Mack, but where Connie is somewhat austere and solemn and excessively quiet, Donovan is a rare mixer who makes friends at every turn."

Though he was hardly Jacob Ruppert's first choice to manage the Yankees, he quickly became popular in New York, and if anyone could coax Home Run Baker off his farm, and gently facilitate a deal between strong figures like Ruppert and Baker and Mack, surely Wild, Smiling Bill Donovan would do it.

"It isn't my policy to act as a slave driver and build up an aggressive team spirit by cursing my men," Wild Bill once said. "I don't believe in invective or profanity on the field as directed by a manager to his men. If I have a player who can be goaded into work by being cursed and abused, I'd rather have another man in his place."

Everyone wanted him to succeed, but for now, Wild Bill was saddled with essentially the same cast that had failed Frank

Chance. When Donovan checked in to the DeSoto Hotel in Savannah, Georgia, Grantland Rice was on the ear.

"A stranger blew in and spoke to the clerk about as follows," Rice wrote, "'Well, I see Bill Donovan had brought his bunch in. He's got his nerve. A guy like Donovan has got a swell chance to make good where a man like Frank Chance couldn't handle the job.'"

Typically, Wild Bill flashed his great smile and played along. "You're right, I've often wondered why they got a dub like that to handle the club. I know Donovan pretty well and he's a joke."

Then someone came along and called Donovan by name, and the unnamed blowhard turned red and retreated.

Wild Bill faced an uphill battle, all right. As the unpromising bunch of Yankees ballplayers gathered down South in March of 1915, Donovan had heard enough to know Baker could be enticed. But when the Yankees contacted Mack, he asked for $50,000, and discussion was still raging between Ruppert and Huston as to how high to go.

"We offered Mack $25,000 for Baker," Ruppert said on March 1. "We decided to make this liberal offer after consulting with manager Donovan the other day. We expect Baker would be a great drawing card at the Polo Grounds and would gladly pay $25,000, but not a cent more. If Mack insists on the unheard-of sum of $50,000 for Baker, it will simply prevent him from coming to New York."

On Opening Day, Baker traveled to Philadelphia and sat in the stands behind third base to watch as the A's beat Boston 2–0 behind young Herb Pennock. After the game, Baker asked Mack if he would object to his playing for a local team. Mack said he had no problem, so long as it was not near Philadelphia. He later became infuriated when Baker signed to play weekends and holidays with a team in Upland, Pennsylvania, right outside the city.

"I have never said that I would blacklist Frank Baker and never shall blacklist him," Mack told reporters in Boston on April 27, "But I want to say right now that I hope I never see him again. He has treated the club unfairly and I have no time for a man who is not fair in his dealings. A man who breaks his word once is likely to do it again. Once and for all, I do not want him on my club. We miss him terribly and need his service, but I would prefer to have a losing club than have a man whose words are unreliable."

Mack and Baker met again at the Philadelphia rail station, where Baker expressed his resentment over Mack's public statements, making Philadelphia fans believe he was being greedy and a "contract jumper." In June, Baker said he'd return to the A's if Mack would take back what he said. There was no meeting of the minds. So Baker toiled on the farm all summer, hit .377 for Upland, which won the Delaware County League, and Mack refused to sell his rights for less than $50,000.

It was a wasted season for all involved. Mack's new-look A's went 43–109, as he sold off his remaining star players, part of one of the worst teams in baseball history. To further rub salt in it, the crosstown Phillies won the NL pennant for the first time. The Yankees, now wearing the blue pinstripes and interlocking *N-Y*

combination they would wear ever after, finished fifth, 69–83, though everyone, even Ruppert, seemed to agree Donovan had done the best he could with what he had. Fritz Maisel, who hit .281 with 51 steals, was the only regular to have a decent year.

When the season ended, Donovan and the Yankees resumed their pursuit of Frank Baker. Now there was urgency—Baker had been another season out of the game, and his skills and marketability would likely erode and his contract expire, affecting leverage. Baker made it clear that he would not report to Chicago or St. Louis, other destinations about which there had been speculation. The now-dying Federal League was still trying, hoping to build a New York franchise around Baker.

In late November, Donovan and Huston traveled to Wilmington to meet Baker and make certain they could make terms with him but came home empty. On December 11, Baker interrupted his favorite pastime, shooting ducks at the farm, to tell a reporter by phone, "I am willing to come back and play the game but only if my terms are met. I do not need to play baseball for a living anymore." Donovan, though, made one more trip to the farm with a sweetened offer, and Baker agreed. Now it was again up to Connie Mack, who, nudged by Ban Johnson, began to soften his demands. On February 16, 1916, one year to the day of the Philadelphia writers dinner, Mack and Ruppert emerged from a meeting at the Brewery in Manhattan and announced a deal was done. There was wide variance in the reporting of the terms, but the best estimate is Mack and Ruppert met in the middle. Mack got $37,500 and agreed to give Baker a piece of the sale price to get him to agree to report to New York. Baker then agreed to between $7,500 and $10,000 per year through 1918.

"I am pleased that Baker is a member of the Yankees," Mack said. "When we came to a parting of the ways, I realized that it would be to my advantage to place Frank with the New York club if possible. Everyone can appreciate the value of a winner in New York."

Ruppert: "I am satisfied that the Yankees should lift themselves this year out of the joke class, anyhow. Our crying need was hitters."

And Baker: "I see that out-of-town papers have been saying that I am all in. Just wait and see 'Bake' hit that ball if I come back. I am in great shape and will be just as good as ever."

Donovan had his man, and another, Lee Magee, a hard-hitting outfielder, to bring optimism for 1916. But it was destined to be yet another ill-starred Yankees team. Before leaving the farm, Baker had a minor accident, his hand smashed by a heavy piece of wood, injuring two fingers. He would get a late start.

Baker's presence as a tall, left-handed batter taking aim at the right-field porches of the league made him an ideal mentor to first baseman Wally Pipp, and with them hitting back-to-back, the Yankees would have more home runs than ever before. On May 9, Baker settled into the box in the first inning against the White Sox lefty Claude "Lefty" Williams and drove one over the Polo Grounds grandstand, hitting the ornate frieze crowning the second deck, his first home run as a Yankee. "Now that the lid is lifted," wrote the *Sun*, "the fans are willing that he jostle bas-relief friezes or any other fair territory ornamentation that catches his eye."

By late June, "Bake" indeed looked as good as, or better than, ever—homering on three consecutive afternoons against Washington, "all sonorous swats," as Rice wrote. All of them fell onto the short right-field porch at the Polo Grounds, June 24, 25, and 27. "It's almost as hard for Baker to drive a ball into those right field seats as it is for President Wilson to write notes or a Mexican bandit to start trouble," Rice concluded. Wilson was known to write a lot of memos, and Pancho Villa was on the loose that summer.

Home run number 7 came on the Fourth of July, and another on July 11. On July 13, the Yankees beat Cleveland, 6–2, to move into first place by half a game, though the top six teams were within 5 ½ games. The next day the Tigers came to New York, and every-thing changed. In the second game of the doubleheader, Baker crashed into a low wall chasing a foul pop toward the grandstand and was knocked out cold; when he came to, he had a wrenched back, serious bruises on his chest, and, probably, broken ribs. He didn't play again until August 29, by which time the Yankees had fallen to fifth place, having gone 19–24 with Baker, and several other starters, including Magee and Maisel, out injured.

No Yankee had ever hit more than 6 home runs in a season before, but Baker, batting .269, had hit 10 in only 100 games, and Pipp set a new franchise record with 12. The Yankees had improved to fourth, above .500, and out of Col. Ruppert's "joke class" anyhow.

"I have seen many teams," Donovan said after the season, "but never a team so game in the face of repeated reverses as the Yankees of 1916."

One more time, accolades and optimism were on the Yankees' side. They had a star in the prime of his career, Home Run Baker, a young star in the making in Wally Pipp, owners with the money to back up their ambitions, and the right manager at the right time. Donovan had brought Ray Caldwell back in the fold and was molding a young pitching staff in his own making. To a banquet audience in New York after the season, Wild Bill talked about how to build a pitcher's confidence (offering to sell him for a penny wasn't part of it).

"To me, victory means more than it does to any fan in the stands," Donovan said, a week before signing a new contract for 1917, "but there is another side to be considered. I cannot break a pitcher's spirit for the sake of one ball game. I don't mean by that a young pitcher should never be taken out. I mean there are occasions when it may be better for the club to have him stay in, though he is being batted hard. If I took . . . any young pitcher out any time a few hits were made, how long would they have confidence in themselves?"

Bob Shawkey, a 25-year-old right-hander acquired from Mack, won 25 games, and Donovan liked Slim Love, Urban Shocker, Nick Collup, Ray Keating, Allen Russell, and George Mogridge, all young and promising. Wild Bill himself, who threw an inning at age thirty-nine, was the only Yankees pitcher in 1916 who was above twenty-eight.

There was the smattering of second-guessers in the grandstand in 1916, as surely as there were in 2016. "There are many angles to a ballgame that escape the fan in the stands, yet he would have his judgment guide the manager," Donovan said.

Huston was around the team most often, and enjoying himself, Ruppert back at the brewery was satisfied with the progress—the

Yankees drew 469,211 fans in 1916, a large increase from the 256,035 in 1915, justifying the investment in Baker and the faith in Donovan.

"Little complaint or discontent was reported from Bill Donovan's camp; the manager and the genial owners think that only hard luck and accidents knocked the club out of a high position in 1916, and that even a moderate break of better fortune will be all that's needed for next summer," wrote *Baseball Magazine* as spring training approached in 1917.

But as the Yankees were gathering for spring training in Georgia that March, the world around them was changing. The United States' entry into World War I now seemed inevitable, and Huston arranged for drill sergeants to put ballplayers through their daily paces, using bats in place of rifles.

As camp broke, Donovan thought he was one pitcher away from competing for the championship.

"Give me one more pitcher of the Shawkey variety," Donovan, the ex-pitcher, said, "and I'll make the rest of the league acknowledge I have a real ballclub."

Mogridge, a twenty-eight-year-old lanky left-hander from Rochester, made the rotation and, early in the season, threw the first no-hitter in the franchise's history at Fenway Park on April 24. It wasn't a shutout—the World Champion Red Sox scored a run on a walk, an error, and a sacrifice fly—but the Yankees scratched out a run in the top of the ninth and Mogridge completed the no-hitter to win, 2–1. New York papers opined that

Mogridge had pitched himself into the "Hall of Fame," though such a thing was only mythical at the time.

"It means that he has established himself in his own mind," Bozeman Bulger wrote for the *Evening World*, "that he has passed through the fire and is a genuine all wool-a-yard big leaguer. That's what George Mogridge is today."

Lefty George Mogridge pitched the first no-hitter in Yankees history. *Bain News Service, courtesy of the Library of Congress*

Mogridge went 9–11 despite a 2.98 ERA in 1917 and went on to win 132 games, though only 48 for the Yankees. Shawkey, Caldwell, and Mogridge all had sub-.500 records despite sub-3.00 ERAs. The Yankees of 1917 just couldn't hit.

Shortly after the season began, Huston departed to join the army's engineers in Europe, removing the buffer between the brusque

Ruppert and the affable Donovan. The team also endured more injuries and bad breaks, as well as underperformance. Baker played 146 games, hitting .282 with six homers and 71 RBIs. Pipp hit nine homers and knocked in 70 but batted only .244. The Yankees hit .239 as a team. Magee was traded for outfielder Armando Marsans, who got hurt almost upon his arrival.

"Bill has done as well as he could under the circumstances," said Ruppert in mid-July, as he was already contemplating a change, "and I am at a loss to account for the report that came out of Chicago that Bill's head was going to be chopped off. The boys like Bill and they play their heads off for him. They have received the worst break of any team in the American League."

As the season neared its end, and talk of suspending baseball and players entering the service grew prevalent, the Yankees tanked, going 7–20 in August. The Giants won the NL pennant in 1917, and the Yankees' attendance fell to 330,294.

On September 16, Baker failed to accompany the Yankees to Bridgeport for a Sunday exhibition game, and Donovan benched him the next day. When Baker dressed and went home, the manager suspended him. "I'm going to buy and draft all the ballplayers I can," Ruppert said, fed up with Baker's lackluster play, "and get rid of some of my old ones." Home Run sat until the 25th, then finished the season with 2 hits in his last 29 at-bats.

During Baker's suspension, the *New York Globe* reported that Donovan was turning disciplinarian, requiring his players to rise early for 9 a.m. team breakfast, perhaps an indication that the root of problems in Ruppert's mind was that Wild Bill had been just too darned nice.

By the end of September, there were already reports from United Press and syndicated columnist Christy Mathewson that

Ruppert had decided to fire Donovan and, at Ban Johnson's urging, had his eye on Cardinals manager Miller Huggins, who was not denying it. Huggins had, in fact, let Ruppert and Ban Johnson know of his availability and interest during the season and again during the World Series.

Donavan went to the brewery on October 23 to ask Ruppert how he stood and found the Colonel wasn't willing to chalk up a third empty season to bad luck. After some hemming and hawing, Ruppert said, "I like you, Donovan, but there needs to be some changes around here."

Donovan: "I know it, Colonel."

"If I live 50 years more," Ruppert said a few days later, when Donovan's successor was named, "I hope I never have to face such a painful task as confronted me when I was forced to tell Bill I had decided upon a change of managers."

Home Run Baker remained a Yankee, though it was clear he was on the decline and he would still have to be cajoled away from the farm in an annual rite of March. After his wife died, he spent the 1920 season down at the farm with his children, in another temporary retirement. He returned to the Yankees as a valuable bench player and clubhouse presence and played in two World Series for them, though decrying the "rabbit ball" that made home runs commonplace. He retired for good to his Trappe farm in 1922.

"I'd like to see them swinging against the spitters, shiners, and emery balls at which we used to look," he told writer Harry Grayson in 1943. "Dozens of balls I hit every year landed within a few inches of the top of the barrier," he said, "a little of that rabbit and they probably would have gone over."

As a minor league manager, Baker discovered Jimmie Foxx and sold him to Connie Mack, starting a new era of championships for Philadelphia. He was inducted into the Hall of Fame in 1955 and died on his farm on which he was born in 1963.

Wild Bill Donovan coached in Detroit in 1918 after leaving the Yankees and managed in Philadelphia in 1921. In 1923, after he managed the New Haven Profs to an Eastern League title, he was on his way to the winter meetings in Chicago, where it looked as though Clark Griffith were going to hire him to manage the Senators for the 1924 season.

Donovan was talking baseball in the lounge car, lamenting that modern pitchers couldn't master the curveball, then retired to his sleeping berth in the rear car.

There was trouble on the tracks, and as Donovan rode in the second of three sections of the 20th Century Limited, it was stopped in Western New York. The third section's powerful locomotive plowed into the rear car where Donovan and New Haven GM George Weiss were sleeping. Weiss, who became the Yankees GM in 1945, survived. Wild Bill Donovan, just forty-seven, was one of nine killed at Forsythe, New York, on December 9, 1923.

"The news hits me very hard," Ruppert said at the meetings in Chicago. "He was still in his prime and one of the greatest managers in baseball. I say this because I know. When he was with the Yankees Donovan had more hard luck that I have ever seen on a ball field. One player after another was injured, but still Donovan kept plugging ahead, and he never forgot how to smile. 'Smiling Bill' is what they should have called him."

CHAPTER 13

THE MIDGET MANAGER

I wish I had the knack of salving newspaper men, but I haven't and that's all there is to the story. I work and if my work won't speak for me, why, I guess I sha'n't make much of a holler myself.
—Miller Huggins, *Baseball Magazine*, December 1921

The unmistakable aroma of yeast, hops, and mass beer producing was always in the air at Lexington and 93rd Street, but visually the office where Jacob Ruppert conducted business hardly reflected a brewery, with marble and mahogany everywhere once visitors made their way past the copper vats.

The new owners had established midtown Yankees offices on 42nd Street in 1916, but the brewery was where the big deals closed. On October 25, 1917, the Colonel had called New York's sportswriters to his inner sanctum for an important announcement at 5 p.m.

"All during the summer, various persons have been appointing new managers for my baseball club," Ruppert began. "I personally preferred to wait until the season was over before I did anything in the matter. Then I decided I would select a man of my own choosing. There were many candidates in the field and I considered each one carefully. Only this morning did I arrive at a final conclusion . . ."

Reporters had been certain for days and weeks who would manage the Yankees in 1918. So they probably had to work to pretend to be in suspense as Ruppert made an awkward stab at theatrics.

"I decided on Miller Huggins. I have not signed him to a contract yet, but I propose to sign him now. The contract has been drawn up during the day, and here is Mr. Huggins."

With that, a door opened, and out from an inner office stepped Miller James Huggins, maybe 5-foot-5, more likely 5-foot-1 or -2, and maybe 125 pounds, wearing a dark business suit, starched collar, and a businesslike expression. Ruppert had been taken aback by Huggins's appearance when they first met, as he'd been wearing a wool cap and smoking a pipe. This was more like it.

Nevertheless, Ruppert had been impressed with Huggins's obvious baseball I.Q., and his all-business approach in handling players, and made an offer. It probably didn't hurt that John McGraw, one whose opinion Ruppert so respected, had once said, "there is no smarter man in baseball today than Miller Huggins."

Reporters began to make their circle around the new manager for questioning when Ruppert noted that he had not signed yet. Ruppert sat, left elbow on his desk, left hand pressed against his cheek with an almost dreamy expression. Huggins leaned over, fountain pen in right hand, half a cigar protruding from the fingers of his left, and as flash bulbs popped he signed the contract, in triplicate, that would make him one of the most revered names in the history of his profession.

Huggins's first move as Yankees manager, characteristically, was to contradict the press, denying that he had, in fact, reached an agreement with Ban Johnson a month earlier.

Miller Huggins was a diminutive man, but with Jacob Ruppert's backing he withstood every challenge to his authority and became the first great manager in Yankees history. *Bain News Service, courtesy of the Library of Congress*

"I did visit Col. Ruppert once last season," Huggins told the newspapermen, "and asked him to consider me if he contemplated changing managers this fall. He told me at that time he did not know whether he would retain Donovan."

One can only imagine the furor that would result today if a manager, under contract with one major league club, applied to the owner of another for a not-yet-vacant position in the middle of a season, but this was the way baseball business was done in 1917, especially when it involved expiring contracts and changing leagues. Like Ban Johnson, Huggins was a Cincinnatian, and a law student, and the AL president, in one of the last times he would advise Yankees ownership, urged Johnson to take a talented man away from the National League.

Still, Huggins wasn't sure he wanted to manage in New York. "He didn't jump at the job," Huggins's sister, Myrtle, would recall for *Collier's* magazine. "For several weeks . . . he turned the offer over in his mind. 'New York is thumbs down on a losing club,' he told me, 'they're too impatient and they may not give me enough time to build a winner all the way from the cellar.'"

Huggins had collected accolades for his five years' work with the low-budget Cardinals, finishing third in 1914, when they lost several players to the Federal League, and third again in 1916, when they refused to take any of those players back. Those were the Cardinals' highest finishes since 1876. When the franchise was sold before Huggins could organize investors to buy it himself, the new team president, Branch Rickey, tried to keep him. But Rickey intended to control player personnel, so Huggins looked to leave, turning down a multiyear deal that included a piece of the profits, such as they were.

"Rickey asked me after the season if there was any truth to the rumors I had signed with Johnson," Huggins explained. "I emphatically told him, 'no.' . . . I went out to St. Louis a week ago to talk over terms with Rickey, but we could not agree. I then accepted an invitation to talk over terms with Col. Ruppert, with the result that I am now his manager. I leave St. Louis and the St. Louis club under the most cordial conditions."

Cap Huston, in France with Company A of the 16th Engineers Regiment, was regularly writing to his sportswriter friends back home, asking for information and offering his opinions on what was happening with the team, and detailing his adventures, the letters often appearing in the papers. Huston adored Bill Donovan and was even more fond of colorful, roly-poly Wilbert Robinson, the Dodgers manager, with whom he went drinking, fishing, and hunting. Huston wanted Robinson, if a change were to be made. Ruppert did invite "Uncle Robbie" to the brewery but told him, in his blunt manner, that he "wouldn't do . . . for one thing, you're too old." Robinson, fifty-four, who had managed the Dodgers to the World Series in 1916, was rather put out.

Huston would never get over his resentment of the Miller Huggins hire, without his knowledge and approval, but Ruppert, now that he was no longer a novice in the baseball business, was ready to take command of the Yankees. He had fired a gregarious, press-friendly, players' manager who had been close to Huston, so he was not about to hire another in the same mold.

No, the taciturn Huggins, thirty-nine, was the Colonel's man, and, after the Yankees had gone through eight managers between 1908 and 1917, the right man. Signed to a two-year deal worth $10,000-$12,000 per year, Huggins would have Ruppert's support, through thick and thin, for the rest of his life.

"I think it's a pretty fair-looking club," Huggins said of his new team. "There seems to be a nucleus of a good ball club in the material that has been turned over to me. Several positions we may try to strengthen, and we may put over a deal or two before the winter is over."

The scribes would have to get used to a new managerial tenor, terse quotes sometimes punctuated with "and that's all there is to the story."

When the press conference broke up, *New York Times* correspondent Harry Cross turned to the others and murmured, "a cold little fish, isn't he?"

When Miller was born in 1878, the family took him to a famous phrenologist, a Dr. Robert Fowler, who examined the baby's head and scribbled in the family bible, "Miller James Huggins will make his livelihood out of athletics." At age sixteen, Huggins read that and became passionate about baseball, though his father thought it frivolous.

When Huggins, as his sister told it, was studying law at the University of Cincinnati at the turn of the 20th century, one of his professors, future president William Howard Taft, himself a baseball fan, told him, "I've seen enough of your classwork to realize you would make a good lawyer. I've also heard enough about your feats outside the classroom to realize you would make a better baseball player. You can become a pleader or a player— not both. Try baseball, you seem to like it better."

Huggins did complete his degree and pass the bar, but he began playing semipro baseball, sometimes under an assumed name, "Proctor," to keep his devout Methodist father from learning he was playing on Sundays.

He made his way to the big leagues with the hometown Reds in 1904, where the larger players—and every player in the majors was larger—hazed him until realizing that he could, and would, stand up to anyone. Huggins, when he mentored a young Leo Durocher with the Yankees in the 1920s, told him players with "strong minds and weak backs" would always have a job in baseball. Even as a young player, Huggins was considered a managerial candidate, and Reds manager Clark Griffith traded him to St. Louis, where he had his best seasons, earning nicknames like "Rabbit" and "Mighty Mite."

"When I first joined the Reds," Huggins told *Baseball Magazine* in 1918, "I was full of energy and pep and roamed all over the infield and outfield. I wanted to play the whole game myself. And the fans soon christened me 'Little Everywhere.' . . . Some years later, I was traded to the St. Louis Cardinals and everything went wrong with me the first couple of weeks. I couldn't get a good start. In a short time, the fans had changed my nickname from 'Little Everywhere' to 'Always in the Way.'"

Huggins hit from a low crouch, choked up on the bat like Willie Keeler, and taught himself to switch-hit. He liked to bunt, to chop the ball and run, and to pull off the hidden-ball trick, and with his superior intellect he absorbed and created strategy as he went.

In July 1911, when the Cardinals were in the rear cars of a train from Philadelphia to Boston, the train took a switch too fast and flew off the track in Bridgeport, Connecticut. Huggins and his teammates scrambled down the embankment to help pull survivors out of the wreckage, Huggins using his small stature to burrow in and pull a man out of the gruesome scene. Two days later, he tied a major league record for second basemen, handling

16 chances, eight putouts and eight assists, in one game, and scored three runs. The next season, Huggins's on-base percentage was .422, and in 1913 it was .432.

The Cardinals were managed by Roger Bresnahan, the gnarly old catcher, who bristled when the team's owner died and control of the club passed to his niece, Helene Hathaway Britton. Huggins, though, ingratiated himself with the new owner, and when Bresnahan tried to trade Huggins back to Cincinnati, she blocked it. In 1913, Britton named Huggins the manager. Writers called him "The Midget Manager," but his teams always played better than they looked on paper, and he therefore earned respect throughout both leagues for getting the most out of modest talent. Huggins put a lot of stock in scout Bob Connery, who had discovered and signed Rogers Hornsby for $600. "I will stake my reputation on Connery," Huggins said, when he brought Connery with him to the Yankees.

In speculating in September of 1917 that Huggins was headed to New York, Christy Mathewson theorized that Ruppert, after the Home Run Baker disappointment, would stop trying to quick-fix the Yankees by purchasing veterans and develop his own talent.

"Desired material will be provided if it can be bought," Ruppert told the *Tribune*, "and if it cannot be bought, I am sure we have the right man to develop it."

This approach wouldn't last, of course. Within weeks, Ruppert was engaged in trying to buy the Browns' young star George Sisler, but rebuffed with a prohibitive price tag. Huggins and Ruppert did manage to acquire second baseman Del Pratt and outfielder Ping Bodie but had largely the same team when spring training convened in Macon, Georgia.

Huggins, like his boss, never married, and he listed it as a regret that he did not have a son to teach the game. He lived much of his life with his sister, Myrtle, who was his confidante and helped manage his nonbaseball affairs. He bought and sold Florida real estate at just the right time, played the stock market and golf, and was once photographed playing a bass saxophone, which was nearly as tall as he. But his main business, his hobby, his life was baseball, and the wins, losses, trades, and player behavior took a heavy toll on his frail constitution.

"I could see," his sister recalled, "year in and year out, the pace of the game was telling on Miller Huggins. He made a record unexcelled by anybody. But he had to pay for it."

When he settled into Donovan's old desk at the Yankees offices, Huggins, wrote the *New York Times*, "can just peek over the plate glass desk top. He can't quite reach the ink well, so he uses a fountain pen when he writes."

But he was a flurry of activity in that winter of 1917–18, getting 17 players signed before he left New York on March 11 for Macon. The Great War continued to rage, now with all-in US involvement. Eleven Yankees would be called for military service during the season, which was cut short, ending Labor Day.

At the end of March, Ruppert traveled to Macon, Georgia, to spend a week observing his new manager conducting spring training.

"What impressed me most was the fine team spirit Huggins has inculcated into the ranks," the Colonel told the *Tribune* when he returned to New York. "His fighting, hustling spirit is imbued into the entire cast."

New York, he assured, would be shocked at the change they would see in the players who were part of the late season tanking the year before. "Can you imagine a fighting, roaring, sod-busting Pipp, or Peckinpaugh or Baker? That is what you will see, all right, when the team gets back."

The Yankees were looking for experienced pitchers, dallying unsuccessfully with former Athletics stalwarts Eddie Plank and Chief Bender. Huggins was sizing up a crop of young players; his most trusted scout, Connery, was touting outfielder Sammy Vick. After Ruppert left Macon, the Yankees won six consecutive exhibition games against George Stalling's Braves, who were training nearby.

The season opened in Washington with a 6–3 victory. Huggins showed he was not as willing as Donovan to leave a pitcher in to build confidence; he removed George Mogridge in the fourth inning, and Allen Russell pitched 5 ⅓ innings of one-hit relief. The Yankees were 3–5 when they returned to New York, but they beat the Senators 5–4, with the rejuvenated Baker getting three hits and Pratt, the cleanup hitter, knocking in three runs. Col. Ruppert was lauded for buying $70,000 worth of Liberty Bonds, the lion's share of the $111,350 sold at the Polo Grounds that day.

"Miller Huggins, the midget manager of the Yankees, made a pronounced success of his local debut," wrote Bill McBeth in the *Tribune*. The Yankees infield deftly foiled a Washington double-steal attempt to end the game with the tying and go-ahead runs on base.

Indeed, Baker, who hit .306 in 126 games, and Pipp, .304 in 91 games, performed much better under Huggins in 1918.

The Yankees were 16–8 in May and after a four-game winning streak during their western trip sat in first place at 27–18, percentage points ahead of the Red Sox, at the close of play on June 8. But as Uncle Sam began to draw players from the game, the 1918 season lost its significance. The Yankees' attendance of 282,047 for 67 home dates was second in the AL. They finished 60–63 when the season was halted, good for fourth place, and the Red Sox went on to win the World Series, their fifth title since 1903—they wouldn't win another for quite some time. Huggins was learning the American League, and much better days were just around the corner.

Much like Joe Torre, a successful Yankees manager of a later generation, Huggins did not believe in calling out players in the press, or berating them publicly, but behind the scenes he was as stern as any situation demanded.

"I have my own ideas about running a club," Huggins said as a young manager in 1914, "I believe I can tell a ballplayer a great deal on the ride home from the park after a game. If he has played a game wrong, I can explain to him personally his mistakes and accomplish a great deal more than I could at an open meeting."

This was far removed from George Stallings or Frank Chance—but, then again, Huggins didn't have to manage Hal Chase. Soon, he would have to handle Babe Ruth.

World War I ended on November 11. Huston returned from France triumphant on January 2, 1919, with a Lt. Colonel's rank. "I'll tell you the truth, boys," Huston told the scribes who gathered to greet him at the Yankees offices on 42nd Street and Madison, including Fred Lieb of the *Sun*. "As soon as that armistice was signed, I concluded I had seen enough of the war. I got

Once the Yankees got Babe Ruth, everything changed. There were championship flags and never a dull moment. *AP Photo*

an awful hankering to have a look at Broadway. . . . I have been so out of touch with baseball affairs that I am not trying to do any reforming. I want to find out what is what first."

What was what? The Yankees had a new manager, not cut from Bill Donovan's or Wilbert Robinson's convivial cloth, and Huston had made it known through his letters to his "little army" of sportswriting friends that Huggins was not his choice.

"During his first year, there were open demands for his removal," Myrtle Huggins remembered, "Col. Huston being outspoken in his opposition to the little manager's remaining. Huston was popular with the newspapermen, and sportswriters were inclined to his side of the argument. It all upset my brother greatly."

What would become an awkward, then difficult, and finally untenable relationship actually began on a good note. Huston and Huggins secretly made the long, tedious trip together by train to Trappe, Maryland, to convince Baker, who was building a new house, to play in March 1919. Their double-team succeeded. "My probable return is prompted by a deep sense of duty to the owners," Baker said, "who have expended a great deal of money for my release from the Athletics and who have not yet received due return for the investment."

The Yankees finished 80–59, third place in 1919, and after the acquisition of Babe Ruth, 95–59 and third in 1920, steady progress that satisfied Ruppert, but not Huston, especially after his buddy, Wilbert Robinson, led the Dodgers to the NL pennant.

"It takes some time to build up a machine of pennant caliber," Huggins wrote for the *Tribune* in 1920, "but once you have one, it will last four or five years."

The Yankees of this period were rowdy veterans, many of whom had won championships elsewhere and were hard for Huggins, still the "midget manager," to control. Huston, with his adulation of ballplayers, rarely helped when trouble brewed, such as vicious conflict with pitcher Carl Mays, which caused a ruckus during spring training in 1922. "The players are aware of differences between the owners," Huggins told his sister. "That's bad for discipline."

Ruppert had his back, and Huggins would survive him-or-me confrontations with Huston, Ruth most famously, and all comers. But he took criticism, which was constant in his early years, very hard, personally, defensively—as evidenced in a long soliloquy with reporters, who found him in a deserted clubhouse, his warm-up jacket thrown over his shoulders like a shawl, after the Giants had clinched the 1921 World Series. As recorded by *Baseball Magazine*:

I have been criticized a good deal this season, but I really have no comments to make. None of us knows it all and I am learning daily. But I have tried by hard work to get results and think the results have equaled expectations. Some of the criticism of me has seemed unjust, but I have no counter-criticisms to make and if I did I shouldn't make them publicly. Some of the blame which has been given me has been on my method of handling pitchers. I guess it is now no secret that I have had an uncertain pitching staff. During the close of the seasons I had but two pitchers who could be depended upon to go the full nine innings and that fact was very evident during the series. I have told people that all I wanted was four pitchers, but two is just exactly half of four.

. . . Handling pitchers is perhaps the most difficult part of a manager's job. Naturally opinions differ on this problem. I have listened to the opinions of my players at times and handled pitchers their way. I am not too set to take good advice or advice that seems to warrant a trial. Then I have handled pitchers my way and it seems to me with better results.

After World Series losses in 1921 and '22, Huggins suffered breakdowns. "Huggins isn't sick," Ruppert told reporters after the 1922 World Series. "He is a delicate man, you know, and he is run down. He needs a rest, that's all."

Huston had tried again to maneuver Robinson from Brooklyn to the Yankees dugout in 1920, when Huggins first thought of quitting for health reasons, and swore to friends at an after-party that Huggins "was through" following the '22 Series. Finally, Ruppert bought Huston's half of the team, rather than allow him to run Huggins out of New York.

"Coming home from a bitterly fought contest," Myrtle Huggins wrote, "he would be downcast, even when he won. It would be Miller's habit to play over every game with me at the dinner table, reviewing each pivotal play and pointing out the spot where the game was won or lost."

"I will be frank with you," Miller told Fred Lieb of the *New York Post* in 1924, "I would not go through those years [with Huston] again for a million dollars. I was a sick man during a good part of the time, perhaps sicker than my friends knew, but I held on and stuck it out."

Huggins rested, recovered, and went on to his greatest victories. In the mid-1920s, he got the chance to rebuild the team by developing his *own* young players—Lou Gehrig, Earle Combs, Tony Lazzeri, Mark Koenig, Bob Meusel among them—and he at last got his due as a great manager. "My system is to run the bases," Huggins had said in 1914. "You can cause more trouble on the bases than in any other method of attack."

He won six AL pennants and three World Series between 1921 and '28, though the game had changed 180 degrees from the game Huggins had played and loved—from reliance on speed and small ball to reliance on home run power. But Huggins, strong mind and weak back, never did let the game pass him by.

"I was on the Yankees before Hug came," said Bob Shawkey, who would one day succeed him as manager, "and I soon learned he was the keenest student of the game baseball has known."

His epic confrontations with Babe Ruth have been well chronicled and came to a head in 1925 in St. Louis, when Huggins fined the greatest of stars $5,000 and told him to get out, he was suspended. As Ruth stalked off, Huggins turned to writer Ford Frick and said, "I'll make a man out of him yet." Again, with Ruppert unwavering in his support, the fine stuck, and the relationship between Ruth and Huggins settled into what, according to Myrtle, was always Huggins's ideal: "friendliness toward his players, but not chumminess."

The Yankees were in the next three World Series, winning in 1927 and '28 with perhaps the greatest teams ever assembled, and assembled largely by Miller Huggins. After the '28 World Series sweep, the New York Baseball Writers chipped in to buy a gold watch and chain, presented to Huggins at their annual dinner. Huggins was so emotional, witnesses said, he had to be helped up to the podium to receive the watch from Bozeman Bulger. Huggins said, "I know when you fellows did me wrong, it was just your opinion. I'd rather have this watch than anything."

Huggins returned to his winter home in St. Petersburg, which became the Yankees' permanent spring training home, for a rest. "His so-called rest was nothing of the sort," his sister said. "He played a little golf but his mind was obsessed, as it always was, by baseball. I knew that Miller was beginning to crack, but he wouldn't tear himself away from the game."

In 1929, the Yankees needed a minirebuild—although, more accurately, Connie Mack had simply built a superior machine that would last three years. The Yankees fell far behind, and Huggins began to suffer physically, almost wasting away.

He developed an ugly red carbuncle below his left eye and kept picking at it, tried to lance it himself. When he was advised to see a doctor, he said, "Who, me? The man who took the spikes of Frank Chance and Fred Clarke?"

It became infected, and Huggins finally was hospitalized, his fever soaring. As he lay on his deathbed at St. Vincent's Hospital, he asked his sister for updates on the Yankees' doubleheader in Chicago.

Miller Huggins died of pyaemia (blood poisoning) at age fifty-one on September 25, 1929. The Yankees were in Boston when the end was near, and Ruth asked a large crowd at the Cambridge Knights of Columbus, and everyone they knew, to pray for his manager. "You all know how I feel about it," Ruth told writers in Providence, the day after Huggins passed. "He was my friend. We will miss him more every day."

The first of the three monuments erected in center field in Yankee Stadium was dedicated to the Midget Manager in 1932.

CHAPTER 14

CHARACTERS

Your pardon, Ping, if I should sing your fame with lack
of moderation. For who am I to modify an inexpressible
elation?
  —Grantland Rice, "The Rte. Hon. Ping Bodie," *New-York*
Tribune, April 30, 1919

Thirty-two years before Mickey Mantle exploded onto the
scene in Arizona, the Yankees had a switch-hitting, lightning-fast,
all-around athlete and physical specimen taking training camp
by storm.

The New York papers, even the understated *Times*, could
hardly contain their enthusiasm:

It is an unusual thing for a college player to jump right
into the big leagues and become a regular in his first season, but this is the thing that [George] Halas threatens
to do. He is swift of foot and is a heady and proficient

base runner. He covers a lot of ground in the outfield, and best of all he has a world of enthusiasm for the game.

Halas had been a football, baseball, and basketball star at the University of Illinois and was the Most Valuable Player of the 1919 Rose Bowl, in which he caught a touchdown pass and returned an interception 77 yards. He arrived at the Yankees' training camp in prime condition—lean, hungry, and still sporting his crew cut—and he brought college football-like intensity to the quiet spring training games in Jacksonville, Florida. "I considered myself in perfect condition," Halas wrote in his memoirs, "ready to astound baseball fans with my speed and desire."

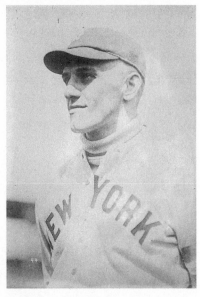

Halas made good on that; Miller Huggins fell in love with him, as did everyone else. Scout Bob Connery; veteran Yankees scout Joe Kelley; Wilbert Robinson and the Dodgers, who were also training in town; and just about everyone else was buzzing about five-tool player George Stanley Halas, "the find of the spring," in 1919. Day after day, the writers sent glowing reports back to New York.

"The experts are all smoked up over young George Halas,"

Big, strong, athletic, and intense, George Halas was the talk of Yankees training camp in 1919, but his destiny was in pro football. *Bain News Service, courtesy of the Library of Congress* said the *Tribune*, "the outfielder who came here direct from the Great Lakes Training Station. Every spring training trip has its phenom, and the ensign has the earmarks of being this season's phenom. He is a Husky youth with 180 pounds of solid stuff to put behind each swing."

"Halas, who comes to the club with a reputation as an all-around athlete, breezed around the outer works like a breath of spring," wrote the *Sun*, after one early workout. "Unless we are very much wrong, this boy is going to stick, for he looks every inch the ballplayer and handles himself like one."

On April 1, Halas drew a walk in an intrasquad game, and when Roger Peckinpaugh bunted, Halas wheeled around second base like a tight end running a crisp pattern. The *Tribune*: "Not content with reaching second base, Halas scurried for third. His audacity shocked [Eddie] Mooers to such an extent he made a wild heave and Halas came all the way from first on a sacrifice."

A player with this kind of talent had not yet been seen in a Highlanders or Yankees uniform. The only thing George Halas, twenty-four, couldn't do on a diamond was hit a curveball, but Huggins was convinced he could be taught. Halas hit .350 at Illinois, and after enlisting in the Navy, he played in the summer of 1918 for the Great Lakes Training Station, where Connery saw him at his best and convinced the Yankees to invite him to spring training. Then he played football; the Rose Bowl matched teams of military personnel in 1919.

"Miller Huggins was a great manager and he thought I had some possibilities," Halas recalled, a lifetime later, in an interview with Chicago sportscaster Brad Palmer.

Writers and scouts were debating whether Halas should continue as a switch-hitter, or stick with hitting right-handed. On

April 2, a day another former college football star, Jim Thorpe, homered for the Giants in Gainesville, Halas stepped in against veteran Dodgers lefty Rube Marquard and blasted the ball far over the outfielders' heads. He motored to third base.

Dan Daniel reported in the *Sun*:

> Halas is all speed, and he takes all sorts of chances on the paths, but is wide awake and not a crazy runner. . . . The three-bagger was perpetrated against a person of no less importance than Rube Marquard. It was a beautiful smash into distant left field. Halas, who hits them from either the port or the starboard, was hitting right-handed this time and showed that he could smite with considerable vim and vehemence from that angle of his front.
>
> . . . The prospective leadoff man seemed to strain his right leg as he rounded second and he slowed up as he reached third.

Okay, stop the music. Here is where it all began to go wrong. Halas seemed to have the team made when, after hitting a long drive over the heads of the outfielders, he pulled up at third base limping, rubbing his thigh.

"Huggins is a bit worried over the enthusiasm of young Halas and has cautioned him to save some of his speed for the big time," Daniel wrote in the *Sun*. "It would not profit the Yankees greatly if Halas should stretch a tendon trying to stretch a two-bagger into a triple on the rough paths of this lot. But Halas is hard to restrain. He is one of those youngsters who has to play for all that is in them all of the time. That is probably the very reason he will win the odd outfield spot and lead off in the Yankees' attacks."

The trainer, Doc Woods, told Huggins he should rest Halas a few days, and he did. But on April 3, Huggins was ready to declare himself ready, with rare effusiveness:

"You may say for me that George Halas will start in right field for the Yankees," Huggins told the writers, to their obvious delight. "Of course, I do not know how he will act against American League pitching, but if I am any judge of a ballplayer, Halas is a star. He has every action of a great player and so far he is hitting. That boy learns faster than any youngster I have tackled, and he is here to stick."

When Halas returned to the lineup April 8, he struck out three times. He singled in one of the last exhibition games on April 15 but again pulled up lame at first base. Halas was not healthy enough to make the Opening Day lineup, but Huggins signed him to a contract calling for $400 a month and introduced him to Ruppert, who handed him a $500 bonus when the team reached New York.

But Halas did not debut for the Yankees until May 6, when he singled in four at-bats in a 3–2 loss to the A's.

The magic had vanished, the bandwagon emptied. Halas started four games, leading off in right field, going 2-for-17, including 0-for-5 in a start against Walter Johnson, a 14-inning scoreless tie on May 11, though Halas remembered hitting two possible home runs just foul before striking out. Then he went to the bench when the Yankees traveled to Detroit on May 14. The veterans on the team urged the fiery football player to vent his intensity from the dugout, try to rile up Ty Cobb when he came to bat. As Halas told the story, perhaps embellished, Cobb heard enough to holler, "I'll see you after the game, don't forget, punk."

Halas hollered back that he would be there. He was among the last to leave the Yankees clubhouse, hoping Cobb would forget the whole thing and leave. But when Halas finally emerged, Cobb was waiting for him. "I like your spirit, kid," Cobb said, extending his hand, "but don't overdo it when you don't have to." Back in New York, they met again and took a long walk together. "Direct your energy positively," Cobb, older and wiser than when he beat up a crippled fan seven years earlier, counseled him. "Don't waste it being negative."

Halas was taking long walks at Woods's suggestion to try to improve his sore hip, but he was hobbling badly, picked off second base in a game on May 30, and on June 5, when he was put in as a pinch-runner, veteran Eddie Cicotte of the White Sox picked him off third. Finally, he asked Huggins for permission to go to Youngstown, Ohio, and see John "Bonesetter" Reece, a trainer/chiropractor well known in athletic circles. Reece told him he dislocated his hip when he slid into third base.

"He pushed his steely finger deep into my hip," Halas said, "and he gave the bone a sharp twist. The pain vanished." He rejoined the Yankees and, he said, "ran like a wild horse."

But on June 19, Huggins decided Halas needed more experience to hit a major league curveball and sent him to St. Paul to play the rest of the season for manager Mike Kelley, a close friend of Huggins. "He was a terrific coach, and he taught me how to hit a curveball," Halas, who hit .274 in 39 games, recalled in the interview with Palmer. "And I thought I was ready for the big leagues the next spring."

But by the next spring, the Yankees had a new right fielder by the name of Ruth and wanted Halas to spend more time in the minors. He would play for St. Paul, if he got the same $400-a-month salary. Kelley said he'd pay it only if the Yankees gave up the rights to Halas, so St. Paul could reap the benefits of developing him. The Yankees refused, and Halas left baseball, putting his engineering to work in the bridge design department of the Chicago, Burlington and Quincy Railroad.

Wherever he went, "Ping" Bodie was always the life of the party. But he didn't really beat an ostrich in a spaghetti-eating contest . . . did he? *Bain News Service, courtesy of the Library of Congress*

Halas played football in industrial leagues, for the Staley Manufacturing Company, and, in September 1920, he led a meeting that included Jim Thorpe in an automobile showroom. The result was what became known as the National Football League.

So George Halas never did become the face of the Yankees, his career over with two singles in 22 at-bats, but rather one of the fathers of pro football; a player, coach, and owner of the Chicago Bears; and a charter member of another Hall of Fame in Canton. "Papa Bear" probably made the right choice, but one can only wonder what a five-tooled switch-hitter might have done with a little more time, roaming the outfield at Yankee Stadium and applying all that football strength to the "rabbit" baseball that was introduced in the 1920s.

Francesco Stephano Pizzola, as his real name has most often been recorded, from the Telegraph Hill neighborhood in San Francisco, was one of the first Italian-Americans to make it to the major leagues. He took the name "Ping," presumably because it was the sound of the ball hitting his lively bat, and "Bodie," because it was the name of a California mining town, now a ghost town, where his uncle once worked.

Early in the 20th century, it wasn't fashionable to play baseball under such an ethnic-sounding name. "Frank L. (Ping) Bodie, the fast and hard-hitting outfielder of the Chicago White Sox, is . . . one of the finds of the 1911 season," wrote *Sporting Life* in January 1912. "There is no truth to the report his real name is Pizzola, that being the name of his stepfather."

Two weeks later, the magazine received a letter from San Francisco.

Frank's real name in our language is Franceto Sanguelitto Pizzola. He took the name of Bodie from our uncle, our mother's brother, when he started to play ball because he thought all the fans would josh him. Frank is a hero now and we both wish you would correct what you said.
Yours truly,
Dave Bodie (Pizzola)

Perhaps Ping took some ribbing at first, but by the time he joined the Yankees, one of Miller Huggins's first acquisitions in 1918, he was one of the most popular players in baseball, at least with the writers, who jotted down all his witticisms. "The only attractions left in this town are I and the Liberty Bell," he had once said, while playing for a poor A's team.

He was boisterous, full of a likeable brand of braggadocio and a lover of practical jokes. During spring training of 1919, an air tank exploded near the Yankees' quarters, the Hotel Burbridge, in Jacksonville, blowing out windows and causing some panic in the dining room.

"Calm yourselves," Bodie bellowed, rising to his feet and motioning for everyone to stay seated, "that noise was only Ping Bodie putting one over the fence. Whenever Ping swings on the old apple, there is not a window for miles around that is safe. I promise not to swing on another today, so there will be no more cause for alarm. I thank you."

That scene was recorded for the *New-York Tribune* on March 25 by W. O. McGeehan, who couldn't seem to get enough of Bodie's hijinks. "That shrinking violet of modesty," McGeehan called him.

With Bodie, McGeehan, and Grantland Rice, also covering that spring for the *Trib*, in one place, one of baseball's everlasting hoaxes was bound to emerge. This was the era of silly stunts in baseball. Catching baseballs dropped from high places, particularly the top of the Washington Monument, as former Highlander Gabby Street had done, was a thing. So was racing horses around the bases.

That in mind, McGeehan and Rice spent a lot of free time at an ostrich and alligator farm that fate had located right across the street from the Yankees camp, and they seemed fascinated by how old alligators got to be, and how much an ostrich could eat. Food was a hot topic that spring, too, with Herbert Hoover administrating the unpopular rationing during the recently ended Great War. Food always seemed to be on Ping Bodie's mind.

"Who's Hoover? That's what I say," Bodie declared one day, "He's the bird that cut down our rations. And I want to ask you, how's a guy going to crash that old apple when he doesn't get enough food to nourish him? I ain't for the ostrich, and I don't go much for alligators."

Yet, those animals seemed to get all they wanted to eat, while poor Ping had to survive on paltry meal money doled out by the Yankees' assistant traveling secretary, Mark Roth.

"I asked that guy for an advance of fifty today," Bodie said, again with McGeehan within earshot, "and he goes and refuses me. I wanted the dough to get some proper food that would nourish me for the season. But he wouldn't come through for me. A guy needs some food before he can crush the old apple."

Bodie couldn't get Ruppert to fork over more meal money when he arrived in camp. Colonel Huston, as always getting a kick out of the ballplayers, was lightheartedly complaining about how much Bodie was eating on the Yankees' tab.

All the ingredients came together. Right around April 1, McGeehan, who wrote a lot about boxing, cooked up an idea for a heavyweight eating bout between the starving Ping and one of the ostriches he'd been spying, and Rice began touting this upcoming match in his columns. Talk about a scoop.

"W. O. McGeehan has completed final arrangements for the spaghetti eating contest between Ping Bodie, the California champion, and Percy, the ostrich champion of the Jacksonville ostrich farm," Rice reported. "Percy is the ostrich who, when all of America was put on a diet during the late war, remarked, 'who the hell is Hoover?'

". . . Those who think we are fabricating or becoming flippant will obtain the correct answer in *Sunday's Tribune*, where our McGeehan will cover the bitter contest by rounds."

Indeed, on Sunday, March 6, 1919, readers of the *New-York Tribune* were treated to one whopper of a story, as McGeehan described 12 rounds of the food fight at the South Side Pavilion. In walked Bodie, with Yankees catcher Truck Hannah as his "second," and he glowered as Percy waddled in, with Dodgers manager Wilbert Robinson as his handler.

"The match was promoted by the Jacksonville Chamber of Commerce," McGeehan explained, "which had advertised Percy as the world's greatest eater. Col. T. L. Huston, who foots the fodder bills for Bodie, laughed at those pretensions."

The match was not advertised because, as McGeehan explained, "it was feared that federal or state authorities might intervene in terms of the brutality of the terms of the match." Yet, somehow the pavilion was packed with spectators, and the press, or at least McGeehan, was allowed to cover it. Right.

Per McGeehan's hilarious plate-by-plate account, the spaghetti was twirled and devoured by Bodie, presumably slurped by Percy. In the sixth round, "many spectators started for the door for humanitarian reasons. They did not want to see the finish." In Round 7, "even strong men began to edge back from the ring. They feared Percy would explode." In Round 9, "even hardened eaters were shouting to Wilbert Robinson to throw in the sponge. 'Do you want your bird killed?' they demanded. 'Not while he is still on his feet,' retorted Robinson brutally."

In the 11th round, the ostrich dropped to his knees as Bodie grinned and the timekeeper began to count. "As the timekeeper muttered the final 'ten,' the ostrich sank back, to rise no more."

It was clearly tongue-in-cheek—wasn't it?—but it was not labeled as such in the paper, and 100 years later one can still find places in print and on the Internet where the story is retold as if it really happened. Of course, an ostrich wouldn't just eat itself to death . . . would it? Nor would spectators with an ounce of heart stand by and cheer as it did so . . . would they? And the Yankees would never have allowed their starting centerfielder to take such a health risk on the eve of a season . . . would they have?

Bodie went along for the laughs and hit .279 for the Yankees in 1919 and .295 in 1920, when he cheerfully conceded Babe Ruth was the new team leader in caloric intake. His best-known line: when asked what it was like to be Babe Ruth's roommate, Ping answered, "I only room with his suitcase."

After leaving the Yankees and the majors in 1921 with a .275 lifetime average, Ping continued to crush the old apple in the minors until he turned 40 in 1928, having helped blaze a trail so that future Italian-Americans coming to the big leagues, like Tony Lazzeri, Frank Crosetti, and Joe DiMaggio, would not feel compelled to change their names. Bodie became an electrician working on movie sets in Hollywood, getting the biggest movie stars to laugh out loud before he passed on to join Percy in 1961.

The Yankees signed Frank O'Doul, better known as "Lefty," on St. Patrick's Day, 1919. "Experts and ivory hunters who watched him on the coast last summer declare the youth is a sure comer,"

the *Sun* explained. "During the joint meetings of the two leagues last January, leading scribes and magnates had an opportunity to see O'Doul in action. He was featured in [a] new style of motion picture which was slowed down to one-thirtieth of normal speed and which allowed the spectator to follow every twist and curve of the ball from the time it left the pitcher's hand until it hit the catcher's glove. . . . Run at full speed, the young man's fastball seems to be a thing of beauty."

So Lefty O'Doul was evidently the first player signed after studying video. Another San Francisco kid, he joined Halas as the talk of training camp. O'Doul injured his arm, but was one of the fastest runners, and he showed a natural hitting ability. "Just about the fastest man who ever wore a Yankee uniform," the *Tribune* exclaimed, "He is possessed of an exceptional eye and never offers at a bad ball." The writers began questioning Huggins about making O'Doul a full-time outfielder.

"I appreciate the fine writers we have on this trip," Huggins told Fred Lieb one day in the lobby of the Burbridge. "But I just can't let you fellows pick my lineup. Furthermore, you fellows have O'Doul confused. I told him regardless of what he reads in the papers, he should consider himself a pitcher and concentrate on pitching. He once showed me a fastball that was as good as any in the big leagues. He has the making of an Eddie Plank, a George Wiltse, a Slim Sallee, and if he can hit, so much the better."

O'Doul stuck with the Yankees as a pitcher, but Huggins could not have been more wrong, as Lefty pitched just a handful of games without distinction. Once O'Doul and outfielder Chick Fewster, thinking a game would be rained out, skipped off to the racetrack and learned later the games were played. They weren't disciplined; Huggins didn't notice they were missing.

He did send Lefty up as a pinch-hitter on occasion. O'Doul loved jokes, too, and became an early running mate of Babe Ruth. Finally, in 1922, Huggins sent Lefty to Boston to complete a deal for Jumpin' Joe Duggin.

After a stint in the Pacific Coast League, O'Doul returned to the major leagues as an outfielder and hit .353 across seven years in the National League, garnering 254 hits in one season for the 1929 Phillies, hitting .398. He is very likely the best hitter who does not have a plaque in Cooperstown.

After retiring, O'Doul did help the Yankees. As manager of the San Francisco Seals, he helped mentor the young Joe DiMaggio. One of the game's most beloved characters and ambassadors, he is best remembered for helping introduce the game in Japan, with tours before and after World War II.

If Halas was the wide-eyed "natural," Bodie the clown, and O'Doul the jovial ambassador, Carl Mays was something else altogether. Here, Huggins and the Yankees knew what they were getting.

Carl Mays came to the big leagues in 1915, delivering nasty pitches from nasty angles few could solve, and a nasty disposition few could understand.

"It was long ago made apparent to me that I was one of those individuals who were not fated to be popular," Mays wrote for *Baseball Magazine* in 1920, in the kind of self-examination one might find today on Derek Jeter's *Player's Tribune* website. "When I broke into baseball, there seemed to be a feeling against me, even from the players on my own team."

Mays, with close-cropped blonde hair, dark eyebrows, and blue eyes, could work up a warm smile for the camera. But he was shy, aloof, with a temper that exploded in the heat of competition and oh, so good at his job, with an underhanded delivery that sent balls to the plate by way of third base, at tremendous velocity. In the era of stained baseballs and unlit ballparks and 3:30 p.m. start times, the ball must've been invisible to right-handed hitters in the late innings. Fastballs up and in set the hitters up for his devastating sinker ball, which felt like a shot-put when contact was made. In five seasons with the Red Sox, he was 72–51 with a 2.21 ERA,

Carl Mays is remembered for throwing the pitch that killed Ray Chapman, and for being a disagreeable teammate. He was, in fact, a complex man. *Bain News Service, courtesy of the Library of Congress*

helping them win three World Series, but winning few friends.

Shortly after the 1918 World Series, Mays married a Boston girl, Marjorie Fredricka "Freddie" Madden, a graduate of the New England Conservatory of Music, and they built a farmhouse in Missouri.

"I put into that home most of my earnings as a ballplayer," Mays wrote, "Furthermore I put into that home all of the little mementos and souvenirs I wished to preserve, and my wife did also. But by the time we had everything settled, the house caught fire and burned to the ground. Everything in it was totally destroyed, but as it was insured for only a fraction of its true value, I found myself practically wiped out."

As the 1919 season wore on, Mays grew increasingly bitter, the loss of his home, the adulation and salary gained by his teammate Babe Ruth, and the taunts of the fans all eating at him, and he came to believe his teammates were purposely tanking games behind him. He tangled with fans in Philadelphia on Memorial Day, firing a ball into the stands and hitting a spectator. Ban Johnson fined Mays $100, and the Red Sox wouldn't pay the fine for him. Then came a series of dreary losses, his team hardly scoring for him and playing poor defense. At one point, he refused to pitch if Jack Barry played second base.

Finally, on July 13, after a comedy of defensive errors, Mays was removed from a game in Chicago, trailing 5–0. He would never pitch for the Red Sox again, he screamed, and when manager Ed Barrow sent players back to the clubhouse to fetch him, they found him sobbing at his locker. Mays dressed, left the ballpark, and caught the next train back to Boston, then went straight to the offices of the *Boston Herald* and sought out writer Burt Whitman, who wrote the story, which was eventually entered into the New York Supreme Court records.

"I'll never pitch another ball for the Red Sox," Mays told Whitman. "I intend to settle my affairs here tomorrow and then go on a fishing trip to upper Pennsylvania. . . ."

A man of his word, that is exactly what Carl Mays did. He was 5–11 despite "pitching better than ever," he moaned. "The team cannot win with me pitching, so I am getting out, and that is all there is to it. . . . Maybe there will be a trade or a sale of my services. I do not care where I go in that event."

The Red Sox played it cool, knowing that there would be plenty of high-paying suitors for Carl Mays. The White Sox, the Indians, and the Yankees all checked in.

On July 30, the Yankees, 6 ½ games behind the White Sox, made the winning bid, sending Allen Russell, Bob McGraw, and $40,000 to the Red Sox for Carl Mays. In stepped AL president Ban Johnson, who suspended Mays indefinitely. If a player could force a trade by quitting a team, the basis of his argument went, then chaos would result. He ordered the deal cancelled as detrimental to baseball.

"I am convinced there must be some misunderstanding on the part of the president of the league," Til Huston said. "Col. Ruppert and myself, I believe, have always shown we are anxious to have discipline maintained in the game. We have the game and its interests at heart as much as anybody in it."

Johnson met with Ruppert and Huston at the Holland House in New York, and when it was over, Ruppert issued a bellicose statement. "We both know that two, possibly three of the clubs Johnson states requested Mays's suspension are clubs which were negotiating for Mays's services up to the very time New York secured him. We will proceed at once to protect our rights by enjoining Johnson from interfering with the club."

It was reported Yankees players, anxious to have Mays take the mound, would strike if the suspension was not lifted. The case went to court. "Ban Johnson brought this fight upon himself," Huston said, "and we will give him all the fight he wants."

It dragged on for months and got ugly, and the AL owners split. The Colonels charged Johnson owned a piece of the Cleveland team and was voiding the deal to help them. Red Sox owner Harry Frazee believed Johnson had long had it in for him. Comiskey was backing the Yankees and Red Sox. Statements flew back and forth, with Ruppert and Huston vowing to curb Johnson's power to manipulate player movement—power, ironically, that had so often benefited New York's franchise in the past. On August 6, Justice Robert L. Luce, of the Supreme Court of the State of New York, issued an injunction. "Huggins has been advised that he may pitch Mays whenever he desires," Ruppert said, triumphantly.

The next day, Mays debuted with a six-hitter, striking out nine to beat the Browns, 8–2. "There were court proceedings and more court proceedings," Mays wrote. "Perhaps if I had been inclined to be swell-headed, I would have got all puffed up about the desperate struggle that was taking place over my own, unimportant self."

Mays went 9–3 with a 1.65 ERA in 13 starts, beginning what would be an even stormier chapter in his career. He was full of surprises, though. Right after his debut with the Yankees, as the controversy raged, Mays and his wife gave a long interview to Jane Dixon of the *Evening Telegram*—one of the first female sportswriters in America. "He seems a harmless-enough looking boy, this Mays lad—in repose," Dixon wrote. ". . .'Come and meet Mrs. Mays,' was his greeting. There was a world of pride in the invitation."

It was easy to see why: Freddie Mays said she got so mad at fans who heckled Carl, "I'd like to sharpen my claws and do some real scratching, only my husband said I must not." The

Mays were planning a postseason hunting and fishing trip to Oregon, then a drive to Missouri to rebuild the home on their 70-acre farm.

On October 25, Justice Robert F. Wagner made the injunction permanent. "[Johnson's] act was, to say the least, not fortified with that perfect appreciation of the facts which evinces a desire to do equity to all parties concerned," Wagner concluded.

Some of the owners backing Johnson tried to withhold the players' third-place shares, about $350 each, but Ruppert and Huston paid them out of their own pockets. Ban Johnson and the National Commission finally recognized defeat and, like Percy the Ostrich, sank back to rise no more.

Mays won 26 games in 1920, but the defining moment of his life, what would be the first sentence of his obituaries in 1971, was the high-and-tight fastball at the Polo Grounds on August 16 that hit Indians shortstop Ray Chapman in the temple, fractured his skull, and ultimately killed him. Teams signed petitions calling for his banishment from the game.

"It is a recollection of the most unpleasant kind which I shall carry with me for as long as I live," Mays wrote, in the aftermath, for *Baseball Magazine*. "It is an episode I shall always regret more than anything that has ever happened to me, and yet I can look into my own conscience and feel absolved from all personal guilt in the affair."

Mays won 27 games for the Yankees in 1921, pitching brilliantly to win the franchise's first-ever World Series games. But by then he was feuding with Huggins. When he was taken out of a *spring training* game in 1922, Mays threw the ball over the grandstand and stalked off. Huggins fined him $200, and Mays threatened to quit if the fine stuck. Huston journeyed south to mediate and, this time, backed Huggins. Mays stayed, but Huggins began phasing him out, and Ed Barrow, who by then was the Yankees' business manager, sent Mays to the Reds in 1924.

"I have been trying for two years to get away from Huggins," Mays snarled, adding that Huggins was to blame for making Lefty O'Doul a bust in pinstripes. Mays, 207–126 with a 2.92 ERA in 15 seasons, remains one of the better pitchers not in the Hall of Fame.

"I have been told I lack tact, which is probably true," Mays wrote, "but that is no crime. I can explain most of my troubles on the grounds of unpopularity. For my own part, I have long since ceased to care what other people think about me."

The Yankees finished the 1919 season, which began with the promise of Halas and ended with the delivery of Mays, with an 80–59 record, a 29-game hitting streak by Roger Peckinpaugh, and, with Sunday baseball at last legal in New York, a franchise-record attendance of 619,194.

They were, you might say, one player away.

CHAPTER 15

AND ALONG CAME . . .

Gee, I'm glad that guy is not going to hit against me
anymore. You take your life in your hands every time
you step up against him. You just throw up anything that
happens to come into your head with a prayer, and duck
for your life with the pitch.

> —Yankees ace Bob Shawkey, on the day the sale of
> Babe Ruth was announced

A small crowd of about 5,000 had settled into the Polo
Grounds to watch the Yankees and Red Sox play on a fair spring
afternoon, the temperature edging toward 70 degrees on that
May 6, 1915. The Yankees had one of their better pitchers going,
Jack Warhop, a journeyman right-hander with a submarine-style
delivery. Boston sent to the mound a rookie left-hander who
was just beginning to cause a bit of a stir around the American
League.

Babe Ruth, batting ninth, where the pitcher belonged, got the fans out of their seats to crane their necks in the third inning, when he launched one of Warhop's offerings into the upper deck in right field.

This was The Babe's first major league home run, the first of 714. Ruth's rise from the streets of Baltimore, his father's saloon, and reform school, to the major leagues to become one of the icons of 20th-century America, has been often told definitively in a number of books and needlessly embellished in a couple of movies. Here, we focus on his route from the Red Sox to the Yankees, unquestionably the most impactful transaction in baseball history.

Ruth had just turned twenty when he first appeared on New York's radar with not only the home run, but two singles. Had the Red Sox not made four errors behind him, he would have won easily. As it was, he was one out away when Daniel Boone doubled to send home Doc Cook with the tying run. Ruth stayed in the game, which he lost in the 13th when Doc singled home the winning run. The 13-inning game took all of 2:35.

Four weeks later, it all happened again. The Red Sox were back in New York on a chilly June 2; Ruth batted against Warhop in the second inning with a man on and launched one even deeper into the upper deck. "We can stand for the Speakers, the Cobbs, the Jacksons, the Bakers doing things like that," Bozeman Bulger wrote the next morning, "but for a pitcher—well, it's against the union rules, that's all."

Now, Ruth was more than a blip on New York's radar. This time, he won 7–1, the first of the 17 wins he would register against the Yankees over the next five seasons. But Ruth, angry at being walked in the sixth and eighth innings, kicked the dugout wall and broke his toe, costing him two weeks. A home run, a brilliant pitching performance, and a temper tantrum resulting in a broken toe, all in one day—perfectly encapsulated what he would become.

Ruth finished 18–8 and helped the Red Sox win the World Series; if the Rookie of the Year Award existed, he probably would have been the top candidate in 1915. Over the 1916 and '17 seasons, Ruth won 47 games, but his home run slugging began to intrigue and then fascinate baseball fans coast to coast. By 1918, he was looking to become a full-time outfielder and feuding with manager Ed Barrow. He led the league in homers with 11 and won 13 games during the regular season as a pitcher, plus another in the World Series. In 1919, Ruth won nine games—and slugged 29 homers, breaking every record researchers could find. The Red Sox captured three titles, and Ruth at one point pitched 29 scoreless innings in World Series play.

There were times it seemed as if he were just plain flirting with the Colonels in New York. Three of his four homers in 1915 were against the Yankees, two of which came at the Polo Grounds; he spared the Yankees in 1916 but hit one of his two in 1917 in New York. In 1918, Ruth hit three of his 11 homers against the Yankees, all at the Polo Grounds, and in 1919 he victimized Yankees pitching five times—four in New York, one completely over the roof in right. So 12 of his 49 homers in a Red Sox uniform came against the franchise he was destined to lift, with 10 in 95 at-bats at the Polo Grounds.

Now Ruth was the biggest draw baseball had ever seen, and he was smart enough to know it and demand a fair share—a Ruthian share, as his name was becoming part of the language as a synonym for colossal. He had a business manager, Johnny

Igoe, lining up revenue streams from barnstorming to vaudeville, and he even opened a cigar factory in Boston. Meanwhile, the owner of the Red Sox, Harry Frazee, was caught between Ruth's bat and a dangerous place. World War I had hampered attendance for two seasons and flooded the franchise with red ink. The previous owner, Joe Lannin, was calling in notes. Ruth could be the Red Sox's ticket to back to solvency, or he could bankrupt them with his demands. He had a signed contract for $10,000 per year, but he wanted it torn up and redrawn at double the salary.

In July of 1919, while they were dickering over Carl Mays, Ruppert and Huston offered $100,000 for Ruth, but Frazee said, "no." The *Tribune*'s Bill McBeth later reported: "This was not an advertising stunt in any way, for no mention was made of the fact at the time."

But by late December, Frazee and the Colonels were talking again. "I refused $100,000 cash for Babe last year, before he became the great home run attraction he became at the end of the year," Frazee told the *Boston Post*'s Paul Shannon on December 22. "There is nothing I have that I wouldn't sell—for the right price, of course—but what do you think, now, I'd take for Ruth? Do you believe anybody in baseball would be foolish enough to give what I would have to get to brave the fury of the Boston fans if I were to let him go?"

The Babe was worth so much, no one in baseball would be foolish enough to pay him for what he was truly worth. That was waving a red flag in front of a couple of bullish New York magnates, who had seen too much of Ruth not to want him. Huston put off his postseason plans and returned to New York to huddle with Ruppert. With the season over, Frazee was concentrating on his Broadway productions from an office on 42nd Street, a few blocks down from the Yankees' offices, so talks, though complex, picked up speed.

The Carl Mays case had made the Yankees and Red Sox allies against Ban Johnson and the establishment, which would have liked nothing more than for Frazee to have to sell the Red Sox and get out of the game. As it came together, the selling price would be $100,000, paid in a series of notes that, with interest, would bump it to $125,000. Then, in the key to the deal, Ruppert would loan Frazee $350,000, for which the Yankees would hold a mortgage on Fenway Park as security.

Now, Ruppert and Huston sent Huggins out to California, where the Babe was barnstorming and playing golf, nearly every day, on the municipal links at Los Angeles' Griffith Park. On January 4, Huggins waited in the clubhouse for Ruth to finish his round, then introduced himself when Ruth roared in.

Huggins offered a lecture, admonishing Ruth it would have to be "all business" in New York. Ruth, waving it aside, wanted to know only what the Yankees intended to pay him. They met again at the Rosslyn Hotel in downtown LA and signed a memorandum of agreement, Ruth to get his $20,000 a year. When he learned that Frazee was telling reporters in Boston that Ruth had become too selfish, too much to handle, Ruth unloaded to a group of reporters out at the golf course.

Frazee is not good enough to own any ballclub, especially one in Boston. On 'Babe Ruth Day' in Boston, people packed the park. He reserved 15,000 seats and forced his ballplayers to pay for their wives; I paid for Mrs. Ruth. After the game, I was called to his office where he handed me a cigar and thanked me. That is a fair sample of his liberality. Because I demanded a big increase in salary, which I feel I was entitled to, he brands me as an ingrate and a troublemaker.

. . . The time of a ballplayer is short, and he must get his money in a few years or lose out. Any fair-minded fan knows my efforts on the Boston ballclub last season warranted a larger salary and I asked for it. I have always hustled as hard as any man on the diamond. When not taking my turn in the box, I played the outfield, doing everything I could to make the club win. I don't like to play for Frazee, I like Boston and the Boston fans. They have treated me splendidly and if not for Frazee, I would be content to play with the Red Sox to the end of my baseball days. Frazee sold me because he was unwilling to meet my demands and to alibi himself with the fans he is trying to throw blame on me.

Opinion in Boston was split, some taking Frazee's side, suggesting he unloaded a selfish player and did what was best for the franchise, others more prophetically noting that he had, instead, ripped the heart from it. You don't have to believe in "curses" to grasp that this single move changed the course of both franchises for generations to come. The Yankees were now on the right side of baseball history.

Once Huggins sent word to New York that Ruth was on board, the Colonels, exultant, announced the deal at the Yankees' offices on January 5, 1920. "I am not at liberty to tell the price we paid," Ruppert chortled, "I can say positively, however, that it is by far the biggest price ever paid for a ballplayer. Ruth was considered a champion of all champions and, as such, deserving of a chance to shine before the sports lovers of the greatest metropolis of the world. We are going to give them a pennant winner no matter what the cost."

As Ruth stayed out in Los Angeles, he entertained reporters with long drives and whimsical quotes. He talked about shortening his swing and trying for a batting title, then about crushing his own home run record. He talked about demanding to play center field, so he wouldn't run into the right- or left-field walls in the Polo Grounds. The Yankees considered trading Wally Pipp to the White Sox for center fielder Happy Felsch, and installing Ruth at first base. And what if Ruth would pitch? The Yankees would have the best rotation in the league.

The Carl Mays case had paved the way for Ruth's sale to the Yankees—about which Ban Johnson was out of the loop, and unhappy. The Babe was keenly aware of all that was going on, far more astute about these things than portrayed in future caricatures.

"Before the battle between Johnson and the 'triple alliance,'" Ruth said, referring to the Yankees, Red Sox, and White Sox, "there was not much chance [of a trade], as Ban would have been against it. Since the war in the American League, anything can be expected. Frazee is through in Boston and he knows it. He has never been a popular magnate. His theatrical tactics have not been a hit in baseball. Frazee cares nothing for the Boston baseball public and his actions show it."

Frazee returned fire, telling the *New York Herald*, "Had Ruth been possessed of the right disposition, had he been willing to take orders and work for the good of the club like other men on the team, I would never had dared to let him go. But lately this idol has been shattered in the public's estimation because of the way in which he refused to respect his contract and his given word. He would not pitch, but insisted on playing the outfield. He had no regard for the feelings of anyone but himself and was a bad influence upon others and younger members of the team."

Then Frazee told the *Tribune*, "Really, the fans of Boston took the sale better than I thought they would. Boston is the greatest baseball city in the country. The fans there are greater students of the game than anywhere else. They appreciated that Ruth was not treating me fairly in his demands for double salary in spite of an unexpired contract."

It was, you might say, grand theater. Ruth left California in early February, saying he wanted a piece of the action—part of the purchase price. "It's no concern of ours," Huston said. "It's between him and Frazee."

Frazee refused Ruth's demand, or to even talk about it. He was the Yankees' problem now. When he finally arrived in New York to meet Ruppert and Huston, waving off another lecture from Huston on his behavior, they came to agreeable salary terms. Day after day, the New York papers brimmed with excitement over the possibilities.

"Why, I don't see any reason that fellow can't knock out 50 home runs playing in the Polo Grounds," Ruppert said. "He surely rapped enough hits into that stand playing against us."

The Yankees led the American League in homers in 1919, with 45, prior to Ruth's arrival. Ping Bodie, who was working as a riveter in a San Francisco shipyard, weighed in on the addition of Ruth: "We'll make life miserable for those pitchers!"

With Babe Ruth, the Yankees were not just relevant, they were bigger than life—and spring training had not even begun.

The Yankees were again training in Jacksonville, but ostriches and alligators would not get much attention this year. Ruth came from Boston and met a group of his new teammates boarding the 6:20 p.m. train at Penn Station in New York on the evening of February 28 for the overnight, coast-hugging ride on the Seaboard Air Line.

"Yes, I'll be pleased when the old season swings round," Ruth told a throng of scribes at Penn Station, where he was photographed wearing a dark suit, a dark, three-quarter-length camel hair coat, and a matching cap. "I think I'll like New York first rate. I've always liked playing here, as most of the fellows do. I figure this is going to be my biggest year."

The season had been expanded to 154 games, and therefore, Ruth pointed out, 77 would be at the Polo Grounds. "I think I'd like to play the outfield regularly. If I do, I'll have more chances to wallop the pill, and I think my work in the field will improve by playing one position regularly. However, if Huggins wants me to shift around, that's all right with me. If I can help the boys bring in the pennant by taking a turn in the pitching box, I'll be happy to do so."

Huggins was the manager, emphasized Babe, who was on his best behavior as he boarded the train with Ping Bodie and Hank Thormahlen, "and what he says, goes."

Wherever the train stopped for more than a few minutes in places like Virginia, the Carolinas, and Georgia, crowds were gathered to get a glimpse of Ruth, who appeared and handed out more cigars from his Boston factory. He may have given more away than were sold.

During a March 2 practice, he pulled on the Yankees' pinstripes for the first time. On the 30-hour train ride, he had already made fast friends with the irrepressible Ping Bodie, who was hitting ground balls to him. "Hit 'em harder," the Babe kept hollering. At the end of the practice, Ruth and Bodie took a jog around the field. First chance he had, Ruth led a group of players out to the golf course, bragging that he shot as low as 76 out in Los Angeles. He broke two clubs during one tough round. "The Babe's club head flew off on the ninth tee, and both the club head and the ball sailed into a lake 70 yards in front," reported the *Sun*.

The next day, Huggins played Ruth in center field, which is where he was to begin. Bodie played right, Sammy Vick left. Scouts Bob Connery and Joe Kelley served as coaches and ran the workouts, and Kelley was assigned to keep Ruth out of trouble at night.

A shipment of Ruth's bats arrived on March 13—and even that made headlines, described as "yellow, large, heavy and formidable-appearing."

The Yankees traveled down to Miami to play the world-champion Reds for a few games. In a game at Palm Beach, Ruth ran into a palm tree chasing a fly ball in batting practice and was knocked out. "I knocked as much bark off the tree as the tree knocked skin off me," Ruth told reporters on the train back to Jacksonville. During batting practice on March 20, Ruth launched one over the center-field fence at South Side Park, a feat no one had ever previously accomplished. Coach Charlie O'Leary and longtime groundskeeper Phil Schenk chased the ball, found it 60 feet beyond the fence, and estimated the drive at 480 feet.

On March 21, during a loss to the Dodgers in Jacksonville, a fan in the stands called Ruth "a big piece of cheese," and when Ruth turned to glare, he invited him up into the stands to do something about it. Ruth began to oblige. When he got close, he saw the man was relatively small and let out a laugh. The heckler subsequently pulled out a knife. "Let me tell you one thing," Ruth hollered, "when you go to ball games, amuse yourself some other way than riding ball players." Yankees pitcher Ernie Shore pulled Ruth back to the field before things got out of hand.

It was all Ruth all the time. The Yankees weren't winning games yet, but the fun was just beginning.

Babe Ruth's first game with the Yankees came in Philadelphia on April 14, 1920. He was batting cleanup and playing center field as he desired, because Bodie had left the team for a time, and rapped out two singles against Scott Perry, who beat Shawkey and the Yankees, 3–1. The goat? Ruth dropped a fly ball in the eighth inning, allowing the winning runs to score.

Twenty thousand showed up at the Polo Grounds eight days later to see Ruth's first home game but were disappointed. Swinging from the heels at a slow ball in batting practice, Ruth injured his rib cage, tearing a muscle from the 11th rib, the X-rays later showed. He was bandaged up tightly and started but doubled over in pain after each swing in a first-inning at-bat. After striking out, he left the game. Ruth, 7-for-31 and homerless, and the Yankees, 4–7 in April, both started slowly.

The fireworks finally began on May 1, against his old mates. Ruth doubled in the fourth inning, then in the sixth, against lefty Herb Pennock, Ruth hit the first pitch over the roof in right field, clearing it, the papers estimated, by 30 feet. Duffy Lewis followed with a home run, and Shawkey pitched a 6–0 shutout. Ruth homered again the next day, off Sad Sam Jones, and the Yankees were at last off and running. The Babe hit 12 homers in May, 12 in June, and 13 in July, surpassing his own one-year-old record, hitting Nos. 30 and 31 off the White Sox's Dickie Kerr on July 19.

The Yankees as a team were riding high on Ruth's unheard-of power, going 44–16 between May 1 and July 3, including a 10-game winning streak between May 25 and June 2. After a nine-game winning streak, the Yankees were in first place, a game ahead of the Indians, when play began on July 4.

By early August, the Yankees, White Sox, and Indians had left the rest behind and were engaged in a three-team struggle for the pennant. The Yankees won four in a row in Cleveland and were a half-game behind the Indians and White Sox when the Indians arrived in New York for a three-game series on August 16. Ruth had 42 home runs at that point.

In the middle of the race, Carl Mays threw his deadly pitch to Ray Chapman and lost a 4–3 decision to Indians ace Stan Covaleski. The controversy raged for a week or so, some teams threatening to strike if Mays was allowed to pitch. Eventually, Mays was allowed to resume, but the Yankees lost seven of nine games and fell four games out by August 26.

All the while, the Polo Grounds was filling at a record pace. Attendance was up all over baseball and the Giants were drawing better than ever, but the Yankees, with Ruth, were setting the pace, pulling in 1,289,442 for the season, or about 16,000 per game. Huston was again a fixture at the ballpark, and now Ruppert was out more often, too.

And as Ruth was slugging home runs and settling in as a rightfielder, he was showing all-around offensive skills, his batting average over .370 all season, with doubles, triples, walks, and stolen bases accumulating. He finished the season with a .376 average, a .537 on-base percentage, a .847 slugging percentage, and a 1.379 on-base plus slugging. He stole 14 bases and was caught 14 times; walked 150 times; and struck out only 80 times in 616 plate appearances. He also threw out 21 runners on the bases. Ruth started a game on the mound, too, pitching the first four innings of a 14–7 rout of Washington on June 1 at the Polo Grounds, where 12,000 came out on for the Tuesday afternoon game.

The Yankees were in first place as late as September 16, when they got to Chicago and lost three in a row to the defending AL champs, who were perhaps sniffing another World Series. Mays won his 25th game, throwing 11 innings to beat St. Louis, 4–3, on September 20, but the Yankees were now three games out. A week later, Mays threw a shutout in Philadelphia, but the Yankees were still three out, with Cleveland on top, leading the White Sox by half a game with a half dozen to play.

The next day, everything changed. Eight White Sox players were indicted for fixing the World Series a year earlier. Former boxer Abe Attell was threatening to "shoot the lid to the sky," according to the *New-York Tribune*. Comiskey, with no choice, suspended all the players. He immediately received a telegram from Ruppert and Huston:

> *Your action in suspending players under suspicion, though it wrecks your entire organization and perhaps your cherished life's work, not only challenges our admiration but excites our sympathy and demands our practical assistance.*
>
> *You are making a terrible sacrifice to preserve the integrity of the game. So grave and unforeseen an emergency requires unusual remedies. Therefore, in order that you may play out your schedule and, if necessary, the World Series, our entire club is placed at your disposal. We are confident Cleveland sportsmanship will not permit you to lose by default and will welcome the arrangement. We are equally certain that any technicalities in carrying it out can be readily overcome by action of the National Commission.*

The idea of Ruth, Mays, Pipp, Shawkey, or any other Yankees being "loaned" to Chicago in the final week of a tight pennant race was politely dismissed. "It's a splendid offer, and one I appreciate from the bottom of my heart, but I'm afraid there is no way I can accept it," Comiskey responded.

The Indians won the pennant by 1 ½ games over the White Sox, three games over the Yankees, who finished 95–59. "I'll never know if we should have won it or not," Roger Peckinpaugh told author Donald Honig. "The White Sox were monkeying around so much during the year you could never tell."

Ruth hit his 54th homer during a doubleheader in Philly on the final day of the season. The Yankees and Giants discussed another October series, which would've packed the Polo Grounds, given the attendance figures of the regular season, but Giants owner Charles Stoneham nixed it. "A good, clean, hard-fought city series would not interfere with the world's series and would be a splendid finale for the season," Huston argued in the *Tribune*. "In these days when organized baseball is on trial, it strikes me as a good time for the promoters to prove their entire good faith with the public."

As the troubling details of the "Black Sox Scandal" unraveled, calls came from all corners for baseball to identify and establish a strong, independent leader to clean it up. "Baseball's greatest need is for a commanding officer," Huston told reporters on October 1. Meanwhile, Cleveland beat the Dodgers, who won the NL pennant for Wilbert Robinson, further emboldening Huston to take on Ruppert and go after Huggins, who failed to deliver a first-place finish despite all that had been invested.

But amidst all the tumult, this much was clear: the Yankees' day was inexorably coming, the game was radically changing, and the old guard—McGraw, Griffith, Comiskey, Cobb, Ban Johnson, and all the rest –would have to brace for it.

CHAPTER 16
THE MISSING PIECE

The most underestimated man on the professional baseball horizon of the past 75 years is Edward G. Barrow.
He made no statistical records. Of humble birth, he
became baseball's most comprehensive contributor in all
the many departments of the game.
— Branch Rickey, *The American Diamond,* 1965

After nearly two decades in baseball's woods, the Yankees had
nearly every piece in place to establish dominance. They had
a deep-pocketed owner, obsessed with winning and possessed
of smart business sense. They had an astute, forward-thinking
manager. They had a solid roster and the biggest star the game
had ever known.

Yet, despite winning 95 games and narrowly missing the AL
championship in 1920, the Yankees were oddly dysfunctional.

By the end of the season, Babe Ruth, who chafed at any discipline and, having single-handedly hit more homers than any

team in the major leagues except the Phillies, saw no reason he should have to abide by the rules, especially at the hands of "the Midget Manager," Miller Huggins, who was conspicuously unsupported by one of the two owners, Col. Til Huston.

A month after the last game, Ruppert told reporters that Huggins would be back for a fourth season as manager, signed to a one-year contract for $12,000. Huston's favorite manager, Wilbert Robinson, spurned as "too old" by Ruppert in 1917, was riding high as pennant-winning manager in Brooklyn, and shortly after the World Series, it had been speculated throughout October that he was about to jump to the Yankees.

"We have not talked to Robby," Huston said, the day Huggins was reupped, "except that on hunting trips or times in the off-season when we were together, being great friends I may have remarked that I wished he was with us. There is no secret about my having wanted him as manager."

Ruppert prevailed again. Robinson signed a three-year contract with the Dodgers two days before the Yankees committed to bringing Huggins back.

Yet there was still, as Bill McGeehan of the *Tribune* described it, "something of a Ruth problem for next year."

"The Babe and the Midget Manager were reported not to be on the best of terms, especially toward the end of the season. In fact, the Babe was quoted as having said there is not room on the same team for himself and the manager," McGeehan explained.

Ruth had his own idea. Why not make star shortstop Roger Peckinpaugh, who had managed the Yankees for a couple of weeks as a twenty-three-year-old in 1914 and now a sturdy veteran, the permanent player-manager?

Ruppert's mastery of the art of running a business dictated the solution for all this. A strong, full-time executive was needed to bring order to the organization. Harry Sparrow had died in 1920, so the Yankees were looking for a new "business manager." On October 29, 1920, the day Huggins was announced as the manager for 1921, Edward Grant Barrow was hired for the front office role.

The move was relatively low-key, but some immediately caught on to what it meant.

"We have a suspicion his duties will not be entirely along the lines of 'business,'" wrote Dan Daniel in the *Herald*. "In Huggins and Barrow, the New York club will have all the elements necessary for good management.

With so many volatile figures on the scene, Ed Barrow became the Yankees' indispensable executive, defining the modern GM. *AP Photo*

". . . Barrow knows how to run a club after the sun has gone down. He has a commanding personality and physical vigor. As an executive, there are few men in baseball who are his equal."

240

Barrow never played major league baseball but had vast experience as a manager and executive, and, having managed Ruth and Mays in Boston in 1918–19, he knew Huggins needed solid backing to keep Ruth in line and control the ballclub.

Ed Barrow—husky, loud, and demanding, with bushy eyebrows that those who dealt with him found somehow intimidating—was born in Springfield, Illinois, in 1868 and grew up in Iowa. He started in the newspaper business, moving from mail clerk to circulation manager. He was a boxer and a pitcher until hurting his arm, and then he became a baseball impresario. In 1895, he had gathered enough money to buy a minor league franchise in Wheeling, West Virginia. He experimented with night baseball as early as 1896 in Wilmington, Delaware. "They couldn't finish the game," Branch Rickey noted, "but he had it." He hired a woman, Lizzie Arlington, to pitch an exhibition game, and famous prize fighters to umpire, and he supported Harry Stevens's launch of his wildly successful concessions empire.

By 1903, Barrow was managing Detroit and knocking heads with Kid Elberfeld but admitted he was furious, and helpless, when Ban Johnson engineered the Tabasco Kid's eventual trade to the Highlanders. Barrow left Detroit to resume owning and managing minor league clubs. In 1910, he became president of the International League and made his reputation by holding the league together despite the Federal League's raiding of its players and invasion of its territories.

When IL owners cut Barrow's salary, he went to work for Harry Frazee in Boston and managed the Red Sox in civilian clothes and a ubiquitous straw hat, en route to the 1918 World Series championship. He and Ruth had a stormy relationship. Nevertheless, Barrow argued against the sale of Ruth to the

Yankees. Barrow was living in Riverdale, New York, when he got the call from Frazee, who loved calling him "Simon" (as in Simon Legree), telling him Ruth was gone. "You ought to know, you are making a mistake," Barrow told him, as he revealed in his memoirs in 1953. He didn't want any part of players the Yankees might send in return as a token for Boston fans. "This has to be a straight-cash deal, and you'll have to announce it that way."

So it was announced, bringing all the coming disenchantment on Frazee, not Barrow, who was a more sympathetic figure as the depleted Red Sox sank to 72–81 in 1920.

Shortly after the season, Barrow, back in Riverdale, received another call from Frazee, this one out of the blue. "Simon," Frazee said, "Cap Huston of the Yankees is over in Roosevelt Hospital and he wants to talk to you. He isn't seriously sick and you can go right in. I'd advise you to see him. Anything you do is all right with me."

Barrow took Frazee's advice and saw Huston, who immediately began calling him Simon and offered him the business manager's position with the Yankees. "What do you say, Simon, is it a deal?" Barrow knew Frazee was about to sell off whatever was left of his major league talent and plunge the Red Sox into the cellar for years to come.

"It was not a hard decision to make," Barrow would recall. "The Yankee colonels were the richest owners in baseball and they were building. They had Ruth. I knew further that this time I would be on the receiving instead of losing end of Frazee's deals. And it was New York."

Reading the tea leaves perfectly, Barrow saw his own future in New York in a powerful role that would one day be known as "GM," the front office buffer between ownership and the baseball operation. Frazee actually appeared at the Yankees offices on 42nd Street on October 29, as Barrow was introduced and Huggins re-signed.

"And that was where I found little Hug when I arrived on the scene in 1920, caught between two colonels," Barrow recalled. "I could see that one of my first jobs was to extricate him."

Barrow sensed Huggins was wary of yet another strong figure towering over him, but he quickly reassured him.

"You're the manager," Barrow told Huggins, "and you'll not be second-guessed by me. Your job is to win; part of my job is to see that you have the players to win with. You tell me what you need, I'll make the deals—and I'll take full responsibility for any deal I make."

Huggins looked at Barrow as if he couldn't believe his ears, but Barrow was true to his word. After he retired from baseball, Barrow insisted that he never set foot on the playing surface at Yankee Stadium until Lou Gehrig was honored in 1939, a decade after Huggins's death, and never entered the clubhouse unless the manager invited him.

Ruppert and Huston, however, were frequently in the clubhouse and in the manager's office, questioning Huggins after games, as players could well see. In 1922, Barrow wrote both owners a stern letter, demanding they stay out of the clubhouse unless invited. Huston called Barrow in and, tapping a pencil on his desk as he did when he was annoyed, asked, "Simon, do you mean this?" Barrow did and made the demand stick.

Once Barrow was in place, he and Huggins began working to push the Yankees over the top. The opportunity was there. Since the demise of Connie Mack's juggernaut, the Red Sox and White Sox had won every pennant between 1915 and 1919. The defending champion Indians didn't have the look of a dynasty. The Yankees, with Ruth, could fill the power vacuum in the American League.

As Huggins told reporters in the Yankees offices the day after Barrow arrived:

> I have not made up my mind yet as to changes in the lineup. I think, however, we shall have some new and faster men on the team. What the Yanks need is a speeding up. . . . What we need most are a pitcher and an outfielder. It is one thing to want them, and another to go out and get them. But I'm going to make a determined effort to get those two and fully expect to do it. My preference is for a left-handed pitcher, but I am not one of those who thinks a southpaw is essential to a pitching staff. A good right-hander will do if we can't get the other kind, but we must have another pitcher. My outfield hasn't suited me for some time and I hope to change it so as to make it stronger defensively. That's the kind of new outfielder I want, one who can cover ground and make our defense out there better. My second choice, if that kind isn't available, is for one who is fast on the bases and will give us more speed that way.

Barrow agreed with Huggins's assessment of the Yankees' needs. "Hug had done well," Barrow would write, "despite the many handicaps under which he worked. He was building the nucleus of a good ballclub, but he still needed more than he had. I got it for him."

Barrow knew just where to shop—Harry Frazee's Baseball Emporium was always open for business. The Yankees acquired pitcher Waite Hoyt and catcher Wally Schang, pitcher Harry Harper, and infielder Mike McNally in an eight-player trade. Home Run Baker, meanwhile, decided to unretire after a year on his farm. Scout Joe Kelley made the trip down to Trappe to talk to him, and despite a report that the Yankees had sold his rights to the Senators for $30,000, Huston insisted that if Baker wanted to play, it would be with the Yankees. It suggested still more disagreement among the Yankees brass. "I am going to play baseball in New York and no place else," Baker declared.

Baker's return allowed Huggins to move strapping, young Bob Meusel from third base to the outfield, where he became a fixture for 10 years, playing whichever corner had more ground to cover. The search for a legitimate center fielder to cover the vast expanse of the Polo Grounds lasted into the season, when Barrow brought a former Yankee, Elmer Miller, back from the minors.

Things fell perfectly into place, and the Yankees finally won their first pennant in 1921, and again in '22, but lost both World Series to the Giants. The ultimate prize came only after Barrow finally, and fully, established the organizational harmony he craved. The feuding of Huston and Ruppert had continued, especially over Huggins, who, Huston determined, had to go after the 1922 World Series. As if to force Ruppert's hand, he began building a case.

The 1922 season had been a tumultuous one from start to finish, beginning with reports of drinking and partying in spring training in New Orleans, and then Ruth and Meusel under suspension for a barnstorming trip to which commissioner Landis objected. There was fighting and brawling, amongst one another and with fans, and more trouble with Carl Mays.

During the season, a private detective named Kelly joined the Yankees traveling party in St. Louis, posing as a traveling salesman and introducing himself to Schang, who brought him into the circle. It was Huston's idea, a scheme to prove that Huggins had no control over the players. In city after city, as Barrow would later describe it, Kelly showed up, offering players horse racing tips and access to alcohol during Prohibition. In Chicago, Kelly brought the players to a brewery for a night of drinking and revelry. While there, he snapped a picture of the group of players, developed it, had it autographed, and presented it to Barrow.

"I put it in a safe," Barrow wrote, "and it remained there, unseen." He published it with his memoirs three decades later. However, Kelly's report found its way to Judge Landis, who came to read the players a memorable riot act. Kelly later laughed when questioned about the whole affair. "That was one of the softest touches I've ever had," he roared to one writer.

After the Yankees were dominated by the Giants in the World Series, four games to none with one tie, Huston was vowing to get rid of Huggins, while Ruppert refused to budge.

Barrow now began to talk of quitting, perhaps succeeding Ban Johnson as AL president.

"I'm through," Barrow told Ruppert and Huston, according to author Frank Graham, "You brought me here to run this club on a businesslike basis. How can I do that with you two quarreling all the time? I've got to know who's boss around here."

Huston was taken aback. Ruppert knew Barrow was right. "Barrows," Ruppert said, mispronouncing his name, as he always did, "I'm sick of it, too. If I buy Huston out, will you stay?"

Barrow agreed and sat tight. During spring training, Ruppert wired him to come to New York and asked Barrow if he could raise $350,000. To his old friend, Harry Stevens, the now wealthy concessionaire, Barrow made the request to borrow the money needed to close the deal with Huston.

After typically drawn-out drama, Til Huston, who had put up half the $480,000 to buy the Yankees in 1915, walked away eight years later with $1.5 million. Barrow ended up with a piece of the team, and, he said, he asked Ruppert to send a telegram to the team in May 1923:

"I am now the sole owner of the Yankees. Miller Huggins is my manager. Jacob Ruppert."

The orderliness that Ruppert, Barrow, and Huggins craved was now a reality, players fell into line, and the Yankees won the pennant by 16 games and were World Champs for the first time within a few months. By then, Barrow had gone back to Boston and finally got the left-hander Huggins wanted—Herb Pennock, as well as third baseman Joe Dugan.

Barrow remained in control of the Yankees until 1945, retiring only when the Ruppert family sold the team, six years after the colonel died. The Yankees played in 14 World Series, and won 10 by that time; great players and championships were coming as if by conveyer belt.

"He was baseball's modest, but leading entrepreneur," Branch Rickey would write, admiringly, "never afraid of innovations. Ed Barrow was the greatest student and master of team balancing of any man I ever knew."

He loved to hunt and fish when business allowed him a break and later in life displayed an appealing, self-effacing sense of humor. As he took the chore of signing players off the manager's plate, Barrow could be stern—in 1929, he coldly sold Leo Durocher to the Reds after a short, heated exchange of salary in the 42nd Street office. But, Durocher later recalled, Barrow then became one of his best friends in baseball, delivering fatherly advice about managing his money and choosing friends carefully.

Rickey had the highest praise for Barrow's judgment of talent. Fred Clarke had delivered papers for him in Iowa, and Barrow ultimately recruited him for the *Des Moines Leader* company team. As a minor league owner, he spotted Ty Cobb in Augusta, Georgia, and made him an offer, and he also signed Honus Wagner. "Ed Barrow was a player scout, none better," Rickey wrote.

One of Barrow's first moves upon coming to the Yankees was the hiring of Paul Krichell away from Boston. Krichell, and the scouting department he would develop in a few years, ultimately discovered the players and built the farm system that would make Ruppert's aforestated vision—developing their own talent without having to overpay for established stars on the way down—a reality for the Yankees. Krichell worked for the Yankees for 37 years.

When the Yankees finished seventh in 1925, Barrow directed Krichell to find new, young talent. Mark Koenig and Tony Lazzeri came up and formed the double-play combination that made for the great 1927 team. The franchise did not have a losing season again until 1965.

Barrow's handiwork impacted the franchise through 1964, the farm system and culture he established continuing under his protégé, George M. Weiss, who was GM from 1948 through 1960.

Like Rickey, Barrow believed it was better to trade a player a year too early than a year too late. He would dispatch a veteran star just as he was beginning to fade and trust the fans would soon forget once the new kid was established. Though Peckinpaugh believed to the end of his life that he was traded after the 1921 season because he was a threat to Huggins, Barrow insisted it was because he was beginning to lose his range at shortstop. From Lazzeri to Joe Gordon, from Frank Crosetti to Phil Rizzuto, from Ruth to Joe DiMaggio—it was a pattern that repeated itself again and again, as Barrow continued to bargain hard with players, eschew sentiment, and rejuvenate his roster.

"The most efficient baseball business firm ever operated was a one-man organization," wrote Red Smith, "and its central office was under Ed's hat."

Barrow, refusing to entertain Ruth's managerial ambitions, employed only three managers during his long tenure: Huggins until his death, Bob Shawkey for one year, and then Joe McCarthy from 1931 on. Stability, order, and efficiency were the trademarks of Ed Barrow's Yankees. He was inducted into the Hall of Fame in the summer of 1953 and died that December.

"I was always happy and satisfied being the man *behind the Yankees,*" Barrow would write. "Because that was where I belonged. The spotlight should be reserved for the players and players alone."

CHAPTER 17

THE FIRST FLAGS:
WINNING THE HARD WAY

If we don't win this year, I cannot see how we could ever win. With our hitting strength, our attack is stronger than that of any other club. We have a fine fielding team but, of course, pitching is a large percent. Well, it looks to me as if we have the pitchers.

—Til Huston, *New York Herald*, March 21, 1921

On November 19, 1920, the Yankees' now complete brain trust was convened in Jacob Ruppert's office, now at 1638 Third Avenue. Ruppert and Huston would be there, as well as Ed Barrow and Miller Huggins and scouts Joe Kelley, Bob Connery, and Bob Gilks.

As described, the meetings were much like the ones George Steinbrenner would call in Tampa 75 years later, after each season. The Yankees came close to winning it all in 1920, but the air of disappointment hung heavy at the brewery, and the agenda now was geared to getting over the top. Nothing less would do, and Ruppert would sound more like his successor, more like The Boss, than ever before. The Yankees would be aggressive, relentless in pursuit of that elusive first pennant—in pursuit of a club with no apparent weaknesses.

Could Joe Dugan be purchased from the A's to play third base? Was it time to trade Wally Pipp? Ruppert never really got over his fascination with Eddie Collins, still with the White Sox. Barrow thought Babe Ruth should be playing first base, and Ruth, who was playing ball in Cuba for $1,000 a week, sent word he was willing to try first base and take a regular turn on the mound. Huggins was still calling for more speed in the outfield.

The Yankees were also in the market for a new location for training camp, and New Orleans was going all out to bring them to town, but Shreveport would get the double prize—Ruth and the Yankees, plus McGraw's Giants—in March.

The Yankees acquired a young shortstop, Johnny Mitchell, from the Pacific Coast League to push veteran Roger Peckinpaugh. The deal for Dugan didn't come off that winter, but to fill third base, Huggins made the long trek to Trappe, Maryland, to see if Home Run Baker could be talked out of retirement. Eventually, he agreed to return, as the Yankees were discussing elaborate trades with Washington and St. Louis.

On January 1, Ruppert had some writers in his office and declared the Yankees were not done dealing, after acquiring outfielder "Braggo" Roth from the Senators.

"We intend to go right ahead and build up a strong ballclub for next season," Ruppert said. "Not a club that is strong in one or two departments, like catching or pitching, but a team that is well molded. What we need on the Yankees is teamwork and speed. These elements will be added to the club during the remaining weeks of winter and Huggins will perfect them when spring training gets underway in Shreveport.

"Colonel Huston and I have but one objective in mind. That is to win the World's Championship. We will not be not be content to finish second or third. We want that title. New York has shown splendid loyalty to the Yankees. Interest in the game will be greater next year than ever before. Isn't there every reason for us to fight for the limit to win the flag?"

By the end of February, the Yankees were making their way to Shreveport. Huggins was journeying from Cincinnati. A group of rookies, staffers, and newsmen from New York and elsewhere came by way of St. Louis. Ruth journeyed from Hot Springs, Arkansas, where he had gone to drop some weight before camp. No team had won a pennant, the newspapers were always pointing out, without a solid left-handed pitcher. Harper had potential but could be wild. Was Ruth the answer? There was a report, originating in Cincinnati, that Baker had been re-signed and sold to Washington, but Baker and Huston, still an unabashed admirer, immediately squelched that. Baker agreed to come out of retirement, but only to play for the Yankees. "I am going to come back to the game I love this season, but it will be with the New York club and no other," Baker wired to reporters in Shreveport. "I had a conference with Col. Huston and we agreed on everything."

Once Baker arrived, Huggins decided to move Aaron Ward to second base and keep Bob Meusel in left field. He would sort among his outfielders for the best combo in the remaining right-fielder and center-fielder spots. This would not be a camp for unproven young phenoms; the Yankees were going with veterans. On March 7, Babe Ruth arrived, limping with a sore heel, and when word got out, the locals flocked to Gassers Park. He blasted eight homers in one BP session and proclaimed, "I'm in as good a shape now as I was last summer." He was also taking grounders at first base, with Huggins hitting them.

But it was a quiet camp, businesslike, and as the season approached, Huggins and his lieutenants were telling the writers the club was in far better shape than it had been a year earlier.

"The Yankees are wonderfully equipped to make a determined fight of it," Huggins exalted just before Opening Day. "We fear only Cleveland."

On April 13, some 37,000 filled the Polo Grounds for the opener. Ruth, in left field, rapped out 5 hits—2 doubles and 3 singles—as the Yankees routed Philadelphia, 11–1, behind Carl Mays. The Yankees, who compiled 17 hits and held Philadelphia to just 3, looked like Ruppert's ideal, a well-molded club. Mays, Shawkey, and Hoyt were proved to be a triple-aced top of the rotation and spearheaded a five-game winning streak that put the club 10 games over .500 on May 30.

Ruth hit his first home run on April 16, but his five-hit opener was more indicative of the kind of season this would be—an all-around, consistent offensive barrage. After hitting 5 homers in April, he hit 10 in May; 13 in June; and 10 each in July, August, and September.

Off the field, Ruth was in and out of hot water when it came to his driving, which he did as he did everything else—fast and loose. He was in a rollover crash in Pennsylvania, but escaped unhurt, and was arrested more than once for speeding and was sent to jail for a day. "The law is made for the high and mighty as well as the hard-working, everyday chauffeur," the judge told him. "When a man as prominent as you appears before me, I feel cowardly if I [merely] fine him."

Released on June 8, Ruth was late to the Polo Grounds but got in as a pinch-hitter and drew a walk in a 4–3 victory over Cleveland, as the Yankees and Indians split a four-game series.

Huggins wanted to put restrictions on players' driving, but Huston, the story goes, nixed it.

Behind Mays and Shawkey, the Yankees swept a July 4 double-header against the A's, and Hoyt won the next day to cap an eight-game winning streak, but the Yankees (46–28) still trailed the defending champs, the Indians, by two games. Huggins's fear was well grounded.

Waite Hoyt first became widely known as a high school pitcher in Brooklyn, at Erasmus Hall High, and he was only fifteen when he signed with the Giants, his father cosigning. At age nineteen, he debuted with the Giants, pitching a scoreless inning, but he and McGraw butted heads. When McGraw sent him to the minors, Hoyt quit pro baseball, and he stymied all of McGraw's attempts to trade him to a minor league team and get something back.

Finally, the Red Sox purchased his rights, and Hoyt agreed to sign only if they would pitch him in the majors right away. He threw a 12-inning complete game for Barrow on July 31, 1919. He shut the Yankees out a few weeks later, and again in 1920. The Red Sox found Hoyt hard to handle, but Barrow admired

Miller Huggins immediately took a shine to Waite Hoyt, who had a knack for pitching big games. *Bain News Service, courtesy of the Library of Congress*

his moxie, and Huggins soon grew to love it, too.

During the first long road trip in May, Hoyt, blond and burly, pitched consecutive complete-game victories at Cleveland, Chicago, St. Louis, and Washington, and Huggins was sold, ready to trust him with the biggest games.

"The secret," Hoyt later told writer Tom Meany, "was to get a job with the Yankees and joyride along on their home runs."

He didn't pitch a lot of low-hit games, but he was steady and knew how to cruise with a big lead, or bear down to hold a slim one. He was a bulldog. The Yankees were still 2 ½ games behind the Indians at the close of play on August 21. Three days later in Cleveland, Hoyt faced Stan Coveleski, hero of the 1920 World Series, one of those allowed to throw the spitter after it had been outlawed.

Hoyt allowed two early runs and walked six. He had to pitch out of two bases-loaded jams but hung with Coveleski until the Yankees scratched out an unearned run in the ninth and closed out the 3–2 victory, with the help of a game-saving catch by Elmer Miller, putting the Yankees in first place, essentially, to stay.

The Yankees won 30 of their last 41 games in a ferocious pennant race. On September 23, the Indians came to the Polo Grounds for four games, billed as "The Little World Series." Hoyt again outdueled Coveleski, 4–2, in the first game, as Ruth hit three doubles. In the final game of the series, Huggins called together his pitchers and asked for suggestions. He decided to pitch Jack Quinn, with all hands on deck for relief duty.

The Indians scored three in the first inning. Huggins brought Hoyt in, and he threw seven innings of relief as the Yankees came back to win, 8–7, in, the *New York Times* called it, "as desperate a conflict as was ever seen on a major league diamond."

Ruth hit his 57th and 58th homers as well as a double to center field that may have been longer than either, and Miller, the journeyman minor leaguer Barrow picked up for his defense, roamed that cavernous center field at the Polo Ground to rob the Indians of several extra-base hits.

With the Indians threatening in the ninth inning, Ruppert, according to Frank Graham's account, wandered down to the bullpen and paced nervously as Carl Mays came in to strike out the last man and finish the victory before 28,000. The Yankees took three out of four and a two-game lead with five to play. Miller got 3 hits as the Yankees clinched the pennant with a win over Philadelphia on October 1, then Ruth, his spring training offer to take a regular turn on the mound long forgotten, threw four innings of relief the next day. He played left field and first base in the game and stole his 16th base. He had already shattered his own home run record and finished the season with a .378 average, 44 doubles, 16 triples, 59 home runs, 168 RBIs, 177 hits, 145 walks, and an on-base-plus-slugging mark of 1.368.

A FRANCHISE ON THE RISE

The Yankees ended up with 98 victories and a 4 ½-game edge over the Indians. Waite Hoyt's 6–1 record against Cleveland had made the difference.

"It was a long, hard fight," said Roger Peckinpaugh, the longest-suffering Yankees player. "But we came through triumphant, if a little worn."

After 19 seasons, the Yankees had finally reached the top of the American League, and it was only fitting that their remaining rival for supremacy of the baseball world would be John McGraw's Giants. After all, it was the Giants who had tried everything to keep the Yankees from coming into existence in 1903, the angry landlords who were now forcing the Yankees to get out of the Polo Grounds. In this way, the Giants represented the older of the leagues and traditional brand of baseball against the modern power game employed by Ruth and the Yankees.

At last, the Yankees and Giants would be playing, not in an emotional but otherwise meaningless exhibition series, but with *everything* on the line, from the hearts and minds of New Yorkers to the future direction of the game. Huggins, though, had it in mind that the Deadball game could be blended with live ball, and it would eventually take *three* World Series for all of these storylines to play themselves out.

"This one series where there will be no quarter shown," Huggins wrote for *New-York Tribune* on the eve of the series. "For both teams will be fighting all the time on home grounds."

McGraw, in his own column, wrote, "I will say I have one of the greatest teams I've ever managed, and I can assure followers of the Giants that my players will give a good account of themselves in the final test."

After training side by side in Shreveport and sharing the same home ballpark, the players knew one another all too well.

The World Series was a best-of-nine contest in 1921. Huggins had Mays and Hoyt lined up for the first two. Shawkey had an injury-marred campaign but would take the third slot. Huggins didn't trust his other pitchers very much, and the Giants, with seven .300 hitters in their lineup, could wear out a thin pitching staff, one base at a time. The Yankees hit 134 home runs, 52 more than anyone else in the major leagues, but nearly even without Ruth's 59. The Giants were the proponents of "inside baseball," playing for one run at a time, but they hit 75 homers, including 23 from "High Pockets" Kelly, who had emerged as their biggest threat.

The franchise's first World Series game was set for 2 p.m. on October 5, a sunny but chilly afternoon that got progressively chillier. Mays was 27–9 in the regular season, starting 38 games, completing 30, and coming out of the bullpen 11 times, saving seven games. In all, he threw 336 2/3 innings, striking out only 70. His underarm delivery kept the Giants completely off balance in Game One, and he used only 86 pitches to shut them out. "I knew they could not hit the underhand ball," Mays chortled afterward, "and I fooled them with the curve."

Only Frankie Frisch solved Mays, getting four of the Giants' five hits. "I can't imagine why the boys did not kill that Mays pitching," he said, "if he pitches again, we'll soak him all over the lot."

The Giants' Phil Douglas was just as crafty, allowing only 5 hits, but the Yankees resorted to McGraw's style of small ball to win, 3–0, in just 98 minutes. Ruth stroked an RBI single in the first inning. In the fifth, Mike McNally, getting the start at third base, doubled to left and, at third base with two out, saw Douglas going to a full windup, and he lit for home, sliding safely across the plate feet first.

"We surprised them, and we beat 'em," Peckinpaugh shouted. "There isn't a team in the world which will stop us."

Game Two was more of the same, as Huggins turned to Hoyt, who rekindled his old feud with McGraw. "I wanted to go out and show McGraw I was a real pitcher," Hoyt said, "and remind him of a day in 1918."

Hoyt allowed only 2 hits, walked 5, struck out 5, and held a 1–0 lead (he had knocked in the run with a groundout, too) until the Yankees clinched it with two runs in the bottom of the eighth. Bob Meusel had been jawing the entire game with Giants catcher Earl Smith and told him in the eighth, "look out for me when I get around to third, I'll show you a thing or two about guts." Muesel did reach third and made good on his boast, stealing home as Smith dropped the throw.

The Yankees were up, 2–0, and hadn't hit a home run yet. They were beating the Giants at their own game, "inside baseball," and Huggins, in a rare display before the writers, allowed his giddiness to show. "We had more pep, we had more speed, we had greater defense, and we had greater pitching," he said. "Hoyt was a wonder. He exceeded our fondest expectations. With two great pitchers to throw right back at the Giants, we look pretty good, don't we?"

Hoyt, just twenty-two, was still entertaining the writers in the clubhouse. "I guess I had those Giants swinging—and I'll have them swinging when I face them again," he proclaimed, and with that, he clopped off to the showers. The Yankees were sitting pretty.

But this was a nine-game series. They needed three more wins, and the rest of Huggins's staff was spent. McGraw, meanwhile, still had his best pitcher, Fred Toney. When the Yankees scored four runs in the third inning of Game 3, knocking out Toney, the Giants' outlook was at its bleakest. But Jesse Barnes stopped the Yankees cold, and the Giants scored four in their half of the inning before they went on to pummel Yankees pitching, starting with Shawkey and Quinn, for 20 hits in a 13–5 victory.

Worse, Ruth had torn up his elbow with two hard slides and had to leave the game.

Mays had the Giants shut out again, 1–0, until the eighth inning of Game Four but finally caved and allowed three runs. Ruth, his elbow bandaged, hit his first-ever World Series homer in the ninth inning, but Douglas won the rematch with Mays, 4–2, and tied the Series.

Hoyt allowed 10 hits in Game Five but outdueled Art Nehf a second time, winning 3–1, before the Giants hit Harry Harper and Shawkey hard and tied the series again. Ruth's arm was now infected, getting worse, and his knee was sore. The doctors declared him done for the Series.

"How he had been able to do what he had done during the afternoon made me look at him in amazement," Huggins told reporters after Game Five. "It was an exhibition of gameness that will go down through baseball history."

McNally, too, had damaged his shoulder with his aggressive baserunning. Mays and Douglas hooked up again in Game Seven, and the Giants prevailed, 2–1, leaving it to Hoyt to keep the Yankees' hopes alive.

The eighth and final game of the 1921 World Series was played on October 13. Hoyt walked 2 batters in the first inning, though he thought he had one of them struck out and was furious at umpire Ollie Chill, who called it ball four. Next, High Pockets Kelly's hard grounder clanked off Peckinpaugh's glove, through his legs, and into left field—a devastating error by the senior Yankee, the kid whose first tries at shortstop had been mishandled by Hal Chase, enraging Frank Chance, eight seasons earlier.

"Peck's" error resulted in the only run of the game as the Yankees lineup missed Ruth's presence badly. In the ninth, his elbow bandaged, Ruth tried to pinch-hit and grounded out weakly. Nehf walked a batter, and up came aging Frank "Home Run" Baker, in the lineup for McNally. Could he destroy McGraw's Giants again, as he had 10 years earlier? He made a bid, worked the count full, and fouled off four pitches as teammates hollered, "The old stuff, Frank!" and "remember 1911" from the dugout. But Baker's hard smash was snared miraculously by Ross Youngs at second base, the start of a game-ending double play. It was hailed the next day in the papers as the greatest play ever seen in a World Series—better, even, than Bill Wambsganss's unassisted triple play the year before.

Thousands of fans poured out of the grandstand to surround McGraw in front of the Giants dugout. Under the stands, Hoyt sat on a little bench in the middle of the small, dimly lit dressing room, a scene described in the *New-York Tribune* by Jack Lawrence, his finger bandaged due to a cut, his head bowed. One by one, Ruth, Peckinpaugh, and Baker came by to shake his hand and commend him on his three brilliant performances. Ruppert entered and magnanimously congratulated players as if they had won. Then Huston came in, walked quietly to Hoyt, and extended his hand, and the brash, young pitcher broke down and began to cry.

Like Jack Chesbro in 1904, he had given all he had and deserved a better fate.

The Series generated record crowds, revenue, and betting. "Everything considered, I think it was the greatest World Series of all time," McGraw said, "and it will continue to be the greatest until the Giants and Yankees meet in another."

It didn't take long.

The Yankees had passed another milestone, winning the AL championship, but old issues remained as they convened again for spring training in 1922. Huston wanted Huggins out, while Ruppert and Barrow were solidly behind the manager. But the Yankees roster, including Mays, Meusel, Hoyt, and Ruth, was a difficult group to discipline, especially when they sensed the manager was looking over his shoulder.

Ruth, of course, believed he was above discipline and was only partially disabused of that when Landis suspended him and Meusel for the first six weeks of the season for playing on a barnstorming tour without authorization.

Huggins wanted to improve the pitching and defense and had decided Peckinpaugh had lost a step. Barrow traded Peckinpaugh away on December 20 in a complex set of deals involving the Senators and Red Sox that netted the Yankees two pitchers to fill out Huggins's rotation, Sam Jones and Joe Bush, and shortstop Everett Scott, who would continue his streak of consecutive games played until it reached 1,307.

During the first week of March, the Colonels signed off on a two-year contract for Carl Mays, worth $10,000 per year, rewarding him handsomely by the standards of the time for his two monster seasons with the club. Another big contract was drawn up for Ruth, "the greatest drawing card in baseball," according to Ruppert, as well. In Ruppert's words, Ruth was "a team in himself. You cannot conceive what moral effect his presence has with a ballclub."

The Yankees did train in New Orleans this time—hardly the best place for this group—and Huggins blew his stack when word of the players' nightly drinking at "The Little Club" made headlines. There was a lot of tension within the team. Ruth and Mays, never friendly, began a bitter feud that nearly ripped the team apart, as it began to play its way northward, against the Dodgers in one town after another. Huggins and Hoyt got into a shouting match in San Antonio, where the Dodgers had pounded him for seven runs. Baker, back for another season, had lost all of his range at third base, and Hoyt was calling for Huggins to get rid of him.

In a game at Little Rock, Mays was pounded, and, when Huggins came to take him out, he turned and heaved the ball into the grandstand. Huggins fined him $200. "I'm through with the Yankees if that fine is collected," Mays roared. "In all the years I have been with the Yankees, Huggins has never given me the slightest encouragement or thanks." This was patently false, but, Mays asked, why was Hoyt allowed to finish the inning in San Antonio while he, Mays, was humiliated with a midinning hook? Why was Ruth allowed to do what he pleased?

Mays planned to appeal to Ruppert and Huston. "There will be other fines if men don't buckle down to business," Huggins said. "They are taking this exhibition tour far too lightly."

When the Yankees reached Norfolk, Virginia, Huston joined the team, and, the *Evening World* reported, it was split in three factions: Ruth and his friends, Mays and his friends, and players loyal to the manager. The problems showed on the field too, as Brooklyn had beaten the Yankees in seven of 10 games.

"Huggins is the manager of the Yankees," Huston said, "and whatever he says will go. Col. Ruppert and I will support him to the limit."

Huston did the right thing, but he also knew he had new ammunition in building his case against Huggins, who fumed when writers asked him to respond to Mays's charge that he "played favorites." Ruth homered in another loss to the Dodgers in Richmond on April 8, then he and Meusel began their suspensions, which would last until May 20.

Thus began one of the strangest seasons the Yankees, or any team, has ever had. Amidst extensive chaos, they managed to find success. Favored to win the AL championship, they did just that. With two star outfielders missing, Barrow purchased Whitey Witt from the A's for $7,500 on April 17. With a makeshift lineup that included aged Baker still playing regularly at third base, the Yankees won 22 of the first 33 games and were in first place when Ruth returned on May 20. Then, after losing eight in a row, they fell 2 ½ games behind the St. Louis Browns on June 19 and spent the summer in a tense race with the suddenly formidable franchise, led by George Sisler.

Meanwhile, the tumult continued all season. There was Huston's private eye, and escapades he recorded on the first western trip. On July 26, Ruth and Pipp nearly came to blows in the dugout in St. Louis but patched things up after the game. On September 16, Witt was knocked out cold by a soda bottle thrown from the stands, also in St. Louis. Two days later, he returned to the lineup and got 3 hits in a crucial victory over the Browns.

Barrow had been working to patch up the holes in the meantime. At last on July 23, Dugan, by then with the Red Sox, was acquired in a deal that involved seven players and another $50,000 going to Frazee. Dugan, with Scott at shortstop, made for a much tighter infield. The Yankees went 41–19 after Dugan joined the team.

Ruth had 35 homers and 96 RBIs in only 110 games. Mays, brooding the entire season, was 13–14, but Bush won 26 and Shawkey 20 games. Hoyt rounded into form in September, going 5–2. He led the way in beating the Red Sox—for his 19th win—with relief help from Bush, on the second-to-last day of the season to clinch the Yankees' second pennant. They finished 94–60.

"They are inclined to slow down, unless hard pressed," wrote W.B. Hanna after the clinching, "and thereby toss away games. That's the kind of club they are, and what are you going to do about it? None understands their nature better than Miller Huggins, to whom is due the credit for instilling in them the much of the spirit that pulled them through the crises."

The rematch with the Giants was on, but this time it was no contest. The Giants won the opener, beating Joe Bush, 3–2. Game Two was the turning point. Doubles by Ruth and Meusel tied the game, 3–3, in the eighth inning, and the game moved to extra innings, lasting 2 hours and 40 minutes as the sun disappeared behind the Polo Grounds grandstand. At 4:40 p.m., the 10th inning completed, umpires Bill Klem and George Hildebrand ordered the game called on account of darkness. The 38,000 fans nearly rioted, surrounding Commissioner Landis, who thought the game could continue but backed the umpires' decision and promised to give the game's record take of more than $120,000 to charity.

The Giants won the next three games, 3–0, 4–3, and 5–3, and Ruth, 2-for-17 in the series, was considered a goat. McGraw, up to his old tricks, got under The Babe's skin. After one game, Ruth and Meusel went to the Giants clubhouse and nearly started a riot.

When Huggins ordered Bush to intentionally walk a batter in Game Five, the manager found himself in a shouting match with another of his top pitchers. "Bush scowled blackly," wrote W. O. McGeehan for *The Herald*, "and emitted a flood of mumbling protest. He clawed up the dirt around the pitcher's box by way of registering his disapproval."

Bush complied but threw a ball with nothing on it to the next hitter, and Kelly lined it to center field to score the tying and winning runs. "I will not take the blame for losing the game this afternoon," Bush told reporters afterward. A few days later, Bush cooled off and expressed regret.

But in an oft-told tale, Huston arrived at a postgame sorrow-drowning session with players at his current hangout, the Hotel Commodore, shouting for all to hear, "*Huggins has managed his last game with the Yankees ballclub. He is through. Through. Through.*" Rumors hit the papers that the Yankees were yet again trying to acquire Eddie Collins and install him as playing manager, or would perhaps even trade Ruth or other troublesome players, or maybe entice former Red Sox manager Bill Carrigan, whom Ruth liked, to manage the team, or Mike Kelly from St. Paul.

Ruppert, hardly pleased with the series, but less emotional, had read and heard enough. "You cannot blame Huggins for the way things went against the Giants," he said. "Huggins did the best he could and does not deserve the censure which has been heaped on him. He won the pennant for us last year, and he won another this year against pretty tough opposition. That's quite an accomplishment and if he wants to stay he can do so."

Four days after the series, Ruppert had sufficiently strong-armed Huston. And Huggins, notably, was summoned not to the brewery or the team's offices, but to The Commodore— Huston's turf. "My throat is getting dry saying 'no' to all these rumors," Huston told Ruppert, with reporters in earshot. "Let's liquidate the matter with a little ink."

Huggins was handed a new contract and a fountain pen, and he signed for 1923. The quarreling colonels had reached the point where one would have to go, but not before the grandest dreams of both rose from a desolate vacant lot on 161st Street in the Bronx.

CHAPTER 18

THE HOUSE THAT WAS BUILT IN A HURRY

To play 18 years in Yankee Stadium is the best thing that could ever happen to a ballplayer.

—Mickey Mantle, 1969

When Ruppert and Huston bought the Yankees from Frank Farrell, they inherited his grandiose dreams for a new stadium.

Right up to the time of the sale, Farrell had held onto his hopes of a new ballpark in Riverdale, a site on which he had lost a fortune. After the deal with Ruppert and Huston closed, the new owners set about Manhattan looking for a site to build their own ballpark. Before the sale was completed, the *New York Telegram* reported in December 1914, Huston had inspected six sites and eliminated three, including Farrell's spot at 225th Street.

"If we should win the pennant," Huston archetypically told the *New-York Tribune* on February 26, 1915, "we may be able to play the World Series in our own ballpark."

A FRANCHISE ON THE RISE

The story that began when Hilltop Park was shut down in September 1912 and ended with the opening of Yankee Stadium on April 18, 1923, had dozens of twists and turns, fits and starts, yet with all of the setbacks along the way, the timing proved perfect—the end product entirely beyond the wildest dreams of anyone originally involved. Though he wouldn't be part of the Yankees long enough to enjoy the fruits of it, or ever get the credit he deserved, the key figure was Til Huston—a blowhard on many topics, but a legitimate expert indispensable for a project such as this.

"He threw himself wholeheartedly into the building of the new stadium," Ed Barrow would write in 1953, "and as an accomplished and experienced engineer, made invaluable contributions to its construction. When Yankee Stadium was opened, it was the finest ballpark in the country. Cap Huston deserves the credit for that."

But that was years away. In 1915, the new Yankees owners had the same problems Ban Johnson had in finding a place to build in 1903. No site seemed quite right—they were either too big, too small, too expensive, presented too many obstacles, or were too far away. And the ever-quarreling colonels couldn't agree. In July of 1915, Huston wrote to Johnson that he had studied a site in midtown Manhattan, on West 42nd Street, and wanted to talk about it. Nothing came of it. The same happened with a plan to build over railroad tracks on the West Side, an idea that surfaced and died again in the 1990s. Huston also liked sites in the Bronx, presumably where the stadium was eventually built, and Long Island City, just over the Queensboro Bridge.

So the Yankees continued to be the guests that wouldn't go away, re-signing to play at the Polo Grounds in 1916 for a rent of

$55,000. After that season, Huston floated the idea of three sites he liked in Queens, all of which he touted as being short subway rides from Penn Station. It was widely reported in October 1915 that the Yankees had completed plans to build a ballpark in Queens for $900,000, but this, too, proved to be a false alarm.

Ruppert wanted the park in Manhattan. The Yankees again signed on to stay at the Polo Grounds.

Year after year, the Yankees and Giants haggled over rent. When Sunday baseball became legal in 1919, the teams and their leagues also argued over Sundays and holidays, creating a nightmare for the schedulemakers of both leagues.

Then the Yankees acquired Babe Ruth, began outdrawing the Giants, and the relationship became further strained. But the passage of time had worked to the Yankees' advantage. By 1921, Ruppert and Huston, now with a proven profit-making franchise, were ready to think big again, as big as Farrell's dreams for a megastadium and beyond the quaint, little ballparks of the era. The Giants made it clear they would have to leave, but as baseball owners haggled over what to do in the wake of the Black Sox Scandal, the Giants and Yankees came up with one last agreement. The Yankees would play the 1921 season in the Polo Grounds and hold an option for 1922, but that was it. . . . Really. . . . Finally, this time.

"If it were not for an option the Colonels Ruppert and Huston secured on the Giants' grounds during last year's threatened war over election of Judge Landis as supreme baseball head, the Yankees might today be homeless," wrote Vincent Treanor in the *Evening World* on December 3, 1921.

Ruppert was still determined the Yankees would play on Manhattan Island, and another site, along 11th Avenue in the

50s, was surveyed. Then the Yankees began negotiating to buy the sprawling Hebrew Orphan Asylum, between 136th and 138th Street on Amsterdam Avenue. Some streets would have to be closed, though, and the city was balking. Moreover, the site would have made for a rectangular shape that would have made for a deep right field, not good for the franchise's greatest asset—Babe Ruth's ability to hit home runs.

So the owners, at last, returned to an area that was first explored in 1903, a spot in the Bronx, just across the McCombs Dam Bridge from the Polo Grounds, owned by the estate of William Waldorf Astor. It had been a lumberyard, and was desolate, strewn with rubbish and boulders. Ruppert and Huston announced on February 4, 1921, that they had bought it for $500,000 (though varying reports have had the price as high as $675,000). It was 10 acres and easily reached by subways, particularly the Lexington Ave. Line.

Osborn Engineering, founded by Frank C. Osborn in 1892, designed the roads, railways, and bridges to fuel the growth of the nation at the start of the 20th century, then added baseball and college football stadia to its portfolio. From its cluster of rolltop desks in a downtown Cleveland space, the firm had designed Fenway Park and Braves Field in Boston, the rebuilt Polo Grounds, and most other notable sports venues in America.

They put their top man, chief engineer Bernard Green, to work drawing plans for the stadium Huston and Ruppert wanted, for a fee of $223,000. Huston, who had his own ideas, and a friend, Col. Thomas H. Birmingham, worked closely with Osborn.

There would be obstacles to overcome. It would take time to be get guarantees for the necessary street closings, time to clear and level the 10-acre site, to learn for sure where the permanent subway and possible rail stations would be located. The original concept of three tiers would have to be modified; the city would not allow a grandstand higher than 108 feet. Green and his men were able to cut down the height of the massive grandstands by scaling down the middle tier, or what became the "mezzanine."

Originally, the stadium was to be completely encircled by the 2 ½ tiers, the work to be finished later. In October of 1922, Davis J. Walsh of International News Serves reported that the Yankees' grand scheme was for the enormous coliseum to be used as the centerpiece for a New York City bid for the 1928 Olympic Games. A quarter-mile running track with a 220-yard straightaway finish along the south side of the field was planned. The track, designed by Frederick W. Rubien, secretary of the AAU and the American Olympic Committee, was finished in December, his son supervising its construction. The result was a 400-yard lap, with a 120-yard straightaway finish.

"The construction of the track will not interfere with baseball," the INS reported. "A novel method was adopted—the usual curb being sunk below the level of the surface, and the track will be perfectly level with the grass of the infield and bear the same relation to the sod as the running paths between the bases. A temporary curb will be installed when track events are in progress. . . . In the winter the track can be sprayed and make a splendid skating surface."

But to keep costs under control, and have the stadium baseball-ready more quickly, the decks would go only foul pole to foul pole, with wooden bleachers in the outfield. The tiered grandstand would be expanded later, though never completely to surround the field. And though there were many nonbaseball events held at Yankee Stadium, neither the 1928 Olympics nor ice-skating was among them. Though the concept was not new, the term "warning track" was derived from this running track built at Yankee Stadium. And in conceiving a "multipurpose" stadium, Huston proved ahead of his time.

The final ink-on-canvas drawings completed in late 1920 were so impressive, even the quarreling colonels agreed. Extremely accurate drawings of what was to come appeared in the Sunday *New-York Tribune* on February 4, 1921.

They included a copper "frieze" around the top tier of the grandstand, which, to this day, is among the signature elements of Yankee Stadium. The U.T. Hungerford Brass and Copper Company supplied the copper, the cost of which, according to Yankees executives who replicated it for the modern stadium, would be unfathomable in 2009. Kinnear Manufacturing in Ohio fashioned it into the desired Gothic look and, once the 16-foot frieze was bolted in place atop the roof, painted it white, so it would not show when oxidation turned the copper green. The magazine *The American Architect* would pan the frieze as "rather idiotic." But it did, the magazine concluded, give the ballpark a "festive air." It also evoked the image of a cathedral, a term which would eventually be commonly applied to Yankee Stadium.

"The new site embraces 10 acres or more and by every consideration of transportation is the most very accessible spot that could be selected in the metropolis," gushed the *Tribune*. "Colonel T.L. Huston, one of the very foremost civil engineers in the United States, has substantiated a dream of architecture that will be the very last word in baseball construction."

Ruppert was excited, but all business, as always. "You may say," Ruppert told reporters, "we will begin building as soon as the price of materials comes down."

That would be an issue. World War I had put off many projects and placed higher demands on materials and labor. In the fall of 1921, Osborne and the Yankees made favorable deals to secure iron and steel, the most expensive part of the project.

Throughout the year, Ruppert used every measure of his influence to get the city to close the streets that ran across the site. Hearing after hearing was held until, on December 17, 1921, the *Herald* reported:

"The last barrier was removed yesterday when, after a public hearing at City Hall, the Board of Aldermen gave Ruppert and Huston permission to close Cromwell Avenue and 159th Street, which intersect just about where second base would be located. The comptroller will fix the amount the New York club will pay for the privilege of putting the two streets into their playing field."

The Yankees advertised in all the New York papers for bids to begin the construction, beginning January 3, 1922:

> The Yankees baseball club will receive bids for the construction of its new stadium on 161st Street and River Avenue until January 18, 1922. Tenders will be received on the following subdivision of work, but anyone can bid

on the work as a whole. Lump sum bids will be received for each subdivision, or for the whole, but consideration will be given to propositions on any other plan contractors may see fit to make: Excavation, grading, Masonry, sewers and down spouts, reinforced concrete, lathing and plastering, ornamental metal work, tile work, terrazzo floors, carpentry, toilet stalls, roofing, sheet metal, steel sash, painting and wood bleachers.

Huston went hunting at his favorite spot in Georgia, and when he returned he told the press: "It is absolutely essential that we make a real start by [March 1]. Of course, we may strike a blizzardly March and be forced to change our plans.

". . . Another factor that may set us back is bids for the work to be done. If these bids are higher than we had expected, we are not going to rush into contracts. We will wait until the bidders become more reasonable. But at present it does not look as if we are likely to get set back from that direction. Bids for the steel work were not quite as low as we had expected, but they are quite satisfactory."

In all, 40 bids were considered before White Construction Co., headquartered on Madison Ave., was selected to build the grand stadium. They were the concrete experts. On St. Patrick's Day, Mayor John F. Hylan signed the necessary papers, the final green light from the city. He stated, "The city can't afford to disappoint the thousands of rooters who want to see Babe Ruth knock them over the fence."

There were more setbacks, but finally on May 5, officials of Osborn and the White Construction Company met in the Yankees' midtown offices and signed the papers, a jovial front masking behind-the-scenes tensions. White's president, Edward C. Escher, agreed to have the massive project completed in eight months, which would be November of 1922. However, Escher told reporters, "I will say, if the Yankees go ahead to another pennant this year and win their way to the World Series, the White Construction Company will work mighty hard to give them a park of their own to play part of it in during October."

Ruppert immediately interjected. "We'll win the pennant. So the gentleman from the White Construction Company better go ahead and have the stands ready."

Huston estimated that the stands could be sufficiently completed to accommodate at least 50,000 spectators as soon as October. That would be asking a lot, but Huston and his buddy Tom Birmingham would watch over the construction and keep it moving.

During the summer and fall of 1922, the Yankees were keeping their end of the bargain on the field. Despite a myriad of controversies, beginning with Babe Ruth's suspension, they were winning another American League championship. But starting a project the magnitude of this state-of-the-art stadium in May and finishing by early October was, predictably, too ambitious, even if everything went smoothly.

"What an undertaking that was," read White's promotional brochure, circulated after the stadium opened in 1923. "During the course of the construction, the owners made numerous changes in the structure, which necessarily delayed the progress of the work. Strikes on, or away from the site slowed down the work, or stopped temporarily the manufacture of material needed in the building. There was no penalty or bonus attached to the contract."

By mid-September, it was clear there would be no World Series played at 161st and River Avenue in 1922. Osborn had estimated the stadium less than 30 percent complete. There were more than 60 change orders, adding a quarter-million to the costs. As 1922 came to a close, Osborn estimated $886,833 had been spent, roughly 78 percent of the contract to complete. The Yankees asked the American League to delay their home opener.

In mid-March, White Construction was nearly broke, unable to pay subcontractors, and the contract with the Yankees and Osborn had to be amended to allow for Ruppert and Huston to advance money sooner. Ruppert and Escher haggled over money well after the work was completed.

Despite it all, Yankee Stadium was completed in time for the Yankees to play their first home game of 1923, a total of 284 work days. In time, this would come to be appreciated as something of a miracle. For contrast, after nearly a century of technological advances, the building of a 6,000-seat minor league baseball stadium in Hartford, Connecticut, was so fraught with problems, the team had to play the entire 2016 season on the road, the park opening more than a year *late*.

After the Giants embarrassed the Yankees in the 1922 World Series at the Polo Grounds, and Huggins survived Huston's last big drive to run him out of town, Barrow went to work retooling the team for 1923. At the construction site, the work accelerated, with more than 500 workers on the site at peak.

On November 28, 1922, Huston, with a reporter at his side, arrived at the stadium for an inspection. Phil Schenk, the colorful, portly groundskeeper who had forged the original rocky playing surface at Hilltop Park in 1903, was still on the job and hard at work on the infield for the colossal new stadium. He stopped and saluted the Colonel.

"Sir," Schenk said, with great majesty, "I have the honor to inform you that the playing field at this here place is absolutely finished and complete, with no casualties in the course of construction except one teamster that I fired over four rows of bleachers seats, thereby breaking his dignity in three places. I herewith hand you the keys to the diamond."

Schenk had promised to have the field ready before the first snow. Before Huston and John Kieran of the *New-York Tribune* left, it began to snow, covering the field in white.

"Would you think to look at that guy," Huston said, with a laugh, "that he is such a marvel of precision and accuracy? He promises something months ahead and, by jingoes, or words to that effect, he comes through with all of 10 minutes to spare."

Schenk had searched New York, New Jersey, Pennsylvania, and New England to find sod to his liking and finally settled on a spot on Long Island he would not divulge. As it was, Schenk pronounced the field a work of perfection.

"I've worked night and day on it," he said, "and I'm glad it's over. I am going to bed and leaving a [wake-up] call for February 4."

Winter weather made for more delays, and some work had to be redone. The frigid day after Christmas, a pit had to be reopened for the city to inspect a water main. A worker from Daily Brothers, one of White's subcontractors, dropped something into the pit intended to be a good luck charm.

On Valentine's Day 1923, Babe Ruth, after a winter rededicated to conditioning on his Massachusetts farm, arrived in New York for a stopover on his way to Hot Springs, Arkansas, for a period of intense conditioning.

Accompanied, typically, by a gaggle of writers, Ruth swung for the first time in what would become known as The House That Ruth Built. A stiff, chilling wind whistled through the empty cavern as Ruth and his retinue shlepped through four inches of slush to the spot where Schenk told them the mound would be. "The Babe shed his fur-lined flogger and his imported skimmer," Marshall Hunt wrote, "and stepped nimbly to where the plate is to be. He was wearing a skillfully tailored suit of blue serge."

The Babe, not about to swing hard enough to risk an injury, missed a couple of Hunt's feeble tosses, then hit a couple to the outfield, the ball disappearing in the snow.

"He admitted he could have socked 'em into the stands if he had wanted to," Hunt concluded. "The slugger spent two hours inspecting the Yankees plant. He leaves for Hot Springs tomorrow. . . . "

With the coming of March, the on-site supervisors were seeing as many as 10,000 curious spectators stopping by the construction site, as the anticipation of the stadium's opening gripped the city. Mind-boggling numbers appeared in the newspapers, like the *Morning Telegraph* on April 1, 1923: 30,000 yards of concrete; from Thomas Edison's Portland Cement company, 45,000 barrels of cement; 15,000 yards of sand; 2,500 tons of structural steel; 1,000 tons of reinforced steel; 500 tons of iron;

four miles of piping for railings; and lumber—2 million board feet, with 600,000 linear feet, transported from the West Coast through the Panama Canal, for the seats, which were painted grass green.

The home opener was set for April 18 against the Red Sox. From all approaches, the McCombs Dam Bridge, the Grand Concourse, and the slowly rising subway cars emerging from just to the south, the profile was huge, imposing. Except for the Bronx County Courthouse, nothing nearly that high was in the area. The descriptions from reporters, who were allowed to tour, were filled with the colorful, inflated prose of the times.

From the Harlem River, *Baseball Magazine* wrote, "It looms up like the Pyramid of Cheops from the sands of Egypt."

Just as visitors to New York from overseas were greeted by the Statue of Liberty, noted F.C. Lane, visitors arriving by rail were "confronted by the imposing pile of Yankee Stadium. To the visitor from other parts of America, New York is the amusement center of the continent. And that spirit of diversion finds fitting expression in the colossal monument of athletic sport."

"This new structure," wrote John B. Foster for the *New York Sun*, "is not a stadium in any sense. It is half of a colossal amphitheatre, its western side mounting toward Mars, its eastern half climbing 60 feet or more from the playing surface toward the elevated extension of a subway railroad."

On the morning of the 18th, as Babe Ruth rose from bed at the Ansonia, professing to his ghostwriter to be as nervous as he was before his debut on the vaudeville stage, the *New York*

Times wrote of the long road from Hilltop Park, where the old Highlanders left in that flurry of low comedy at the end of 1912, to this majestic day and the "skyscraper among ballparks" that was about to open its gates.

"From a small stand of wood to the greatest steel and concrete park in baseball is a long jump, even when it takes 11 years to do it."

The long road about complete, the Colonels were exultant—each in his own way. Huston brought some cronies up to the top tier, pointed out the vistas, and chortled, "The Bronx are not so wild when you get used to them."

Ruppert, sober and cold as usual, uttered a line that would one day appear in his obituary: "Yankee Stadium is a mistake—not mine, but the Giants'."

It was not a field, not a park, nor a grounds. The grand coliseum would not be named for Ruth, Ruppert, or Huston but would be called "The Yankee Stadium" until, eventually, it would simply be known in all its renovated and reincarnated forms, as "Yankee Stadium." But then, as now, all anyone needed to call it was "The Stadium." And for the New York American League club, that ragtag franchise created by Ban Johnson, Frank Farrell, and Bill Devery, the last of the pillars was now in place to support a long-lasting dynasty.

CHAPTER 19

TOP OF THE WORLD

The Ruth is mighty and shall prevail.

—Heywood Broun

As one could easily imagine it, the phone jangled on the nightstand and the big man rolled over, pushed aside an empty glass and an ashtray filled with cigar butts, and picked it up. Bill Slocum was Babe Ruth's "ghostwriter" and wanted his thoughts to organize into that day's syndicated column. Slocum, Ruth said, knew his thoughts better than he, himself did.

Ruth usually gave his rambling stream of consciousness from his room at the Ansonia, and "Sloke" churned it out for the afternoon papers. "You know that old gag about never putting off to tomorrow what you can do today?" this April 18, 1923, edition would begin. "The pennant race starts today and I'll be in there swinging with all my might trying to get a homer. I'll let tomorrow take care of itself. Maybe I'll christen the opening of the Yankees' new stadium with a homer, and maybe I won't."

Ruth, in prime condition, was promising to stay out of trouble, hit for a better batting average, and deliver the Yankees back to the World Series—to win it this time. That 2-for-17 performance against the Giants was on his mind all winter at the farm in Sudbury, during his early training sessions at Hot Springs, and all of spring training.

But he was all about *The Big Moment,* and Ruth knew that the police escort that would be needed to get him through the snarled traffic to the new ballpark that afternoon would land him onstage before the biggest crowd ever to watch a baseball game.

He knew what all those people wanted. Dare he disappoint?

Given the fact that it was opening day at the new stadium, Ruth was going to do his best to try not to.

The final touches had been applied to Yankee Stadium. It was ready and so were the Yankees.

The Yankees had nearly pulled off that long-coveted deal to land Eddie Collins in a trade that would have sent longtime Yankees nemesis, lefty Dickie Kerr, and Collins to New York for Aaron Ward and one of the Yankees' starting pitchers. But the White Sox didn't want Mays, and the Yankees would not send Waite Hoyt instead, so the deal fell through in December. Ward would be the second baseman, and Barrow would look again to Boston, sending four players and $50,000 to get the left-hander the Yankees had lacked, Herb Pennock. In the majors as a teenager, he helped pitch Connie Mack's Athletics to the World Series in 1914, then went to Boston where he became a steady starter as the team was dismantled. Pennock was 10–17 in 1922, but with the Yankees' run support and the lefty-friendly dimensions of the new stadium, he couldn't miss. He went 19–6 and began building a Hall-of-Fame résumé. "He had superb control and made pitching look easy," Barrow would write.

Once word got out that Ruppert was buying out Huston, Barrow and Huggins had the leverage to establish some discipline, and despite the temptations and past incidents in New Orleans, this time spring training was relatively quiet. Ruth had profited from his time in Hot Springs and was down to about 210 pounds, but fighting off a serious influenza and a paternity suit that was later dismissed, as he reported to camp in early March. The acquisition of other pitchers marginalized Mays, though he could still distract. Barrow's request that the owners stay out of the clubhouse began to stick, though Huston made his usual inspection tour of spring training.

Wally Schang was solid behind the plate, while Wally Pipp, Aaron Ward, Everett Scott, and Joe Dugan formed the infield. Ruth, Meusel, and Witt were in the outfield. Huggins had what he was calling his "big six"—Shawkey, Hoyt, Bush, Pennock, Sam Jones, and Mays—available to pitch. "The biggest job for Huggins is to arrange some kind of working schedule that will keep them all fit for duty," wrote Henry L. Farrell during spring training.

"Now, we were set at every position," Barrow later wrote. The Yankees broke camp on March 27 and began another town-by-town journey north with the Brooklyn Dodgers, winning seven of 12 games. "It didn't go very well on the trip from New Orleans," Ruth said. "I got a lot of wild and loose swinging out of my system." After the last game, in Springfield, Missouri, the teams made the day-long journey to New York for three more games at Ebbets Field beginning on April 14. Ruth went 5-for-6, portentous of the kind of season he wanted to have, in a 15–2 Yankees victory in the first game. He was quiet, 2-for-8 , in the last two games, the first of which the Yankees rallied to win, 9–8, in 11 innings. The Dodgers won the third game, 9–6.

With the season about to start, it became clear that George Sisler, the Browns' best player, would be out long-term with serious eye problems. That took the closest contender out of the picture. Maybe Ty Cobb, now a player-manager, could lead the Tigers upward to challenge. Maybe the White Sox had another run in them. Then there were the Red Sox, who had lured Frank Chance out of retirement, nine years after he left the Yankees in disgust, to manage.

The prognosticators, the consensus of the country's top baseball writers, were predicting another Yankees-Giants World Series. On April 17, the Yankees and Red Sox took turns practicing in the brand-new ballpark. "Looks pretty far out to that right-field fence," Ruth said. Much farther, it was, than the 250-foot porch at the Polo Grounds.

As workers drilled, hammered, and painted the new stadium to completion, as Barrow and Huggins were completing the roster, and as Ruth was living his one-of-a-kind life, Jacob Ruppert was busy acting on his promise to Barrow, buying out his partner. Like all dealings between the two, it would be hampered and delayed by squabbling.

A $3 million offer for the entire franchise had been made by Edward Simms, an oilman and horse racing enthusiast from

Kentucky, and was used to appraise the franchise. Ruppert offered $1.3 million for Huston's half.

On December 11, 1922, Huston rose at an Elks Club dinner and announced he was ready to sell his half of the team to the highest bidder and retire from baseball, the *New-York Telegram* reported. He had received "several splendid offers," he said, "and I thought it was no more than fair to Colonel Ruppert to tell him of these offers and give him the first chance to buy my half of the club. Ruppert then named a very fine price.

"I am getting old and tired and I want a rest. We started with practically nothing when he took over the New York American League franchise. We now have won two pennants and have the finest stadium in the country. Why shouldn't I get out now?"

But negotiations were just beginning. Simms was offering to buy Huston's half, and so was a group headed by the boxing promoter Tex Rickard, backed by John Ringling. These prospects backed Ruppert into a corner—he wanted no more partners, and he would either buy or sell the entire club.

There were liabilities on the cost of building the stadium to be sorted out, and Ruppert wanted Huston to agree not to buy into any other New York franchise for at least 10 years. The agreement fell apart, and Huston, as always, was doing all the talking and playing coy.

"Yes, I am still a baseball magnate and will be for some time to come," Huston told reporters in the Yankees offices on January 4, 1923. "Colonel Ruppert and I agreed on the price to be paid for my interest in the club. But when we got deeper into negotiations there was a disagreement over certain details. Jake wanted to do one thing and I wanted to do another, so we compromised and decided I ought to stay in baseball."

There was no such compromise. Ruppert wanted Huston out and had no choice but to scrape up close to $1.5 million and agree to Huston's terms. Barrow was on a hunting trip when he received a wire from Ruppert to come to New York. "Can you raise any money? Ruppert asked him. Barrow asked how much. "About $300,000 . . . or better, make it $350,000."

Barrow, who had started out in the concession business, called Harry Stevens, the legendary concessionaire, and asked to borrow $350,000. According to Barrow, Stevens was one in and around baseball who had no love for Huston. "The Stevens family will hock everything it has to get rid of that man," Stevens told Barrow.

Barrow delivered the money to Ruppert and would own 10 percent of the Yankees when the deal closed. "The deal was on and off two or three times after that," Barrow recalled.

Huston remained with the Yankees long enough to bask in the opening of the stadium he created, until they had rushed out to an impressive lead in the standings. In May 22, 1923, the deal was at last done and announced.

"Colonel Til Huston, warrior, engineer and one of the most picturesque characters on the sporting screen, has sold his half interest in the Yankees," wrote Fred Lieb in the *Telegram*.

Ruppert gave up the clause keeping Huston out of baseball. Huston remained nominally as a "director" on the Yankees' board, and he could buy the Dodgers or Giants if he wanted, but he never did get back in the game. Huston made a bid to buy the Dodgers in 1937 but did not get the franchise. He died in March of 1938.

"Now that Huston has retired," Ruppert said as the sale was announced, "it is my hope the club will hold the same position it has enjoyed heretofore. There will be no change in our policy. We adopted a winning policy from the start, and I hope we will be able to maintain it."

The aforementioned telegram from Ruppert—"*I am now the sole owner of the Yankees. Miller Huggins is my manager.*"— reached the visitors' clubhouse in Chicago.

"Peace came to the Yankees after that," Barrow said.

The automobile was still in its first generation, but there were enough cars on the road to create a traffic jam. The rumbling roadsters and sedans of 1923 lined up along the dusty roads outside the new stadium made for an iconic photo on April 18. The Red Sox, caught in traffic, had to walk the last mile or so, over the Macombs Dam Bridge.

Up to that point, the largest crowds ever to see a ballgame were in Boston during the 1916 World Series, when the Red Sox borrowed the Braves' bigger stadium to host the Dodgers. Babe Ruth pitched 14 innings to win one of those games, 2–1, before roughly 42,000.

One and a half times that amount—or 63,000—would fill the three tiers of "The Yankee Stadium," as it was generally called, its price tag now estimated at $2.5 million, more than would see the other three American League openers in Philadelphia, St. Louis, and Cleveland combined.

"A super-World Series atmosphere pervaded the atmosphere of the formal dedication of the huge new home of the Yankees," read the wire service account. "The record crowd, which jammed every nook and corner of the triple decked grandstand and packed all but a few corners of the bleacher sections, far exceeded all expectations."

The "official count," as reported in the *New York Times* and other newspapers, was 74,200, but the real attendance has most commonly been estimated at something over 60,000. The 18,000 reserved seats were long sold, with 52,000 unreserved grandstand and bleacher seats held for day-of-game sales through 36 ticket windows. "Outside the park," the *Times* reported, "flattened against doors that had long since closed, were 25,000 more fans who finally turned around and went home, convinced that ballparks are not nearly as large as they should be. The dream of a 100,000 crowd at a baseball game could easily have been realized if the Yankee colonels had only piled more concrete on concrete, more steel on steel."

There were arrests made for scalping tickets, too. But with the gates opening at noon, three hours before the first pitch, most everyone with a ticket was able to make their way through the bedlam and into their seats. The subway system proved most efficient for the challenge. Even flinty old commissioner Landis arrived by subway and was caught in the crowd trying to get in at 1 p.m., when police recognized and escorted him inside.

The weather started out overcast and blustery but transitioned to be more agreeable, warm, and fair. Phil Schenk, who had worked a miracle 20 years earlier in getting Hilltop Park more or less ready for baseball, came through in a big way. This playing field, his creation from scratch, drew nothing but rave reviews.

John Phillip Sousa's Seventh Regiment Band gathered in front of the Yankees dugout and marched all around the field, finally stopping in front of the Yankees dugout. Then it marched both teams out to the flagpole in distant center field, where Huggins and Chance, resplendent in a wool sweater, hoisted the flags, including the Yankees' heavy flannel 1922 championship pennant. Then the band marched them back to the plate. Before Alfred E. Smith, the popular governor who would run for president in 1928, took his box seat, he threw a perfect strike to Schang for the first pitch.

"Governors, generals, colonels, politicians, and baseball officials gathered solemnly to dedicate the biggest stadium in baseball," the *New York Times* reported. "But it was a ballplayer who did the real dedicating."

When Ruth arrived at the stadium in his Pierce Arrow, he checked to make sure that the police who escorted him and a couple of kids he had met near the Ansonia were given tickets. Inside, he was more specific in his proposal to the Baseball Gods than he had been in his column. He would give "a year off his life" to hit a home run on this day. He was presented with a pre-game gift—a large bat in a case.

Bob Shawkey's first pitch to former Yankee Chick Fewster at 3:30 p.m. was a ball, low and away, so far as umpire Tom Connolly was concerned. The Red Sox's George Burns got the first hit, a single in the second inning. In the bottom of the third inning, Aaron Ward singled and Everett Scott, playing in his 987th consecutive game, bunted him to second. Ward was caught in a rundown on Bob Shawkey's bouncer back to the mound. Then, back to the top of the order, Whitey Witt, who led the league in walks in 1922, drew one. Joe Dugan singled to center, and Shawkey scored.

Up came Ruth. Chance and his pitcher, Howard Ehmke, had decided to work Ruth the way the Giants had in the '22 World Series—set him up for slow stuff outside. With The Babe so determined to hit a home run on Opening Day, it seemed the perfect plan. Ruth and Ehmke battled to a 2–2 count, and the right-hander lobbed a slow curve to the outside. Ruth, as he promised, swung with all his might.

"A white streak left Babe Ruth's bludgeon," Grantland Rice wrote, "On a low line it sailed, like a silver flame, through the gray, bleak April shadows and into the right-field bleachers."

Ruth followed Witt and Dugan around the bases, and cameras caught him grinning as he touched the plate with his left toe and greeted batboy Eddie Bennett. Former teammate Al DeVormer, catching for Boston, stood silently with his hands behind his back as Ruth doffed his hat to the crowd that, again in Rice's words, had given "the greatest vocal cataclysm baseball has ever known."

"The big slugger is a keen student of the dramatic," the *Times* said, "in addition to being the greatest home run hitter."

He later gave the bat to a Los Angeles newspaper, which presented it as first prize in a high school home run contest to Victor Orsatti. In 2004, the bat sold at auction for $1.26 million, Sotheby's announced.

The Yankees followed "the script," which would become the franchise's habit. The rest of the day belonged to Bob Shawkey, the senior Yankee who drew the start in part for sentimental reasons on Huggins's part. He fashioned a 3-hitter, walked 2, struck out 5, and had the massive crowd streaming back to the subway platforms after 2 hours, 5 minutes. Bush, Jones, and Mays followed with victories as the Yankees started out 4–0.

On April 24, President Warren G. Harding, who had been unable to attend the opener, made his way up from Washington to watch the Yankees and Senators. Wearing a long overcoat and hat, he stood up in his bunting-draped box and greeted Ruth, a self-proclaimed Democrat, who came to sheepishly shake the Republican president's hand.

Harding had once called on Americans to "strive for production the way Babe Ruth strives for home runs." Ruth obliged that day, with his second home run as Sad Sam Jones threw the shutout.

Pennock got his first win the next day, and the Yankees were off and running, 8–4 in April and 21–6 in May. The Yankees were in Chicago on the day Ruppert's deal to buy out Huston was made public. Ruth hit a two-run homer in the top of the 15th inning to give the Yankees a 3–1 win over the White Sox, allowing the team to barely make its train and aging traveling secretary Mark Roth to breathe easy. When Ruth learned of the danger of missing the train, he told Roth, "don't worry, I'll get us out of here," and he promptly homered. "Why didn't you tell me about that before?" Ruth playfully asked Roth once the team was on board.

On May 31, Shawkey beat the Red Sox again at Yankee Stadium, and the Yankees led the rest of the league by seven games. By the end of July, the Yankees were 65–30, and 14 games ahead of the pack. They clinched the pennant on September 20 and finished 16 games in front.

One day in May 1921, a teenager named Lou Gehrig lugged his gear to the Polo Grounds to try out for John McGraw. But when a ground ball went through his legs, Gehrig was told to go home. McGraw was in a foul mood, but Giants scouts convinced Gehrig to play under an assumed name—Lou Lewis—for Hartford to get some pro experience. Two months earlier, Gehrig, playing for Columbia University, had hit two long homers in an exhibition game against the Senators in Hackensack, New Jersey; the *Hartford Courant*, spelling his name as "Gahrig," called him "a home run hitter of the Babe Ruth type." So when he returned, Hartford reporters recognized him, though still misspelling his name. "'Lefty' Gahrig, hard-hitting semi-pro from Brooklyn, has been signed up by Arthur Irwin to play first base for the Senators," the *Hartford Courant* reported on June 3, 1921.

Apparently, Irwin, Frank Farrell's man, and the Senators prevailed upon the newspaper to join the conspiracy and keep the secret, for the next day the *Courant* reported, "Lou Lewis, Arthur Irwin's latest discovery, was placed on the initial sack. The youngster, who is only 18 years old, appeared to be a bit nervous. . . ."

Columbia coach Andy Coakley, who had given Gehrig a scholarship, wasn't fooled. Tipped off, he came to Hartford, dragged Gehrig back to New York, and freed him from any contractual ties.

Gehrig, who had played 12 games for Hartford, was suspended from collegiate athletics for 1922, but on April 18, 1923, the day Yankee Stadium opened, he pitched for Columbia and struck out 17 Williams College batters. The head Yankees scout, Paul Krichell, was on Gehrig by then—enamored by his powerful bat—and by June signed him to a contract for the Yankees, who played him in seven games, then sent him to Hartford, where he hit 24 homers in 59 games.

In late September, the Yankees called Gehrig back up to the big leagues. Before the start of the last series of the regular season,

Wally Pipp twisted his ankle getting off the train in Boston. Huggins sat him out and started twenty-year-old Gehrig at first base for the first time on September 27, hitting him cleanup behind Ruth. In the first inning, Ruth doubled and Gehrig hit his first major league home run. Gehrig had three doubles, a single, and 4 RBIs the next day, and finished the four-game series 9-for-19.

Pipp had hit .304 with 109 RBIs, but only 6 home runs in 1923, and Huggins now envisioned a lethal one-two punch that could surprise and overwhelm the Giants, who clinched their pennant on September 28, in the World Series. By Judge Landis's ruling, the Yankees would need the opposing manager's permission to make a late roster change, and McGraw was not about to oblige. "These are the hazards of the games," he said. "If the Yankees have had an injury, that is their tough luck." Pipp, gimpy ankle and all, played in the World Series.

The next time Gehrig, who returned to Hartford and had a monster 1924 season, filled in for Pipp, it would play out a little differently.

For the time being, the combative tone was set for the third Yankees-Giants showdown. If one believed the Yankees wouldn't achieve true supremacy in baseball until they dethroned McGraw, this would be the time.

McGraw had a new wrinkle of his own. "This is the way old Casey Stengel ran yesterday, running out his home run," wrote Damon Runyan for the *New York American*, in one of the most famous baseball leads ever typed. "His mouth wide open. His warped old legs bending beneath him at every stride. His arms flying back and forth like those of a man swimming a crawl stroke. His flanks heaving, his breath whistling, his head held back." And when he reached home plate, "his warped old legs collapsed."

Stengel, a colorful outfielder schooled in the minors by Kid Elberfeld, joined the Giants in 1921 but was a bit player and didn't appear in the World Series. In 1922, he started Game One but pulled a leg muscle and missed the rest of it. Now Stengel, thirty-three, having hit .339 in 75 games, was in the Giants lineup for the first World Series game to be played at Yankee Stadium.

The Yankees and Giants were tied, 4–4, when Stengel stepped up with two out in the top of the ninth against Joe Bush, who had pitched shutout ball since Hoyt was knocked out in the third. He smoked a line drive to left center, and it bounded between Meusel and Witt and out to the far reaches of the Stadium. Running on a sore heel, Stengel made it around the bases, sliding feet first into Schang with the winning run. Grantland Rice was also covering the game. "Mudville is avenged at last," he wrote, in reference to the Mighty Casey. "For Casey Stengel had climbed the purple heights of glory."

McGraw, in his own syndicated column, wrote, "I don't think I have ever felt such a thrill on the bench as when Casey Stengel hit that home run in the ninth."

The next day, at the Polo Grounds, it was Babe Ruth's turn. With Herb Pennock on the mound, Ruth homered in the fourth and fifth innings, finding his old, familiar porch, to stake the Yankees to a 4–2 victory. Now, Heywood Broun, that rumpled member of the Algonquin Round Table, penned another famous lead for the *New York World*.

"The Ruth is mighty and shall prevail. He did yesterday. Babe made 2 home runs and the Yankees won from the Giants at the Polo Grounds, 4–2."

In this heavyweight battle of baseball and prose, Stengel again answered. This time, he could jog after lofting Sam Jones's pitch into the right-field bleachers in the seventh inning, the only run of the game. Art Nehf again shut out Ruth and the Yankees.

As Frank Graham later recounted, "a press box wag said, 'Stengel has won two games, the Yankees have won one. When are the Giants going to win one?'"

The Yankees won the next three, outscoring the Giants, 22–9. In Game Six, Pennock was losing 4–1 when the Yankees erupted for five runs in the top of the eighth. Two runs scored on bases-loaded walks, and after Ruth struck out, Bob Meusel singled to score the tying and winning runs, another racing home on an error. Sam Jones closed the game with two scoreless innings, and the Yankees were the champions.

In the same tiny dressing room where tears had dropped the previous two series, Huggins now "danced a jig as old man Dugan, proud parent of 'Jumping Joseph,' patted time with his hands and feet," according to an AP account. Ruth was looking back at his eighth-inning strikeout and laughing, while Meusel was hugged and kissed by the little mascot, Eddie Bennett. And Wally Schang "kicked off his spiked shoe and it flies clear through a window pane."

McGraw had walked Ruth 8 times, but the Babe hit .368 with 3 homers. Meusel had 8 RBIs, and Pennock had 2 wins and a save. Casey Stengel would one day have his own laughs in a Yankees uniform.

"The Yankees beat us cleanly," McGraw told his ghostwriter, "beat us off better pitching and harder hitting. They earned the crown they wear."

Ruppert joined the press at The Commodore that evening, beaming ear to ear, a drink thrust into his hands.

"Ruppert must have felt as though he were sitting on top of the world," Graham would write. "His team—and his alone—playing in his ballpark, were the champions."

On that shaky foundation established by Ban Johnson, Big Bill Devery and Frank Farrell, Clark Griffith and Jack Chesbro, and Hal Chase and Kid Elberfeld and Roger Peckinpaugh, the Yankees emerged. On the old lumberyard Ruppert had purchased, where his troublesome partner, Til Huston, saw to the construction, a towering baseball cathedral would stand until 2008. Organized by Ed Barrow and Miller Huggins and powered by Babe Ruth, the Yankees now stood alone at the summit, looking down on the baseball countryside.

And the rest is . . . well, you know the rest.

EPILOGUE
THE ENDURING BRAND

In the history of this country, there are, arguably, a number of myths that define who we are as people. One is the frontier. One is the New England town meeting. One is New Orleans Jazz. Another is the New York Yankees.

—Tony Kornheiser

The full effectiveness of the Yankees' galvanized, in-harness approach to winning didn't take hold until 1926. By that time, Huggins had brought Ruth under control, Gehrig had established himself at first base, and Barrow had jettisoned aging, objectionable characters and developed long-term solutions for second base (Tony Lazzeri), shortstop (Mark Koenig), and center field (Earle Combs). In 1928, Bill Dickey came up to catch.

And there, with the championships of 1927 and '28, the Yankees dynasty was firmly affixed on baseball, and the "top of the world" sensation Ruppert experienced on October 10, 1923, would become the norm. The word "dynasty" is overused in sports, but to the Yankees brand it accurately applies, because its preeminence in professional sports spanned several generations. It needn't be chronicled here that any list of greatest teams of all time must include, if not begin, with the Yankees of 1927, 1939, 1961, and 1998.

It took the original franchise 19 seasons to reach its first World Series, and 21 to win its first championship. To this day, no generation of Yankees fans has had to wait so long. That the 12 seasons without a World Series appearance, from 1964–76, and the 15-year gap between 1981 and 96, *seemed* like forever is testament to the strength of what Ruppert, Barrow, and Huggins built. Never has there been a need to rebrand or reinvent.

The Yankees were among the first franchises to establish a "farm system," which at its peak included roughly 30 minor league affiliates. With no draft, and no free agency, the Yankees were able to cherry-pick nearly all of the best amateur prospects year after year and stockpile them in their endless chain of farm teams for as long as they chose, or trade clusters of them for one prized player.

Only the establishment of the amateur draft in 1965, and half-hearted ownership by CBS beginning in 1964, put a drag on the Yankees' dominance—and then only until George Steinbrenner eventually ushered in a new, different era of success.

The voices of the formative years chronicled in this book speak today to those interested in modern baseball. The uniform and the insignia remain virtually unchanged since 1915. When Ruppert assumed full control, he furnished the team with three sets of uniforms, so they would always have a clean suit of pinstripes. Ballplayers of the era considered it a badge of honor to wear dirty uniforms day after day, but Ruppert wanted the

Yankees to look neat. The modern ownership's ban on facial hair below the lip in an era of long, thick beards is an historical descendant of that philosophy.

The idea that the manager must have control, and that no player can be bigger than the franchise, was born with Miller Huggins's struggle to gain control of the early Ruthian teams, and the Yankees had their greatest successes in eras in which owners *owned*, general managers ran the front office, managers *managed*, and players simply *played*—just the way Jake Ruppert laid it out.

The future Yankees would show their flaws. It took too long for baseball to integrate, and once Jackie Robinson broke the racial barrier, it took the Yankees too long, until 1955, to do the same. As of 2017, the Yankees still have not employed an African-American manager. Bob Watson did break the glass ceiling at the GM level, putting together the Yankees' 1996 champions.

The Yankees' tendency to overspend and try to quick-fix by acquiring past-their-prime stars, dating back to Willie Keeler, Frank Chance, and Home Run Baker, has cropped up now and again with hit-and-miss results. And the desire for the Yankees to have the biggest, best stadium—or, at least, the most expensive one—drove the opening of a new, $1.5 billion Yankee Stadium in 2009, in the midst of a severe recession.

To this day, the Yankees retain the characteristic firmly established when they completed the 20-year journey from the hastily constructed wooden ballpark and rocky, swampy grounds of Hilltop Park and moved into Yankee Stadium in 1923—a symbol of wealth and of supremacy.

That all of this began in the shadows, on the brothel- and poolhall-lined streets of the Tenderloin District, with a graft-happy policeman who collected coins on the sidewalk and a bartender who knew how to keep secrets, and their ability to grease the right political palms, may be ironic—but it is one of the most archetypically American of stories. And for that, one can bet Big Bill Devery and Frank J. Farrell are somewhere still enjoying the last laugh.

BIBLIOGRAPHY

Alexander, Charles. *Ty Cobb*. Oxford University Press. Oxford, U.K. 1984.

Appel, Marty. *Pinstripe Empire: The New York Yankees From Before the Babe to After the Boss*. Bloomsbury, USA. New York, N.Y. 2012.

Barrow, Edward Grant, with James. M. Kahn. *My Fifty Years in Baseball*. Coward-McCann, Inc. New York, N.Y. 1953.

Breslin, Jimmy. *Branch Rickey: A Life*. Viking Penguin. New York, N.Y. 2011.

Chase, Hal. *How to Play First Base*. American Sports Publishing Company. New York, N.Y. 1917.

Cobb, Ty, with Al Stump. *My Life in Baseball, The True Record*. Doubleday. New York, N.Y. 1961.

Creamer, Robert. *Babe: The Legend Comes to Life*. Simon and Schuster, New York, N.Y. 1974.

Dewey, Donald, and Nicholas Acocella. *The Black Prince of Baseball. Hal Chase and the Mythology of the Game*. University of Nebraska Press. Lincoln, Nebraska, and London. 2004.

Durocher, Leo, with Ed Linn. *Nice Guys Finish Last*. Simon and Schuster. New York, N.Y. 1975.

Gallagher, Mark, and Walter LeConte. *The Yankee Encyclopedia (Fourth Edition)*. Sports Publishing Inc. Champaign, Illinois. 1999.

Graham, Frank. *The New York Yankees: An Informal History*. G.P. Putnam and Sons. New York, N.Y. 1943.

Halas, George Stanley. *Halas By Halas*. McGraw-Hill. New York, N.Y. 1979.

Honig, Donald. *The Man in the Dugout*. Follett Publishing Company. Chicago, Illinois. 1977.

Kohout, Martin Donnell. *Hal Chase: The Defiant Life and Turbulent Times of Baseball's Biggest Crook*. McFarland and Company. Jefferson, N.C. 2001.

Leavengood, Ted. *Clark Griffith: The Old Fox of Washington Baseball*. McFarland and Company. Jefferson, N.C., and London. 2011.

Linn, Ed. *The Great Rivalry: The Yankees and the Red Sox, 1901-1990*. Ticknor and Fields. New York, N.Y. 1991.

Mack, Connie. *My 66 Years in The Big Leagues*. John C. Winston Company. Philadelphia, Pennsylvania. 1950.

Mathewson, Christy. *Pitching in a Pinch: Baseball from the Inside*. G.P. Putnam and Sons. New York, N.Y. 1912.

McKenna, Brian. *Clark Griffith: Baseball's Statesman*. Lulu.com 2010.

Mead, William B., and Paul Dickson. *Baseball: The Presidents' Game*. Walker and Company. New York, N.Y. 1993.

Montville, Leigh. *The Big Bam*. Doubleday. New York, N.Y. 2006.

Polner, Murray. *Branch Rickey*. Signet. The New American Library. New York, N.Y. 1982.

Reisler, Jim. *Before They Were Bombers*. McFarland and Company. Jefferson, N.C., and London. 2002.

Rickey, Branch, with Robert Riger. *The American Diamond*. Simon and Schuster. New York, N.Y. 1965.

Ritter, Lawrence S. *The Glory of Their Times (Enlarged Edition)*. Quill William Morrow. New York, N.Y. 1995.

Roosevelt, Theodore. *Theodore Roosevelt: An Autobiography*. Macmillan. New York, N.Y. 1913.

Solomon, Burt. *Where They Ain't*. The Free Press, a Division of Simon and Schuster. New York, N.Y. 1999.

Sowell, Mike. *The Pitch That Killed*. MacMillan. New York, N.Y. 1989.

Spatz, Lyle. *New York Yankee Openers*. McFarland and Company. Jefferson, N.C. 1997.

Spatz, Lyle, with Steve Steinberg. *1921: The Yankees, The Giants and the Battle for Baseball Supremacy in New York*. University of Nebraska Press. Lincoln, Nebraska, and London. 2010.

Spatz, Lyle, with Steve Steinberg. *The Colonel and Hug: The Partnership That Transformed the New York Yankees*. University of Nebraska Press. Lincoln, Nebraska, and London. 2015.

Steffens, Lincoln. *The Autobiography of Lincoln Steffens*. Harcourt, Brace and Company. New York, N.Y. 1931.

Stout, Glenn. *Yankees Century*. Houghton Mifflin Company. Boston, Massachusetts, and New York, N.Y. 2002.

Stout, Glenn. (Editor) *Top Of The Heap: A Yankees Collection*. Houghton Mifflin Company. Boston, Massachusetts, and New York, N.Y. 2003.

Swanson, Harry. *Ruthless Baseball: Yankees Purified by Fire Stadium Construction.* AuthorHouse. Bloomington, Indiana. 2004.

Vaccaro, Mike. *Emperors and Idiots. The Hundred-Year Rivalry Between the Yankees and Red Sox.* Doubleday. New York, N.Y. 2005.

Vass, George. *George Halas and his Chicago Bears.* Henry Regnery Company. Chicago, Illinois. 1971.

Weintraub, Robert. *The House That Ruth Built.* Little, Brown and Company. New York, N.Y., Boston, Massachusetts, London. 2011.

White Construction Company. *The Yankee Stadium* (promotional booklet). 1923.

Magazine Articles

Appel, Marty. "Roger Peckinpaugh." *The National Pastime Museum*, Aug. 3, 2014.

Bodet, Gib. "The Life and Times of Prince Hal Chase" (unpublished biographical essay).

Cobb, Ty. "Ty Cobb on The Batting Art." *Literary Digest,* June 27, 1914.

Elias, Al Munro. "Miller J. Huggins." *Baseball Magazine,* March 1918.

Ford, Russell W., as told to Don E. Basenfelder. "Ford Tells Inside Story Of His 'Emery Ball' After Guarding His Secret For A Quarter Of A Century." *The Sporting News,* April 25, 1935.

Fullerton, Hugh S. "Baseball on Trial." *The New Republic,* Oct. 20, 1920.

Grant, Lester. "Hal Chase, Broke And Ill at 58, Recalls Life's Errors." *The Sporting News*, Sept. 18, 1941.

Grant, Lester. "Hal Chase, Who Plunged from Glory to Gloom, Recalls Greatest Thrills And Players From His Days On The Diamond." *The Sporting News*, Sept. 25, 1941.

"Home Run Baker's Rise." *Literary Digest*, April 6, 1912.

Huggins, Myrtle, as told to John B. Kennedy. "Mighty Midget." *Collier's*, May 24, 1930.

"Kid Elberfeld Opens his Scrapbook." *The Sporting News*, Feb. 19, 1942.

Lane, F.C. "The Man Who Led The Yankees To Their First Pennant." *Baseball Magazine*, December 1921.

Mays, Carl. "My Attitude Toward the Unfortunate Chapman Affair." *Baseball Magazine*, November 1920.

McDermott, J.R. "Miller Huggins, The Midget Manager." *Baseball Magazine*, October 1913.

Phelon, William J. "The Great American Fan, A National Institution." *Baseball Magazine*, September, 1915.

Sehorn, J.W. "Hal Chase Replays His 'Costliest Error'." *The Sporting News*, April 23, 1947.

Stallings, George T. "The Miracle Man's Own Story." *Collier's*. November 28, 1914.

"Taps for Huggins. A Great Little Bear-Tamer." *Literary Digest*, Oct. 12, 1929.

"The Famous Frank Chance Trade." *Baseball Magazine*, March 1913.

Archival Newspapers, Magazines

Baseball Magazine, Collier's, Literary Digest, Sporting Life, The American Architect, The Atlanta Journal, The Boston Globe, The Boston Post, The Bridgeport Evening Farmer, The Brooklyn Daily Eagle, The Buffalo Courier, The Chicago Examiner, The Chicago

Tribune, The Deseret News, The Des Moines Register, The Hartford Courant, The Los Angeles Times, The New-York Tribune, The New London Day, The New Republic, The New York Clipper, The New York Daily News, The New York Evening Telegram, The New York Evening World, The New York Herald, The New York Post, The New York Sun, The New York Times, The Oakland Tribune, The Philadelphia Inquirer, The Pittsburgh Gazette, The Pittsburgh Press, The Providence Evening News, The Salt Lake Tribune, The Sporting News, The St. Louis Globe-Democrat, The Washington Evening Star, The Washington Herald, The Washington Post.

Websites

www.appelpr.com
www.baseball-reference.com
www.chroniclingamerica.loc.gov
www.fultonhistory.com
www.govtrack.us
www.kidelberfeld.com
www.LA84.org
www.newspapers.com
www.nytimes.com
www.retrosheet.org
www.sabr.org/bioproject (various pages)
www.youtube (Brad Palmer channel)